EIGHTEENTH CENTURY WAIFS.

EIGHTEENTH CENTURY WAIFS

BY

JOHN ASHTON

IN ONE VOLUME.

Essay Index Reprint Series

 BOOKS FOR LIBRARIES PRESS
FREEPORT, NEW YORK

First Published 1887
Reprinted 1972

**LIBRARY
FLORIDA STATE UNIVERSITY
TALLAHASSEE, FLORIDA**

Library of Congress Cataloging in Publication Data

Ashton, John, b. 1834.
  Eighteenth century waifs.

  (Essay index reprint series)
  Reprint of the 1887 ed.
  1. Gt. Brit.--Social life and customs--18th century.
I. Title.
DA485.A79   1972   914.2'03'7   71-38741
ISBN 0-8369-2634-X

PRINTED IN THE UNITED STATES OF AMERICA
BY
NEW WORLD BOOK MANUFACTURING CO., INC.
HALLANDALE, FLORIDA 33009

PREFACE.

It was probably Solomon, who, in Ecclesiastes, cap. 12, v. 12, said, 'Of making many books there is no end.' But, if this book had to have been written by him, he might, probably, have modified his opinion.

I have read some books in my life-time, *re* the sixteenth, seventeenth, and eighteenth centuries, and therefore was not taken aback when I was advised by a learned friend, whom I consulted as to the subject of a new book, to try the 'Musgrave Tracts,' in the British Museum. I thanked him, and wrote for them, when I was politely asked, 'Did I want them all?' 'Of course,' was my reply; when I was told, with the courtesy that particularly distinguishes the establishment, that I had better come into an inner room, and have them down shelf by shelf.

The books came in a continuous stream, until I asked if there were any more. 'Oh, yes,' was the reply; and, when I had finished my job, I found I had gone through more than 1760 volumes. Add to this over 200 other books and newspapers used for reference, &c., and that will represent some amount of the labour employed in writing a book.

I have strung together a series of chapters of different phases of social life and biography of the last century, none of which have (as far as I am concerned) appeared in any magazine, but which have all been specially written for this book. And this I have done so that the book may be taken up at any time, and laid down again at the end of an article; and perhaps the best reason for my publishing this book is, that it gives the reader a brief *resumé* of each subject treated, taken from sources, thoroughly original, which are usually inaccessible to the general public, and known but to few students.

They are diverse, to suit all tastes; and if this, my venture, is successful, I may bashfully hint that my store is not yet exhausted.

JOHN ASHTON.

CONTENTS.

	PAGE
A Forgotten Fanatic	1
A Fashionable Lady's Life	17
George Barrington	31
Milton's Bones	55
The True Story of Eugene Aram	83
Redemptioners	112
A Trip to Richmond in Surrey	131
George Robert Fitzgerald	135
Eighteenth Century Amazons	177
'The Times' and its Founder	203
Imprisonment for Debt	227
Jonas Hanway	254
A Holy Voyage to Ramsgate One Hundred Years Ago	278
Quacks of the Century	287
Cagliostro in London	333

EIGHTEENTH CENTURY WAIFS.

A FORGOTTEN FANATIC.[1]

NE of the most curious phases of religious mania is that where the patient is under the impression that he is divinely inspired, and has a special mission to his fellow-men, which he is impelled to fulfil at all costs and under all circumstances.

From the earliest ages of Christianity *pseudo-Christoi* or false Christs, existed. Simon Magus, Dositheus, and the famous Barcochab were among the first of them, and they were followed by Moses, in Crete, in the fifth century; Julian, in Palestine, *circa* A.D. 530; and Serenus, in Spain, *circa* A.D. 714. There were, in the twelfth century, some seven or eight in France, Spain, and Persia; and, coming to more modern times, there was Sabbatai Zewi, a native of Aleppo, or Smyrna, who proclaimed himself to be

---

[1] It may be objected that this story pertains more to the seventeenth than the eighteenth century; but, as the man Roderick was alive in the last century, I claim him as belonging to it.

the Messiah, in Jerusalem, *circa* 1666. The list of religious fanatics is a long one. Mahomet, Munzer, John of Leyden, Brothers, Matthews, Joanna Southcott, 'Courtenay,' or Thomas, and Joe Smith are among them, and are well-known; but there are hundreds of others whose work has not been on so grand a scale, or whose influence has not been of the national importance of the above; and it is of one of these forgotten fanatics that I now treat.

Well out in the Atlantic Ocean, far west, indeed, even of the Western Isles, stands the lonely island of St. Kilda, or Hirta, as it used to be called, from *h-Iar-tir*, the Gaelic for West land, or West country. Its rocky sides are inaccessible, except at one landing-place, at a bay on the south-east, and it is the home and breeding-place of millions of sea-birds, whose flesh and eggs form the main supply of food for the inhabitants, and whose feathers, together with a few sheep and cattle, and what little barley can be grown, or butter can be made, pay the trifling rent required, and help to provide the bare necessaries of civilized existence.

The inhabitants are not healthy, so many dying, as young children, of a disease locally known as the 'eight day sickness,' a disease which generally attacks them on the eighth or ninth day after birth, and mostly proves fatal in the course of a day or two. From this and other causes, including falls from cliffs, the population has remained nearly stationary, as is evidenced by the fact that for the last hundred years the inhabitants have averaged under a hundred. Indeed, at one time, in 1724, small-pox attacked the islanders, being imported by one of them on his return from a visit to Harris, and all the adults died except four, who were left to take care of twenty-six orphans, all that were left of twenty-four families.

Lying out of the ordinary track of boats, even of yachts, it is, even now, seldom visited, and in the last century no one except the steward of Macleod (whose family have been the possessors of St. Kilda for hundreds of years), who made an annual pilgrimage to collect the rent, ever came near the place. Its loneliness was proverbial, so much so that it was an article of faith that the arrival of strangers brought with them a kind of influenza called boat-cough, which was sometimes fatal. This singular disease does not seem to be confined to St. Kilda, for Bates, in 'The Naturalist on the River Amazon,' mentions certain tribes near Ega who are gradually becoming extinct from a slow fever and cold, which attacks them after they have been visited by civilised people. And in the 'Cruise of H.M.S. Galatea,' in 1867-68, it says, 'Tristran d'Acunha is a remarkably healthy island; but it is a singular fact that any vessel touching there from St. Helena invariably brings with it a disease resembling influenza.'

This belief is amusingly illustrated in Boswell's 'Journal of a Tour to the Hebrides.' 'This evening he (Dr. Johnson) disputed the truth of what is said as to the people of St. Kilda catching cold whenever strangers come. "How can there," said he, "be a physical effect without a physical cause?" He added, laughing, "The arrival of a ship full of strangers would kill them; for, if one stranger gives them one cold, two strangers must give them two colds, and so on in proportion." I wondered to hear him ridicule this, as he had praised McAulay for putting it in his book,¹ saying that it was manly in him to tell a fact, however strange, if he himself believed it. They said it was annually proved by Macleod's steward, on whose arrival all the inhabitants caught cold. He jocularly remarked, "The steward always comes to demand something from them, and so they fall a-coughing. I suppose the people in Skye all take a cold when——" (naming a certain person) "comes." They said he only came in summer. *Johnson*—"That is out of tenderness to you. Bad weather and he at the same time would be too much."'

The first printed account of this poor lonely island is, probably, in a little book by Donald Monro, High Dean of the Isles,² 1594. He there says, 'The inhabitants therof ar simple poor people, scarce learnit in aney religion, but McCloyd of Herray,³ his stewart, or he quhom he deputs in sic office, sailes anes in the zeir ther at midsummer, with some chaplaine to baptize bairns ther, and if they want⁴ a chaplaine, they baptize their bairns themselfes.'

At the end of the seventeenth century, when Roderick, the religious impostor, or fanatic, lived, things spiritual were somewhat improved, although they only had the annual clerical visit. There were three chapels on the island, to serve a population of one hundred and eighty. One was called Christ's Chapel, hardly discernible from one of their dwellings, being built and thatched in a similar manner; but it con-

---

¹ 'The History of St. Kilda,' etc. By the Rev. Mr. Kenneth Macaulay. London, 1764.

² ' Description of the Western Isles of Scotland, called Hebrides,' etc.

³ Harris.   ⁴ *Scottice*, are without.

tained one of their chief treasures, a brass crucifix, which lay upon an altar therein. They paid no adoration or worship to this, but it was their most precious possession, being used, as are the gospels elsewhere, for the purpose of solemn asseveration, and it was also made use of at marriages and the healing of strife.

The people observed as Holy-days Christmas, Easter, Good Friday, St. Columba's Day, and All Saints. They ceased all work at midnight on Saturday, and kept the Sabbath, in this respect, very strictly, only resuming their ordinary avocations on Monday morning. They believed in the Trinity, and in a future state of happiness and misery, and that God ordains all things. They took great care with their churchyard, which they fenced round with stone, so that no cattle should desecrate God's Acre, and they had a peculiar belief in the embodiment of spirits, and fancied that they could, at will, incorporate themselves with the rocks, hills, etc.

Of the three chapels, one only seems to have been used, and this, not being large enough to accommodate the islanders, the whole of the inhabitants would assemble, on every Sunday morning, in the churchyard, and there devoutly say the Lord's Prayer, the Creed, and the Ten Commandments. This form of worship was simple enough; but it seems to have been of recent introduction—*i.e.*, about the beginning of the seventeenth century; when, somehow or other, there was a man upon the island who passed for a Roman Catholic priest, but who was so ignorant that he did not know the Lord's Prayer, the Creed, or the Decalogue correctly; and, consequently, he taught the poor people an incorrect version, but to him they owed the crucifix, and the observance of the Holy-days before mentioned, and with this teacher they were content until the year 1641, when one Coll McDonald, or Ketoch, fled from Ireland, and, with a few men, landed at St. Kilda, where he lived in amity with the inhabitants for nearly a year. He rebuked the so-called priest for his ignorance, and he taught the poor simple folk the correct version of the text of their very primitive worship—in fine, he was considered so far superior to the priest, that the natives would fain have deposed the latter; but this McDonald would not suffer.

Martin Martin,[1] writing in 1698, describes the happy condition of the islanders at that date. 'The Inhabitants of St. Kilda are much happier than the generality of Mankind, as being almost the only People in the World who feel the sweetness of true Liberty: What the Condition of the People in the Golden Age is feign'd by the Poets to be, that theirs really is; I mean, in Innocency and Simplicity, Purity, Mutual Love, and Cordial Friendship, free from solicitous Cares and anxious Covetousness; from Envy, Deceit, and Dissimulation; from Ambition and Pride, and the Consequences that attend them. They are altogether ignorant of the Vices of Foreigners, and governed by the Dictates of Reason and Christianity, as it was first delivered to them by those Heroick Souls whose Zeal moved them to undergo danger and trouble, to plant Religion here in one of the remotest Corners of the World.'

This Eden, however, was doomed to have its

[1] 'A Late Voyage to St. Kilda, the Remotest of all the Hebrides,' etc., London, 1698.

Serpent, and these simple folk were fated to be led into error by a man who seems to have been physically above the average of the islanders, for he is described as 'a Comely, well-proportioned fellow, Red-hair'd, and exceeding all the Inhabitants of St. Kilda in Strength, Climbing, &c.' Naturally he was illiterate, for the means of culture were altogether lacking in that lonely isle; but he was above his fellows, inasmuch as he was a poet, and, moreover, he claimed to have the gift of 'second sight,' a pretension which would naturally cause him to be looked up to by these Gaelic islanders. These qualifications which Roderick (for such was his name) claimed, naturally pointed to his becoming a leader of some sort; and he seems to have entered upon his vocation early in life, for, when we first hear of him in his public capacity, he was but eighteen years of age.

We have read how strictly the islands kept the Sabbath, and Roderick seems to have been the first to break through their customs—by going fishing on that day. As, according to all moral ethics, something dreadful will surely overtake the Sabbath breaker, it is comforting to know that Roderick formed no exception to the rule. One Sunday he committed the heinous and, hitherto, unknown sin of fishing —and, on his return, he declared that, as he was coming home, a 'Man, dressed in a Cloak and Hat,' suddenly appeared in the road before him. Needless to say, this apparition frightened him, and he fell upon his face before the supernatural being, but the Man desired him not to be afraid, for he was John the Baptist, who had come specially from Heaven, the bearer of good tidings to the inhabitants of St. Kilda, and with a divine commission to instruct Roderick in religious matters, which instruction he was to impart to his neighbours for their spiritual welfare.

Roderick diffidently objected to thus being made a medium, and alleged his incapacity to receive such revelations and act upon them; but the pseudo-saint cheered him, and bade him be of good courage, declaring that he would immediately make him fit for his predestined purpose, and, according to the poor fanatic's account, gave him the following instructions:

It was to be of primary importance, and as a visible sign of their belief, that his followers should observe Friday as a strict fast—so strict, indeed, that not a particle of food of any description must pass their lips on that day, nor might they even indulge in a pinch of snuff—a small luxury which they dearly loved. He next promulgated the comforting assurance that many of the deceased islanders were Saints in Heaven, and there interceded for those living; that everyone had his own particular advocate, and, on the anniversary of the day peculiar to each Saint, his *protégé* on earth was to make a feast to his neighbours of the very best of his substance, such as mutton, fowls, &c., Roderick, of course, to be the chief and honoured guest on the occasion.

A sheep was to be sacrificed on the threshold of each house by every family (presumably only once a year), and this was to be done in a specially cruel manner, for no knife was to touch it, but its throat was to be hacked with the crooked spades they used in husbandry, whose edges were about half-an-inch thick. This was to be done at night, but no one might partake of the mutton that night under penalty of similarly slaughtering a sheep the next day for every person that had eaten of it. It is difficult to see what was his object in these ordinances—except to make sure of good living at the expense of his poor dupes, who, if they turned refractory, and disobeyed his injunctions, were threatened with the most awful Judgment to come.

That he was keen enough in his own interests is exemplified in one of his promulgations. He picked out a bush upon a rising ground, which he christened 'John the Baptist's Bush,' for there, he declared, the Saint had appeared to him; and this he ordered should be holy ground, which must never be defiled by the tread of sheep or cattle. He also built a wall —certainly not a high one—round it: and should, by chance, any unhappy sheep, in the lightsomeness of its heart, or succumbing to the temptation of the herbage, overleap this wall, and dare to browse upon the sacred soil, it was staightway to be slain—and Roderick and its owner were to eat its carcase. But, as the Saint evidently foresaw that some stiff-necked, and not properly-converted proselyte, might object to this disposition of his personal property and might refuse to have the sheep slaughtered, he commanded that such a recusant should be ANATHEMA, cast out, and excluded from all fellowship, until such time as he saw the error of his ways, recanted, and expiated his sin by permitting the sacrifice.

For discipline must be maintained in a religious body, as well as in a purely secular society; and Roderick had no intention of having his authority disputed. For minor offences he had a cheerful penance. No matter what was the weather, the sinner must strip, and forthwith walk or jump into the water, there to stand until the divinely-inspired one chose to release him, and, if more than one were thus punished at the same time, they were to beguile the moments, and somewhat increase their penance, by pouring cold water upon each other's heads.

He was for no half-measures. This new Divine revelation must thoroughly supersede and root out the old superstitions; so he forbade the use of the Lord's Prayer, the Creed, and the Ten Commandments—the whole formulary of the islanders' simple faith—and substituted forms of his own. His prayers are described as rhapsodical productions, in which, in spite of the abolition of the old form of worship, he introduced the names of God, our Saviour, and the immaculate Virgin, together with words unintelligible either to himself or his hearers, but which he declared to have received direct from the Baptist, and delivered to his hearers, as in duty bound.

He kept up his connection with St. John, and used to assert that every night, when the people were assembled, he heard a voice, saying, 'Come you out,' and then he lost all control over himself, and was constrained to go. Then would the Baptist meet him, and instruct him in what he was to say to the people. St. John evidently expected his disciple to exercise all his intelligence, for he would only say his message once, and never could be got to repeat it. On one occasion, Roderick could not understand it, or hardly remember a sentence; so he naturally inquired of the Saint how he was to behave. He got no comfort, however, only a brusque, 'Go, you have it,' with which he was fain to be content, and, wonderful to relate, on his return to his flock, he remembered every word he had been told, and could retail it fluently—but, as a rule, his discourses were discursive, and apt to send his auditors to sleep.

Naturally the women flocked to him, and he took them specially (some said too specially) under his protection. To them he revealed that, if they followed him faithfully, eternal bliss should be their portion, and that they should go to heaven in glorious state, riding upon milk-white steeds. For them he exercised his poetic talents (for he composed long, rhapsodical rhymes, which he called psalms, and which were sung by his flock), and he taught them a devout hymn, called the 'Virgin Mary's,' which he declared she had sent specially to them, and that it was of such wonderful efficacy, that whoever could repeat it by heart would not die in child-bearing; but, of course, so valuable a gift could not be imparted gratis, so every scholar was mulcted in a sheep before she was instructed in the potent hymn.

Yet, as with many another, a woman was the primary cause of his downfall. It was his behaviour to a woman that first opened the eyes of his deluded followers, and showed them that their idol was fallible, and that his feet were 'part of iron, and part of clay.' The wife of Macleod's representative found favour in his sight; but, being a virtuous woman, she told her husband of the Prophet's wicked advances; and these two laid a little trap, into which the unsuspecting, but naughty, Roderick walked.

It was very simple: the husband hid himself until he judged proper to appear—confronted the guilty man—spoke burning words of reproof to him— thoroughly disorganised him, and brought him very low—made him beg his pardon, and promise he would never so sin again. But although a hollow peace was patched up between them, and the injured husband even gave the greatest sign of friendship possible, according to their notions (*i.e.*, taking Roderick's place as sponsor at the baptism of one of his own children), yet the story leaked out. The Prophet's father plainly and openly told him he was a deceiver, and would come to a bad end; and the thinking portion of the community began to have serious doubts of the Divine origin of his mission.

These doubts were further confirmed by one or two little facts which led the people to somewhat distrust his infallibility, especially in one case in which his cousin-german Lewis was concerned. This man had an ewe which had brought forth three lambs at one time, and these wicked sheep actually browsed upon the sacred bush! Of course we know the Baptist had decreed their slaughter, and Lewis was promptly reminded of the fact—but he did not see it in that light. His heart was hard, and his sheep were dear to him. He argued that, from his point of view, it was unreasonable to kill so many animals, and inflict such serious damage to their proprietor, for so trivial a fault—and, besides, he would not. Of course there was nothing to be done with such an hardened sinner but to carry out the law, and excommunicate him; which was accordingly done—with the usual result. The poor simple folk, in their faith, looked for a speedy and awful judgment to fall upon Lewis and his sheep.

> 'But what gave rise
> To no little surprise,
> Nobody seem'd one penny the worse!'

And then they bethought them that, if it were

their own case, they might as well treat the matter as Lewis had done—seeing he was none the worse, and four sheep to the good; and so his authority over them gradually grew laxer and laxer: and, when the steward paid his annual visit in 1697, they denounced Roderick as an impostor, and expressed contrition for their own back-slidings.

The chaplain who accompanied the steward, and who was sent over from Harris by Macleod, purposely to look into this matter, made the Prophet publicly proclaim himself an impostor, compelled him to commence with his own hands the destruction of the enclosure round the sacred bush, and scatter the stones broadcast—and, finally, the steward, whose word was absolute law to these poor people, took him away, never to return. The poor credulous dupes, on being reproved for so easily complying to this impostor, with one voice answered that what they did was unaccountable; but, seeing one of their own number and stamp in all respects endued, as they fancied, with a powerful faculty of preaching so fluently and frequently, and pretending to converse with John the Baptist, they were induced to believe in his mission from Heaven, and therefore complied with his commands without dispute.

Of his ultimate fate nothing is known, the last record of him being that, after having been taken to Harris, he was brought before the awful Macleod, to be judged, 'who, being informed of this Fellow's Impostures, did forbid him from that time forward to Preach any more on pain of Death. This was a great mortification, as well as disappointment, to the Impostor, who was possessed with a fancy that *Mack-Leod* would hear him preach, and expected no less than to persuade him to become one of his Proselytes, as he has since confessed.' He was sent to Skye, where he made public recantation of his errors, and confessed in several churches that it was the Devil, and not St. John, with whom he conversed —and, arguing from that fact, he probably was docile, and lived the remainder of his life in Skye— a harmless lunatic.

In October, 1885, public attention was particularly directed to St. Kilda, and the story cannot be better told than by reproducing some contemporary newspaper paragraphs.

Morning Post, October 9, 1885.—' A letter has been received by Principal Rainy, Edinburgh, and has been forwarded to the Home Secretary from St. Kilda. The letter was found on the shore of Harris, having been floated from St. Kilda in a little boat made of a piece of plank. The letter was written by the clergyman of St. Kilda, by direction of the islanders, asking that the Government should be informed that their corn, barley, and potatoes were destroyed by a great storm, in the hope that Government would send a supply of corn-seed, barley, and potatoes, as the crop was quite useless.'

Ibid, October 21, 1885.—' The steamer from Glasgow, carrying supplies to the starving people of St. Kilda, reached the island on Monday, and safely landed the stores. The islanders were in good health, but their crops have been swept away, and, but for the supplies sent by the steamer, they would have been in very perilous straits for food. Intelligence of the distress of St. Kilda was first made known by bottles thrown into the sea.'

Times, April 8, 1886.—' A Parliamentary paper has been issued containing a report of Mr. Malcolm McNeill, inspecting officer of the Board of Supervision, on the alleged destitution in the island of St. Kilda, in October, 1885, with supplementary reports by Lieutenant Osborne, R.N., commanding officer, and by the medical officer of H.M.S. *Jackal*. The report shows that, news from St. Kilda having reached Harris by means of letters enclosed in a small boat a yard long, found on the shore, to the effect that the corn, barley, and potatoes of the inhabitants had been destroyed by a great storm that had passed over the island early in September, and that, in consequence, the crofters of St. Kilda were suffering great privations, a steamer, the *Hebridean*, was despatched from Glasgow to the island with stores on the 13th of October, and, by arrangement with the Admiralty, H.M.S. *Jackal*, conveying Mr. McNeill, left Rothesay Bay for St. Kilda on Wednesday, October 21, 1885. Mr. McNeill reported that, so far from being destitute, the inhabitants of the island were amply, indeed luxuriously, supplied with food, and in possession of sums of money said to average not less than £20 a family. Dr. Acheson, of H.M.S. *Jackal*, reported that the inhabitants of St. Kilda were well-clad and well-fed, being much better off in these respects than the peasants in many other parts of Great Britain.'

Another newspaper paragraph not only confirms this, but adds to our knowledge of the island and its inhabitants. ' Mr. Malcolm McNeill . . . reported on the 24th of October that the population of St. Kilda—seventy-seven souls in all—were amply, "indeed, luxuriously," supplied with food for the winter. The supplies included sheep, fulmar, solan geese, meal, potatoes, milk, fish, tea, and sugar ; and a large sum of money, said to average not less than £20 a family, was known to be hoarded in the island—a large profit being derived from tourists. Mr. McNeill states that a former emigrant, who returned from Australia for a few months in 1884, spread discontent among the people, who now showed a strong desire to emigrate, and in this he suggested that the Government should assist them. Dr. Acheson of the *Jackal*, reporting on visits paid both then and in 1884, notes that the people seemed to be better clad and fed than the peasants of many other parts of Great Britain. He was struck by the comparatively large number of infirm persons—by the large number of women compared with men, and by the comparatively small number of children. The food was abundant, but lacked variety; was rather indigestible, and was nearly devoid of vegetables for six months each year. He saw no signs of vinegar, pepper, mustard, pickles, or other condiments, but there was a great liking for tobacco and spirits. The diet he pronounces quite unfit for children, aged persons, or invalids; and, to remedy this, he suggests that an endeavour should be made to grow cabbages, turnips, carrots, and other vegetables on the island; that fowls should be introduced, and that pressed vegetables and lime juice might be issued when no fresh vegetables are procurable. Judging from the amount of clothing worn, the doctor thinks the people are more likely to suffer from excess than from the other extreme, for, on September 14th, 1884, with the thermometer sixty-eight degrees Fahrenheit in the shade, he found a healthy adult male wearing "a thick tweed waistcoat, with flannel back and sleeves, two thick flannel undervests, tweed trousers, a flannel shirt, flannel drawers, boots, and stockings, Tam o' Shanter cap, and a thick, scarlet worsted muffler around his neck." The furniture he found scanty, and very rough, and the houses very dirty. St. Kilda is not a desirable retreat, for Dr. Acheson reports that at present there are no games nor music in the island, and—strangest fact of all in this official document—"whistling is strictly forbidden."'

A FASHIONABLE LADY'S LIFE.

HERE is a little poem by Dean Swift, published by him in Dublin, in 1728, and reprinted in London, in 1729. Its price was only fourpence, and it is called, 'The Journal of a Modern Lady, in a Letter to a Person of Quality.' It is so small, that it is absolutely lost in the Dean's voluminous works, yet it is very amusing, and, as far as I can judge (having made an especial study of the Social Life of the Eighteenth Century), it is not at all exaggerated; and for this reason I have ventured to reproduce it. It is borne out in similar descriptions both in the early and latter portions of the century; as, for instance, in 'The English Lady's Catechism,' 1703, of which the following is a portion:

HOW DO YOU EMPLOY YOUR TIME NOW?

'I lie in Bed till Noon, dress all the Afternoon, Dine in the Evening, and Play at Cards till Midnight.'
'How do you spend the Sabbath?'
'In Chit-Chat.'
'What do you talk of?'
'New Fashions and New Plays.'
'How often do you go to Church?'

'Twice a year or oftener, according as my Husband gives me new Cloaths.'

'Why do you go to Church when you have new Cloaths?'

'To see other People's Finery, and to show my own, and to laugh at those scurvy, out-of-fashion Creatures that come there for Devotion.'

'Pray, Madam, what Books do you read?'

'I read lewd Plays and winning Romances.'

'Who is it you love?'

'Myself.'

'What! nobody else?'

'My Page, my Monkey, and my Lap Dog.'

'Why do you love them?'

'Why, because I am an English lady, and they are Foreign Creatures: my Page from Genoa, my Monkey from the East Indies, and my Lap Dog from Vigo.'

'Would they not have pleased you as well if they had been English?'

'No, for I hate everything that Old England brings forth, except it be the temper of an English Husband, and the liberty of an English Wife. I love the French Bread, French Wines, French Sauces, and a French Cook; in short, I have all about me French or Foreign, from my Waiting Woman to my Parrot.'

'How do you pay your debts?'

'Some with money, and some with fair promises. I seldom pay anybody's bills, but run more into their debt. I give poor Tradesmen ill words, and the rich I treat civilly, in hopes to get further in their debt.'

Addison, in the *Spectator* (No. 323, March 11th, 1712), gives Clarinda's Journal for a week, from which I will only extract one day as a sample.

'WEDNESDAY. *From Eight to Ten.* Drank two Dishes of Chocolate in Bed, and fell asleep after 'em.

'*From Ten to Eleven.* Eat a Slice of Bread and Butter, drank a Dish of Bohea, read the *Spectator.*

'*From Eleven to One.* At my Toilet, try'd a new Head.[1] Gave orders for *Veney*[2] to be combed and washed. *Mem.* I look best in Blue.

'*From One till Half an Hour after Two.* Drove to the Change. Cheapened a couple of Fans.

'*Till Four.* At Dinner. *Mem.* Mr. Frost passed by in his new Liveries.

'*From Four to Six.* Dressed, paid a visit to old Lady Blithe and her Sister, having heard they were gone out of Town that Day.

'*From Six to Eleven.* At Basset.[3] *Mem.* Never sit again upon the Ace of Diamond.'

Gambling was one of the curses of the Eighteenth Century. From Royalty downwards, all played Cards—the men, perhaps, preferred dice, and 'Casting a Main'—but the women were inveterate card-players, until, in the latter part of the century, it became a national scandal, owing to the number of ladies who, from their social position, should have acted better, who kept Faro-tables, and to whom the nickname of *Faro's Daughters* was applied. There were Ladies Buckinghamshire and Archer, Mrs. Concannon, Mrs. Hobart, Mrs. Sturt, and others, whose houses were neither more nor less than gaming-houses. The evil was so great, that Lord Kenyon,

---

[1] Head-dress.   [2] Venus, her lap dog.
[3] A game at cards introduced into France by Signor Justiniani, Ambassador of Venice in 1674. The players are the dealer or banker, his assistant, who looks after the losing cards—a *croupier*, in fact—and the punters, or anyone who plays against the banker.

in delivering judgment in a trial to recover £15 won at card-playing, said that the higher classes set a bad example in this matter to the lower, and, he added, 'They think they are too great for the law; I wish they could be punished. If any prosecutions of this kind are fairly brought before me, and the parties are justly convicted, whatever be their rank or station in the country—though they be the first ladies in the land—they shall certainly exhibit themselves in the pillory.'

The caricaturists got hold of his Lordship's speech, and depicted Lady Archer and 'others in the pillory, and Lady Buckinghamshire being whipped at a cart's-tail by Lord Kenyon. With the century this kind of play died out; but some mention of it was necessary in order to show that Swift's description of ladies gambling was not exaggerated.

THE JOURNAL OF A MODERN LADY.

SIR,
 It was a most unfriendly Part
 In you who ought to know my Heart;
 And well acquainted with my Zeal
 For all the Females' Common-weal.
 How cou'd it come into your Mind
 To pitch on me of all Mankind,
 Against the Sex to write a Satire,
 And brand me for a Woman-Hater?
 On me, who think them all so fair,
 They rival Venus to a Hair:
 Their Virtues never ceas'd to sing,
 Since first I learn'd to tune a String.
 Methinks I hear the Ladies cry,
 Will he his Character belye?
 Must never our Misfortunes end?

And have we lost our only Friend?
Ah! lovely Nymph, remove your Fears,
No more let fall those precious Tears,
Sooner shall, etc.
(Here several verses are omitted.)
The Hound be hunted by the Hare,
Than I turn Rebel to the Fair.
. . . .

'Twas you engaged me first to write,
Then gave the Subject out of Spite.
The Journal of a Modern Dame,
Is by my Promise what you claim;
My Word is past, I must submit,
And yet perhaps you may be bit.
I but transcribe, for not a Line
Of all the Satire shall be mine.
Compell'd by you to tag in Rhimes
The common Slanders of the Times,
Of modern Times, the Guilt is yours
And me my Innocence secures:
Unwilling Muse, begin thy Lay,
The Annals of a Female Day.

By Nature turn'd to play the Rake well,
As we shall shew you in the Sequel;
The modern Dame is wak'd by Noon,
Some authors say not quite so soon;
Because, though sore against her Will,
She sat all Night up at Quadrill.[1]

---

[1] To understand the numerous allusions to the game of cards called Quadrill, it is necessary that the principles of the game should be given. It was played by four persons, each having ten cards dealt to them.

The general laws of this game are, 1. It is not permitted to deal the cards otherwise than four by three, the dealer being at liberty to begin with which of those numbers he pleases. 2. If he who plays either *sans prendre*, or calling a king, names a trump of a different suit from that his game is in, or names two several suits, that which he first named must be the trump. 3. He who plays must name the

She stretches, gapes, unglues her Eyes,
And asks if it be time to rise.
Of Head-ach and the Spleen complains;

trump by its proper name, as he likewise must the king he calls. 4. He who has said 'I pass,' must not be again admitted to play, except he plays by force, upon account of his having Spadille. 5. He who has asked the question, and has leave given him to play, is obliged to do it: but he must not play *sans prendre* except he is forced to do it. 6. He who has the four kings may call the queen of either of his kings. 7. Neither the king nor queen of the suit which is trumps must be called. 8. He who has one or several kings may call any king he has in his hand; in such case, if he wins, he alone must make six tricks; if he wins, it is all his own, and if he loses, he pays all by himself. 9. Everyone ought to play in his turn, but for having done otherwise, no one must be beasted. 10. He, however, whose turn is not to play, having in his hand the king the ombre has called, and who shall tramp about with either spadille, manille, or basto, or shall even play down the king that was called, to give notice of his being the friend, must not pretend to undertake the vole; nay, he must be condemned to be beasted if it appears that he did it with any fraudulent design. 11. He who has drawn a card from his game, and presented it openly in order to play it, is obliged so to do, if his retaining it may be either prejudicial to his game, or give any information to his friend, especially if the card is a matadore; but he who plays *sans prendre*, or calls upon his own king, is not subject to this law. 12. None ought to look upon the tricks, nor to count aloud what has been played, except when it is his turn to play, but to let everyone reckon for himself. 13. He who, instead of turning up the tricks before any one of his players, shall turn up and discover his game, must be equally beasted with him whose cards he has so discovered, the one paying one half, and the other the like. 14. He who renounces must be beasted, as many times as he has so done, but, if the cards are mixed, he is to pay but one beast. 15. If the renounce prejudices the game, and the deal is not played out, everyone may take up his cards, beginning at the trick where the renounce was made, and play them over again. 16. He who shows the game before the deal is out must be beasted, except he plays *sans prendre*. 17. None of the three matadores can be commanded down by an inferior trump. 18. If he who plays *sans prendre* with the matadores in his hand, demands only one of them, he must receive only that he mentioned. 19. He who, instead of *sans prendre*, shall demand matadores, not having them, or he who shall demand *sans prendres* instead of matadores, cannot compel the players to pay him

And then to cool her heated Brains,
Her Night-gown! and her Slippers brought her,
Takes a large Dram of Citron Water.
Then to her Glass; and, Betty, pray
Don't I look frightfully to-Day?
But, was it not confounded hard?
Well, if I ever touch a Card;
Four Mattadores, and lose Codill;
Depend upon't I never will!
But run to Tom, and bid him fix
The Ladies here to-Night by Six.
Madam, the Goldsmith waits below,
He says his Business is to know
If you'll redeem the Silver Cup
You pawn'd to him.   First, shew him up.
Your Dressing Plate he'll be content
To take for Interest Cent. per Cent.
And, Madam, there's my Lady Spade
Hath sent this Letter by her Maid.
Well, I remember what she won;
And hath she sent so soon to dun?
Here, carry down those ten Pistoles
My Husband left to pay for Coals:
I thank my Stars they are all light;
And I may have Revenge to-Night.
Now, loitering o'er her Tea and Cream,
She enters on her usual Theme;

what is really his due. 20. Matadores are only paid when they are in the hands of the ombre, or of the king his ally, whether all in one hand, or separately in both. 21. He who undertakes the vole, and does not make it, must pay as much as he would have received had he won it. 22. He who plays and does not make three tricks is to be beasted alone, and must pay all that is to be paid; and, if he makes no tricks at all, he must also pay to his two adversaries the vole, but not to his friend.'—*The Oxford Encyclopædia*, 1828.

1 Dressing-gown.

Her last Night's ill Success repeats,
Calls Lady Spade a hundred Cheats.
She slipt Spadillo in her Breast,
Then thought to turn it to a Jest.
There's Mrs. Cut and she combine,
And to each other give the Sign.
Through ev'ry Game pursues her Tale,
Like Hunters o'er their Evening Ale.
  Now to another Scene give Place,
Enter the Folks with Silks and Lace;
Fresh Matter for a World of Chat,
Right Indian this, right Macklin that;
Observe this Pattern; there's a Stuff,
I can have Customers enough.
Dear Madam, you are grown so hard,
This Lace is worth twelve Pounds a Yard;
Madam, if there be Truth in Man,
I never sold so cheap a Fan.
    This Business of Importance o'er,
And Madam, almost dress'd by Four;
The Footman, in his usual Phrase,
Comes up with: Madam, Dinner stays;
She answers in her usual Style,
The Cook must keep it back a while;
I never can have time to Dress,
No Woman breathing takes up less;
I'm hurried so, it makes me sick,
I wish the dinner at Old Nick.
At Table now she acts her part,
Has all the Dinner Cant by Heart:
I thought we were to Dine alone,
My Dear, for sure if I had known
This Company would come to-Day,
But really 'tis my Spouse's Way;
He's so unkind, he never sends
To tell, when he invites his Friends:

I wish ye may but have enough;
And while, with all this paultry Stuff,
She sits tormenting every Guest,
Nor gives her Tongue one Moment's Rest,
In Phrases batter'd stale and trite,
Which modern Ladies call polite;
You see the Booby Husband sit
In Admiration at her Wit.

    But let me now a while Survey
Our Madam o'er her Ev'ning Tea;
Surrounded with her Noisy Clans
Of Prudes, Coquets, and Harridans;
When frighted at the clamorous Crew,
Away the God of Silence flew;
And fair Discretion left the Place,
And Modesty with blushing Face;
Now enters over-weening Pride,
And Scandal ever gaping wide,
Hypocrisy with Frown severe,
Scurrility with gibing Air;
Rude Laughter seeming like to burst,
And Malice always judging worst;
And Vanity with Pocket-Glass,
And Impudence, with Front of Brass;
And studied Affectation came,
Each Limb and Feature out of Frame;
While Ignorance, with Brain of Lead,
Flew hov'ring o'er each Female Head.

    Why should I ask of thee, my Muse,
An Hundred Tongues, as Poets use,
When, to give ev'ry Dame her due,
An Hundred Thousand were too few!
Or how should I, alas! relate,
The Sum of all their Senseless Prate,
Their Inuendo's, Hints, and Slanders,
Their Meanings lewd, and double Entanders.[1]

[1] Entendres.

Now comes the general Scandal Charge,
What some invent, the rest enlarge;
And, Madam, if it be a Lye,
You have the tale as cheap as I:
I must conceal my Author's Name,
But now 'tis known to common Fame.
  Say, foolish Females, Old and Blind,
Say, by what fatal Turn of Mind,
Are you on Vices most severe,
Wherein yourselves have greatest Share?
Thus every Fool herself deludes,
The Prudes condemn the absent Prudes.
Mopsa who stinks her Spouse to Death,
Accuses Chloe's tainted Breath:
Hircina, rank with Sweat, presumes
To censure Phillis for Perfumes:
While crooked Cynthia swearing, says,
That Florimel wears Iron Stays.
Chloe's of ev'ry Coxcomb jealous,
Admires[1] how Girls can talk with Fellows,
And, full of Indignation, frets
That Women should be such Coquets.
Iris, for Scandal most notorious,
Cries, Lord, the world is so censorious;
And Rufa, with her Combs of Lead,[2]
Whispers that Sappho's Hair is Red.
Aura, whose Tongue you hear a Mile hence,
Talks half a day in Praise of Silence:
And Silvia, full of inward Guilt,
Calls Amoret an arrant Jilt.
  Now Voices over Voices rise;
While each to be the loudest vies,
They contradict, affirm, dispute,
No single Tongue one Moment mute;

---

[1] Wonders.
[2] These leaden combs were used for darkening the hair.

A FASHIONABLE LADY'S LIFE.

All mad to speak, and none to hearken,
They set the very Lap-Dog barking;
Their Chattering makes a louder Din
Than Fish-Wives o'er a Cup of Gin;
Not School-boys at a Barring-out,
Raised ever such incessant Rout:
The Shumbling (sic) Particles of Matter
In Chaos make not such a Clatter;
Far less the Rabble roar and rail,
When Drunk with sour Election Ale.

Nor do they trust their Tongue alone,
To speak a Language of their own;
Can read a Nod, a Shrug, a Look;
Far better than a printed Book;
Convey a Libel in a Frown,
And wink a Reputation down;
Or, by the tossing of the Fan,
Describe the Lady and the Man.

But, see the Female Club disbands,
Each, twenty Visits on her Hands:
Now, all alone, poor Madam sits,
In Vapours and Hysterick Fits;
And was not Tom this Morning sent?
I'd lay my Life he never went:
Past Six, and not a living Soul!
I might by this have won a Vole.
A dreadful Interval of Spleen!
How shall we pass the Time between?
Here, Betty, let me take my Drops,
And feel my Pulse, I know it stops:
This Head of mine, Lord, how it Swims!
And such a Pain in all my Limbs!
Dear Madam, try to take a Nap:
But now they hear a Foot-Man's Rap;
Go, run, and light the Ladies up;
It must be One before we Sup.

The Table, Cards, and Counters set,
And all the Gamester Ladies met,
Her Spleen and Fits recover'd quite,
Our Madam can sit up all Night;
Whoever comes, I'm not within,
Quadrill the Word, and so begin.

How can the Muse her Aid impart,
Unskill'd in all the Terms of Art?
Or, in harmonious Numbers, put
The Deal, the Shuffle, and the Cut?
The Superfluous Whims relate,
That fill a Female Gamester's Pate:
What Agony of Soul she feels
To see a Knave's inverted Heels;
She draws up Card by Card, to find
Good Fortune peeping from behind;
With panting Heart and earnest Eyes,
In hope to see Spadillo rise;
In vain, alas! her Hope is fed,
She draws an Ace, and sees it red.
In ready Counters never pays,
But pawns her Snuff-Box, Rings, and Keys.
Ever with some new Fancy struck,
Tries twenty Charms to mend her Luck.
This Morning when the Parson came,
I said I could not win a Game.
This odious Chair, how came I stuck in't?
I think I've never had good Luck in't.
I'm so uneasy in my Stays:
Your Fan, a Moment, if you please.
Stand further, Girl, or get you gone,
I always lose when you look on.
Lord! Madam, you have lost Codill;
I never saw you play so ill.
Nay, Madam, give me leave to say
'Twas you that threw the game away;

When Lady Tricksy play'd a Four,
You took it with a Matadore;
I saw you touch your Wedding-Ring
Before my Lady call'd a King.
You spoke a Word began with H,
And I know whom you mean to teach,
Because you held the King of Hearts;
Fie, Madam, leave these little Arts.
That's not so bad as one that rubs
Her Chair to call the King of Clubs,
And makes her Partner understand
A Matadore is in her Hand.
Madam, you have no Cause to flounce,
I swear I saw you twice renounce.
And truly, Madam, I know when
Instead of Five you scor'd me Ten.
Spadillo here has got a Mark,
A Child may know it in the Dark:
I Guess the Hand, it seldom fails,
I wish some Folks would pare their Nails.

  While thus they rail, and scold, and storm,
It passes but for common Form;
Are conscious that they all speak true,
And give each other but their due;
It never interrupts the Game,
Or makes 'em sensible of Shame.

  Time too precious now to waste,
The Supper gobbled up in haste:
Again a-fresh to Cards they run,
As if they had but just begun;
Yet shall I not again repeat
How oft they Squabble, Snarl, and Cheat:
At last they hear the Watchman Knock,
A frosty Morn . . . *Past Four a-clock.*
The Chair-men are not to be found,
Come, let us play the t'other Round.

Now all in haste they huddle on
Their Hoods, their Cloaks, and get them gone;
But first, the Winner must invite
The Company to-morrow Night.
　Unlucky Madam left in Tears,
Who now again Quadrill forswears,
With empty Purse and aching Head,
Steals to her sleeping Spouse to Bed.

GEORGE BARRINGTON.

HERE is much and curious food for reflection, in the tendency that mankind has ever shown to sympathise with the daring and ingenious depredators who relieve the rich of their superfluity, which may possibly be owing to the romantic adventures and hair-breadth escapes which the robbers, in their career, have undergone. But, be the cause what it may, it is certain that the populace of all nations view with admiration great and successful thieves: for instance, what greater popular hero, and one that has been popular for centuries, could be found than Robin Hood?

Almost every country in Europe has its traditional thief, whose exploits are recorded both in prose and poetry. In England, Claude Duval, Captain Hind, Dick Turpin, Jonathan Wild, and Jack Sheppard have each in their turn occupied a prominent place in the annals of crime; whilst in France, amongst the light-fingered heroes that have, from time to time, extorted respect from the multitude, Cartouche and Vidocq take first rank. Germany is proud of its Schinderhannes, the Robber of the Rhine, the stories of whose generosity and courage still render his memory a favourite on the banks of that river, the travellers on which he so long kept in awe. In Italy and Spain, those homes of brigands and banditti, the inhabitants have ever-ready sympathy for the men whose names and exploits are as familiar among them as 'household words,'

Cartouche, however, is the only rival to Barrington in their particular line, and Barrington, certainly, was no mere common pick-pocket, only fit to figure in the 'Newgate Calendar,' but he possessed talents which, had they been properly directed on his first setting out in life, might have enabled him to have played a distinguished part either in literature or in business. But, unfortunately, very early in his youth, poverty led him to adopt theft as his professed vocation; and, by his ingenuity and constant practice, he contrived to render himself so expert, as almost to have conducted his depredations on systematic rules, and elevated his crime into a 'high art.' Barrington, too, by his winning manners, gentlemanly address, and the fair education he contrived to pick up, was a man eminently fitted (if such an expression may be allowed) for his profession! his personal appearance was almost sufficient to disarm suspicion, and this, in all probability, contributed greatly to the success which he met with in his career.

George Barrington, or Waldron (for it is not known which was his right name), was born on the 14th of May, 1755, at the village of Maynooth, county Kildare, in Ireland, now famous for the Royal College of St. Patrick, which is there situated. His reputed father was Henry Waldron, who was a working silversmith, and his mother, whose maiden name was

Naish, was a dressmaker, or mantua-maker, as it was then called (also occasionally acting as midwife), in the same village; but, whether they had ever been legally united, is a matter open to doubt.

To have their parentage disputed is a fate which the great ones of the earth have frequently to undergo, and George Barrington, or Waldron, is an instance of this, for more than one of his historians assert that he was the son of a Captain Barrington, an officer in a marching regiment quartered at Rush, and the date of his birth is given as 1758; but the most trustworthy evidence places it on record as above stated.

His parents' characters stood high among their neighbours for integrity and industry, but they were, unfortunately, always behindhand with the world, and never able to extricate themselves from the state of abject poverty in which they were sunk, in consequence of unsuccessful litigation with a wealthy relation. This want of means prevented them from giving George any education until he was seven years of age, when he was sent to the village school, and there was taught to read and write. A benevolent surgeon in the neighbourhood afterwards instructed him in arithmetic, geography, and grammar; but, if the anecdote related of him is true, he repaid the kindness by the blackest ingratitude in stealing some coins from his benefactor's daughter.

Young Waldron was lucky enough to attract the notice of the Rev. Dr. Westropp, a dignitary of the Church of Ireland, who placed him, when he was sixteen years of age, at a grammar-school in Dublin, and this patron proposed that he should fit himself for the university. But fate had decreed otherwise and he enjoyed the benefits of this gentleman's kindness but a short time, for, in a moment of passion, when quarrelling with another boy, he stabbed his antagonist with a pen-knife, wounding him severely. Instead of making the matter one for legal investigation, the boy received a thorough good flogging, a degradation he could by no means forgive, and he resolved to run away from school, and leave family, friends, and all his fair prospects behind him. But, previous to carrying his plan of escape into action, he found means to appropriate ten or twelve guineas belonging to the master of the school, and a gold repeating-watch, which was the property of his master's sister. Not content with this booty, he took a few shirts and pairs of stockings, and safely effected his retreat, one still night in 1771, starting off for Drogheda.

There happened to be staying at the obscure inn at which he put up, on his arrival at Drogheda, a set of strolling players, whose manager was one John Price, who had once been a lawyer's clerk, and had been convicted of some fraud at the Old Bailey. He soon wormed the boy's whole story out of him, and persuaded him to join the theatrical company, which he did, and he applied himself to study so diligently that he was cast for the part, and played, four days after his enrolment, Jaffier in Otway's tragedy of 'Venice Preserved,' in a barn in the suburbs of Drogheda. Both he and Price were of opinion that it would be dangerous for him to remain so near the scene of his late depredations, but were unable to move for want of money. To overcome this difficulty, Waldron, who had assumed the name of Barrington, gave Price the gold repeater he had stolen, which was sold for the benefit of the company, and they set out for Londonderry.

But it was found that the expenses of travelling for so numerous a body, with their *impedimenta*, were too great to be balanced by the receipts of rural audiences, and, on their arrival at Londonderry, their finances were found to be at a very low ebb indeed. Under these circumstances, Price insinuated that Barrington, with his good address and appearance, could easily introduce himself to the chief places of resort in the city, and, by picking pockets, might refill their empty exchequer. This scheme he at once put into practice, with such success that, at the close of the evening, he was the possessor of about forty guineas in cash, and one hundred and fifty pounds in Irish bank-notes.

The picking of pockets being a crime almost unknown in that part of Ireland, the town took the alarm, and a great stir was made over the matter; but it being fair-time, and many strangers in the city, neither Barrington nor Price were suspected; still they thought it but prudent to leave as soon as they could with propriety, and, after playing a few more nights, they moved to Ballyshannon. For some time he continued this vagabond life, travelling about the North of Ireland, acting every Tuesday and Saturday, and picking pockets every day in the week, a business which he found more lucrative and entertaining than that of the theatre, where his fame was by no means equal to the expectation he had raised.

At Cork, Price and he came to the conclusion never to think any more of the stage, a resolution which was the more easily executed, as the company to which they originally belonged was now broken up and dispersed. It was settled between them that Price should pass for Barrington's servant, and that Barrington should act the part of a young gentleman of large fortune and of noble family, who was not yet quite of age, travelling for his amusement. They carried out their scheme well, purchasing horses and dressing up to their parts, and, during the summer and autumn of 1772, they visited all the race-courses in the South of Ireland, making a remarkably successful campaign. Pocket-picking was a novel experience to the Irish gentry, and their unsuspicious ways made them an easy prey to Barrington's skill and nimble fingers; so much so that when, at the setting-in of winter, they returned to Cork, they found themselves in possession of a large sum of money (over £1,000), having been fortunate enough to have escaped detection or even suspicion.

At length their partnership was rudely dissolved, as, at the close of winter, Price was detected in the very act of picking a gentleman's pocket at Cork, and for this offence he was sentenced to be transported to America (as was customary then) for seven years. Barrington immediately converted all his moveable property into cash, and beat a precipitate flight to Dublin, where, for a time, he lived a very private and retired life, only stealing out occasionally of a dark night to visit some gaming-house, where he might pick up a few guineas, or a watch, etc., a mode of life which was by no means congenial to his ambitious nature, and he again frequented the race-courses. He met with his first check at Carlow, where he was detected in picking a nobleman's pocket. It was a clear case; the stolen property was found on his person, and immediately restored to its owner, who did not prosecute, preferring to let the rascal receive the treatment known as 'the discipline of the course,' a punishment very similar to that meted out to 'Welchers' at the present day. But Ireland was getting too warm for him, and, having realised his property, he set sail for London, where he arrived in the summer of 1773, a remarkably precocious youth of eighteen.

On his voyage across the Channel, he became acquainted with several persons of respectability, with one of whom he travelled post to London, having gulled him with a specious tale about his family and fortune; and, having gained his confidence, he procured by his means introductions into the politest circles, from whom, for a long time, he extracted abundant plunder. But, in order to do this, he had to dress well, and live extravagantly, so that he very soon had to cast about for the means wherewith to supply his needs. Among the earliest visits he paid, after his arrival in London, and in his friend's company, was, of course, Ranelagh, where he found two of his acquaintance on the Irish packet talking to the Duke of Leinster. Bowing to them, and stationing himself near them, he soon eased the duke of above eighty pounds, a baronet of five-and-thirty guineas, and one of the ladies of her watch; and, with this plunder, he rejoined his party as if nothing had happened out of the ordinary course of things.

But his proceedings had been watched by another member of the thieving fraternity, who was in the gardens, and who took a speedy opportunity of letting Barrington know that he had witnessed his crime, and threatened to denounce him to the plundered parties, unless a division of the spoil was made between them. His manner being very impressive, left Barrington no alternative but to comply; and the lady's watch and chain, with a ten-pound note, fell to his share. The two supped together, and it ended with their entering into a mutual alliance, which, for the time, suited Barrington well, as his companion knew town much better than he did, and was especially well-informed in the knowledge of those places where the plunder could be disposed of: but this partnership only continued for a short time, in consequence of their quarrels, there being nothing in common to bind these two rogues together save their crime.

In the course of his depredations, he visited Brighton, or, as it was then called, Brighthelmstone, which was beginning to be the resort of the wealthier classes, but, as yet, had not dreamed of the rise it was to take under George the Magnificent—and no conception could have been formed of the present 'London-on-the-Sea.' Here, thanks to his pleasant manners and address, as well as to the company he frequented, he became acquainted, and intimate, with the Duke of Ancaster, Lord Ferrers, Lord Lyttleton, and many other noblemen, who all considered him as a man of genius and ability (which he certainly was), and were under the impression that he was a gentleman of fortune and family.

His manners were good, and he had a pleasant wit —so that it is not difficult to imagine that his society was welcome. As a specimen of his wit, I may relate an anecdote told of him when on a visit to Chichester from Brighton. In company of several noblemen, he was shown the curiosities and notable things in the town and cathedral. In the latter, their attention was directed to a family vault for the interment of the Dukes of Richmond, which had been erected by the late duke, and which was inscribed 'Domus ultima' (the last house). On this inscription he is said to have written the following epigram:

> 'Did he, who thus inscribed this wall,
> Not *read*, or not *believe*, St. Paul?
> Who says, "There is, where e'er it stands,
> *Another* house, not made with hands;"
> Or shall we gather, from the words,
> That *House* is not a *House* of Lords.'

After living at the expense of the pockets of his new-found friends as long as he deemed it prudent, he returned to London, and began a dissolute and profligate career; but, though his time was pretty well employed between his infamous occupation and his amusements, he yet found opportunity for intervals of study and literary pursuits, and composed several odes and poems, which are said to have been not devoid of merit.

As before stated, he broke with his partner, who retired to a monastery, where, in all probability, he ended his days in penitence and peace. But, in the winter of 1775, Barrington became acquainted with one Lowe, whom he first employed in the useful capacity of receiver of stolen goods, and afterwards went into partnership with. This Lowe was a singular character. Originally he had been a livery-servant, and after that he kept a public-house for some time, when, having saved some money, he turned usurer or money-lender, in which business he accumulated a small fortune, when he assumed the character of a gentleman, and lived in a genteel house near Bloomsbury Square, then a fashionable neighbourhood. Here he passed for a very charitable and benevolent person, and was appointed treasurer or manager of a new hospital for the blind in Kentish Town, in which capacity, it is said, he contrived to become possessed of some five thousand pounds, when he set fire to the institution. Being suspected thereof, he was apprehended at Liverpool, in 1779, when he committed suicide by taking poison, and was buried at a cross-road, in the neighbourhood of Prescott in Lancashire.

On forming his partnership with Lowe, it was resolved on between them that Barrington should repair to Court on the Queen's birthday, disguised as a clergyman, and there endeavour not only to pick the pockets of the company, but, what was a far bolder and more novel attempt, to cut off the diamond stars of the Knights of the Garter, Bath, or Thistle, who on such days generally wore the ribands of their respective orders over their coats. In this enterprise he succeeded beyond the most sanguine expectations that could have been formed, either by himself or his partner; for he managed to take a diamond star from a nobleman, and to get away from St. James's unsuspected. But this prize was too valuable to dispose of in England, and it is said to have been sold to a Dutch Jew, who came over from Holland twice a year on purpose to buy stolen goods, for eight hundred pounds. This haul only whetted his appetite for yet more profitable plunder, and a chance of his skill shortly presented itself.

In the course of the winter of 1775, Prince Orloff, a Russian nobleman of the first rank and consequence, visited England. The splendour in which he lived, and the stories of his immense wealth, were frequently noticed and commented on in the public prints, and attention was particularly drawn to a gold snuff-box, set with brilliants, which was one of the many marks of favour showered upon him by Catherine, Empress of Russia, and which was generally valued at the enormous sum of between thirty and forty thousand pounds. This precious trinket excited Barrington's cupidity in an extraordinary degree, and he determined to exert himself, in order, by some means or other, to get it into his possession.

A favourable opportunity occurred one night at Covent Garden Theatre, where he contrived to get near the prince, and dexterously conveyed the treasure from his excellency's waistcoat pocket (in which, according to Russian custom, it was usually carried) into his own. This operation was not, however, performed with sufficient delicacy to escape detection, for the prince felt the attack that was so impudently made upon his property, and, having reason to entertain some suspicion of Barrington, he immediately seized him by the collar. During the confusion that naturally ensued upon such an unusual scene, Barrington slipped the box into the hand of the prince, who, doubtless, was only too rejoiced to recover it with so much ease. The thief, however, was secured, and committed to Tothill Fields Bridewell.[1]

When examined before Sir John Fielding, Barrington trumped up a story that he was a native of Ireland, of an affluent and respectable family; that he had been educated for the medical profession, and had come to England to improve himself by means

[1] Pulled down 1885.

of his connections. This story, which was told with extreme modesty and many tears, induced the prince to think of him more as an unfortunate gentleman than a guilty culprit, and he declined to proceed against him, so that he was dismissed, with an admonition from Sir John to amend his future conduct; and he must have left the court congratulating himself on his narrow, but lucky, escape. The publicity which was given to this attempt lost him the society of most of his friends, as he was held up to view in the disgraceful light of an impostor; and it also was the means of giving him a further taste of prison discipline.

In the pursuit of his peculiar industry, he frequented both Houses of Parliament, where he acquired considerable plunder. Some weeks after the Covent Garden affair, he was in the House of Lords during an interesting debate that attracted a great number of people, amongst whom was a gentleman who recognised Barrington, and who informed the Deputy Usher of the Black Rod of his probable business there. That official promptly ejected him, though, perhaps, not with the gentleness that he considered his due, and he uttered such threats of vengeance against his accuser that the latter made application to a magistrate, who granted a warrant to take Barrington into custody, and to bind him over to keep the peace. But his credit was now sunk so low that none of his former companions would come forward with the necessary sureties, and Barrington, in default, was relegated to his former place of detention, Tothill Fields Bridewell, where he remained a considerable time before he was released.

During his incarceration, the story of his misdeeds

was industriously circulated, and his character as *bon camarade* was completely destroyed, so that the entry to all decent company was absolutely shut against him, and from this time forward he was obliged to abandon the *rôle* of a 'gentleman' pickpocket, and descend to all the mean artifices of a common pilferer. Even in this humble branch of his infamous industry, his good fortune seems to have deserted him, for he was detected in picking the pocket of a low woman at Drury Lane Theatre in December, 1776, and, though he made a remarkably clever speech in his defence, he was sentenced to three years of ballast-heaving, or hard labour in the hulks at Woolwich. Here, herded with the vilest of the vile, he kept as much as possible from them, and, by his good conduct, attracted the attention of the superintendents of convicts, and by their intervention he was set free, after having sustained an imprisonment of somewhat less than twelve months.

On his liberation, he lost no time in re-commencing his vicious occupation, under various disguises, sometimes as a quack doctor, or as a clergyman; or he would assume the character of a grave commercial traveller, only to appear, a few days later on, as the keeper of a gambling-house, and he had many a narrow escape from capture.

Justice, however, again laid her hands upon him, for, less than six months after his liberation, he was detected in picking the pocket of one, Elizabeth Ironmonger, of a watch, was convicted on the clearest evidence, and, in spite of the very eloquent and skilful defence he made, he was a second time sentenced to the hulks with hard labour, this time for five years. His speeches to the court, which were remarked in the public prints, as well as the letters that he wrote seeking mitigation of his punishment, display such talent that it is a matter of great regret that it was not turned to more honest account. On one occasion, when tried for stealing Sir G. Webster's purse at the opera, in February, 1784, he was able, by his eloquence, to influence the jury to return a verdict of not guilty; and a similar piece of good fortune was vouchsafed to him a year after, when arraigned for the robbery of a gentleman's watch at Drury Lane Theatre, when his most ingenious and well-chosen address to the jury resulted in his acquittal.

He could not stand his second imprisonment on the hulks, and to end it he attempted suicide by stabbing himself in the breast with a pen-knife. Medical aid was at hand, and the wound slowly healed, but he still continued to linger in a miserable state, until he came under the notice of a gentleman of position, who used his influence with the government so successfully that he obtained Barrington's release, subject to the condition that he should leave the country. His benefactor also gave him money for that purpose, and he was soon on the Chester coach, *en route* for Ireland. When he arrived in Dublin, he found his character had preceded him, and he was so closely watched that it was not long before he was again arrested, and acquitted only from want of evidence. The judge admonished him most seriously, which gave Barrington an opportunity of airing his eloquence, and he delivered an oration on the unaccountable force of prejudice that existed against him; but, when once he got away, he came to the conclusion that the Irish capital was not a desirable place of residence for him, so he travelled northwards, and ultimately reached Edinburgh.

However, the police of that city knew all about him, and were more vigilant than their *confrères* in London and Dublin, so that Barrington, finding himself both suspected and watched, came to the conclusion that the air of Scotland was not good for him, and turned his face southward. Unmindful of the terms of his liberation, or careless as to the result of his return, he again sought London, where, once more, he frequented the theatres, the opera-house, and the Pantheon, for some little time, with tolerable success—but he was now too notorious to be long secure; he was closely watched, and well-nigh detected at the latter of these places; and, such strong suspicions of his behaviour were entertained by the magistrates, he was committed to Newgate, though on his trial he was acquitted.

But he only escaped Scylla to be engulphed in Charybdis, for one of the superintendents of convicts had him detained for violating the conditions under which he was liberated, and the consequence was that he was made what was called 'a fine in Newgate,' that is, he had to serve out his unexpired term of imprisonment there. This punishment he duly suffered, and when he was once more set free, he at once re-commenced his old practices, and lived a life of shifts and roguery, until, in January, 1787, he was detected in picking the pocket of a Mrs. Le Mesurier, at Drury Lane Theatre, and was at once apprehended. He was given in charge of a constable named Blandy, but by some means, either by negligence of his custodian, or by bribing him, he made his escape.

For this he was outlawed, and, whilst the offended majesty of the law was thus seeking to vindicate itself, he was making a progress of the northern counties under various disguises, sometimes appearing as a quack doctor, or a clergyman, then in connection with a gaming-table, and occasionally playing the *rôle* of a rider (as commercial travellers were then called) for some manufacturing firm. Although frequently meeting with people who knew him, he was never molested by them, until he was recognised at Newcastle (whilst being examined in the justice-room there, regarding a theft he had committed) by a gentleman from London as being 'wanted' for the robbery at Drury Lane Theatre, and he was promptly despatched to Bow Street once more. On his arrival, he was committed to Newgate as an outlaw, and, miserable and dejected, his spirits sank within him. His friends, however (for even he had friends) made up a purse of a hundred guineas for his defence. His trial took place in November, 1789, when he conducted his own defence, as usual, with extraordinary ability, arguing the various points of law with the judge with surprising acuteness and elegant language, till, eventually, being aided by the absence of a material witness, he made such an impression upon the court that a verdict of acquittal was recorded.

All these escapes, however, seem to have had no deterrent effect upon him, and he again set off for Ireland, where he joined an accomplice named Hubert, who was speedily apprehended, in the act of picking a pocket, and sentenced to seven years transportation. Dublin after this was far too hot for Barrington, so he adroitly made his escape to England, where, after rambling about the country for some time, he re-appeared in London. But he had not been in the metropolis very long before he was apprehended, as his indictment says, for 'stealing on the 1st of September, 1780, in the parish of Enfield, in the county of Middlesex, a gold watch, chain, seals, and a metal key, the property of Henry Hare Townsend.' The case was very clear, but Barrington defended himself very ingeniously, and with a certain amount of oratory, of which the following is a sample:

'I am well convinced of the noble nature of a British Court of Justice; the dignified and benign principles of its judges, and the liberal and candid spirit of its jurors.

'Gentlemen, life is the gift of God, and liberty its greatest blessing; the power of disposing of both or either is the greatest man can enjoy. It is also adventitious that, great as that power is, it cannot be better placed than in the hands of an English jury; for they will not exercise it like tyrants, who delight in blood, but like generous and brave men, who delight to spare rather than destroy; and who, forgetting they are men themselves, lean, when they can, to the side of compassion. It may be thought, gentlemen of the jury, that I am appealing to your passions, and, if I had the power to do it, I would not fail to employ it. The passions animate the heart, and to the passions we are indebted for the noblest actions, and to the passions we owe our dearest and finest feelings; and, when it is considered, the mighty power you now possess, whatever leads to a cautious and tender discharge of it, must be thought of great consequence: as long as the passions conduct us on the side of benevolence, they are our best, our safest, and our most friendly guides.'

But all his eloquence was thrown away on a jury of practical men, and they found him guilty. His trial took place on the 15th of September, 1790, and on the 22nd of September he received his sentence, which was seven years' transportation. He took his leave dramatically, and made a speech lamenting his hard fate throughout life.

'The world, my Lord, has given me credit for abilities, indeed much greater than I possess, and, therefore, much more than I deserved; but I have never found any kind hand to foster those abilities.

' I might ask, where was the generous and powerful hand that was ever stretched forth to rescue George Barrington from infamy? In an age like this, which, in several respects, is so justly famed for liberal sentiments, it was my severe lot that no noble-minded gentleman stepped forward and said to me, " Barrington, you are possessed of talents which may be useful to society. I feel for your situation, and, as long as you act the part of a good citizen, I will be your protector; you will then have time and opportunity to rescue yourself from the obloquy of your former conduct."

' Alas, my Lord, George Barrington had never the supreme felicity of having such comfort administered to his wounded spirit. As matters have unfortunately turned out, the die is cast; and, as it is, I bend, resigned to my fate, without one murmur or complaint.'

Thus ended his life in England, which he was never to see again, and it is with pleasure that we can turn to a brighter page in his history.

In his account of his voyage to New South Wales, he says that it was with unspeakable satisfaction that he received orders to embark, agreeably to his sentence; and it is pleasing to observe that, under his adverse circumstances, the friends he had made in his prosperity did not forsake him in his adversity, for many of them came to bid him adieu, and not one of them came empty-handed; in fact, their generosity was so great, that he had difficulty in getting permission to take all their gifts on board.

His account of their embarkation gives us an extremely graphic description not only of the treatment of convicts, but of the unhappy wretches themselves.

'About a quarter before five, a general muster took place, and, having bid farewell to my fellow-prisoners, we were escorted from the prison to Blackfriars Bridge by the City Guard, where two lighters were waiting to receive us. This procession, though early, and but few spectators, made a deep impression on my mind, and the ignominy of being thus mingled with felons of all descriptions, many scarce a degree above the brute creation, intoxicated with liquor, and shocking the ears of those they passed with blasphemy, oaths, and songs, the most offensive to modesty, inflicted a punishment more severe than the sentence of my country, and fully avenged that society I had so much wronged.'

And there is little doubt but that the moral repugnance to his miserable, and vicious companions was mainly the cause of the reformation which took place in him.

The condition of convicts at that day was not enviable. There were two hundred and fifty of them in the ship with Barrington, all packed in the hold, their hammocks being slung within seventeen inches of each other: being encumbered with their irons, and deprived of fresh air, their condition was soon rendered deplorable. To alleviate their sufferings as much as possible, they were permitted to walk the deck (as much as was consistent with the safety of the ship), ten at a time; and the women, of whom there were six on board, had a snug berth to themselves. But, in spite of this humane and considerate treatment, thirty-six of them died on the voyage.

Barrington, however, was not in such evil case, for a friend had accompanied him on board, and, by his influence and exertions, had not only procured stowage for his packages, but also liberty to walk the deck unencumbered with irons. Nor did his help stop here, for he prevailed upon the boatswain to admit him into his mess, which consisted of the second mate, carpenter, and gunner, on condition that he paid his proportion towards defraying the extra requisites for the mess during the voyage. The boatswain, too, had his hammock slung next to his own, so that his life was made as comfortable as it could be, under the circumstances, and he had not to herd with the convicts.

Soon after leaving the Bay of Biscay, these gentlemen began to give trouble. The captain, very humanely, had released many of the weaker convicts of their galling chains, and allowed them to walk on deck, ten at a time. Two of them, who were Americans, and had some knowledge of navigation, prevailed upon the majority of their comrades to attempt to seize the ship, impressing upon them that it would be an easy task, and that when captured, they would sail to America, where every man would not only obtain his liberty, but receive a tract of land from Congress, besides a share of the money arising from the sale of the ship and cargo.

The poor dupes swallowed the bait, and the mutineers determined that on the first opportunity, whilst the officers were at dinner, those convicts who were on deck should force the arm-chest, which was kept on the quarter-deck, and, at the same time, would make a signal to two of them to attack the sentinels, and obtain possession of their arms, while word was passed for those below to come on deck. And, as they planned, so they carried out the mutiny: when the captain and officers were below examining the stowage of some wine—a cask, in the spirit-room, being leaky—and the only persons on deck were Barrington and the man at the helm.

Barrington was going forward, but was stopped by one of the Americans, followed by another convict, who struck at him with a sword, which luckily hit against a pistol that the American had pointed at him. Barrington snatched up a handspike, and felled one of them, and the steersman left his wheel and called up the captain and crew. For a few moments Barrington kept the mutineers at bay, when assistance came—and a blunderbuss being fired amongst the convicts, wounding several, they retreated, and were all driven into the hold. An attempt of this kind required the most exemplary punishment; and two of the ring-leaders, with very short shrift, were soon dangling at the yard-arm, whilst others were tasting the cat-o'-nine-tails at the gangway.

The mutiny having been thus quelled, and the

convicts re-ironed, the captain had leisure to thank Barrington, and to compliment him on his gallant behaviour in the emergency. He assured Barrington that, when they arrived at the Cape, he would reward him, and that, meanwhile, he was to have every liberty; and orders were given to the steward to supply him with anything he might have occasion for during the voyage. As Barrington observes:

'I soon experienced the good effects of my late behaviour; as seldom a day passed but some fresh meat or poultry was sent to me by the captain, which considerably raised me in the estimation of my messmates, who were no ways displeased at the substitution of a sea-pie of fowl or fresh meat to a dish of lobsconse, or a piece of salt-junk.'

On the ship's arrival at the Cape, the captain gave Barrington an order on a merchant there for one hundred dollars, telling him he might at any time avail himself of the ship's boat going ashore, and visit the town as often as he pleased, if he would only tell the officers when he felt so inclined. It is needless to say he fully availed himself of his privilege, and laid out his money in the purchase of goods most in demand in New South Wales.

On reaching Port Jackson, in consequence of the captain's report, he had a most gracious reception from the governor, who, finding him a man of ability and intelligence, almost immediately appointed him superintendent of the convicts at Paramatta: his business being chiefly to report the progress made in the different works that were carried on there. Here he had ample leisure and opportunities of studying the natives and their habits and customs, and in his 'History of New South Wales,' he gives an interesting account of the aborigines of Australia, now so rapidly approaching extinction. The governor, Philip, made unceasing efforts to win their friendship, and even went to the extent of forcing his acquaintance on them, by the summary method of capturing a few, and keeping them in friendly durance; hoping thus to gain their good-will, so that, on their release, they might report to their friends that the white man was not so bad as he was represented. But it was all in vain; for, beyond a very few converts to civilisation, the savage remained untameable.

By the purchases which Barrington had made at the Cape, as well as the presents he had brought from England, he was enabled to furnish his house in a rather better style than his neighbours, and, moreover, he managed to collect around him a few farm-yard animals, which, together with his great love for horticulture, made his life far from unendurable. His position, as peace-officer of the district, was no sinecure; for the criminal population over whom he had jurisdiction gave him very considerable trouble, more especially after the introduction into the settlement, by some American vessels, of New England rum, the baneful effects of which were very soon apparent: the partiality of the convicts for it being incredible, for they preferred receiving it as the price of their labour to any other article, either of provisions or clothing.

Barrington's tact and good management in the numerous disturbances that arose, as more convicts were poured into the station, were very conspicuous, and his conduct was altogether such as compensated, in a great measure, for his former misdeeds. His domestic matters improved by degrees, so that his situation was equal, if not preferable, to that of most of the settlers there, and, to crown all, in September, 1799, the Governor—Hunter—presented him with an absolute pardon, complimenting him on his faithful discharge of the duties which had been entrusted to him, and the integrity and uniform uprightness of his conduct, and, furthermore, said that his general behaviour, during his whole residence, perfectly obliterated every trace of his former indiscretions.

Barrington was further appointed a principal superintendent of the district of Paramatta, with a permanent salary of £50 per annum (his situation having been, hitherto, only provisional) and, eventually, the confidence he inspired was such that he was raised to the office of Chief of the constabulary force of the Colony, on the principle, it may be presumed, of 'setting a thief to catch a thief.' In this post he gave great satisfaction, and died, much respected by all who knew him, at Botany Bay.

He wrote 'The History of New South Wales,' &c. London, 1802; a most valuable and interesting book. 'An Account of a Voyage to New South Wales,' London, 1803. 'The History of New Holland,' London, 1808; and a book was published with his name as author, 'The London Spy,' which went through several editions.

MILTON'S BONES.

N the first series of *Notes and Queries*, vol. v. p. 369 (April 17, 1852), is a note from which the following is an extract: 'In vol. v, p. 275, mention is made of Cromwell's skull; so it may not be out of place to tell you that I have handled one of Milton's ribs. Cowper speaks indignantly of the desecration of our divine poet's grave, on which shameful occurrence some of the bones were clandestinely distributed. One fell to the lot of an old and esteemed friend, and between forty-five and fifty years ago, at his house, not many miles from London, I have often examined the said rib-bone.'

The lines of Cowper's to which he refers were written in August, 1790, and are entitled

STANZAS

On the late indecent Liberties taken with the remains of the great Milton. Anno 1790.

'Me too, perchance, in future days,
The sculptured stone shall show,
With Paphian myrtle or with bays
Parnassian on my brow.

But I, or ere that season come,
Escaped from every care,

Shall reach my refuge in the tomb,
And sleep securely there.'[1]

So sang, in Roman tone and style,
The youthful bard, ere long
Ordain'd to grace his native isle
With her sublimest song.

Who then but must conceive disdain,
Hearing the deed unblest,
Of wretches who have dared profane
His dread sepulchral rest?

Ill fare the hands that heaved the stones
Where Milton's ashes lay,
That trembled not to grasp his bones
And steal his dust away!

O ill-requited bard! neglect
Thy living worth repaid,
And blind idolatrous respect
As much affronts thee dead.

Leigh Hunt possessed a lock of Milton's hair which had been given to him by a physician—and over which he went into such rhapsodies that he composed no less than three sonnets addressed to the donor—which may be found in his 'Foliage,' ed. 1818, pp. 131, 132, 133. The following is the best:—

TO —— —— M.D.,
On his giving me a lock of Milton's hair.

It lies before me there, and my own breath
Stirs its thin outer threads, as though beside
The living head I stood in honoured pride,

---

[1] Forsitan et nostros ducat de marmore vultus
Nectens aut Paphia myrti aut Parnasside lauri
Fronde comas—At ego secura pace quiescam.
Milton in Manso.

Talking of lovely things that conquered death.
Perhaps he pressed it once, or underneath
Ran his fine fingers, when he leant, blank-eyed,
And saw, in fancy, Adam and his bride
With their heaped locks, or his own Delphic wreath.
There seems a love in hair, though it be dead.
It is the gentlest, yet the strongest thread
Of our frail plant—a blossom from the tree
Surviving the proud trunk;—as if it said,
Patience and Gentleness is Power. In me
Behold affectionate eternity.

How were these personal relics obtained? By rifling his tomb. Shakespeare solemnly cursed any-one who should dare to meddle with his dead body, and his remains are believed to be intact.

' Good friend, for Jesus' sake, forbear
To dig the dust inclosed here :
Blest be the man who spares these stones,
And cursed be he who moves my bones.'

But Milton laid no such interdict upon his poor dead body and it was not very long after his burial, which took place in 1674, that the stone which cover-ed it, and indicated his resting-place, was removed, as Aubrey tells us in his 'Lives' (vol. iii, p. 450). 'His stone is now removed. About two years since (1681) the two steppes to the communion-table were raysed, Ighesse, Jo. Speed,[1] and he lie together.' And so it came to pass that, in the church of St. Giles', Cripple-gate, where he was buried, there was no memorial of the place where he was laid, nor, indeed, anything to mark the fact of his burial in that church until, in

[1] John Speed, the historian, died 1629, and was buried in the church of St. Giles', Cripplegate.

1793, Samuel Whitbread set up a fine marble bust of the poet, by Bacon, with an inscription giving the dates of his birth and death, and recording the fact that his father was also interred there.

It is probable that Mr. Whitbread was moved thereto by the alleged desecration of Milton's tomb in 1790, of which there is a good account written by Philip Neve, of Furnival's Inn, which is entitled, 'A NARRATIVE of the DISINTERMENT of MILTON'S coffin, in the Parish-Church of ST. GILES, Cripplegate, on Wednesday, August 4th, 1790; and the TREATMENT OF THE CORPSE during that and the following day.'

As this narrative is not long, I propose to give it in its entirety, because to condense it would be to spoil it, and, by giving it *in extenso*, the reader will be better able to judge whether it was really Milton's body which was exhumed.

A NARRATIVE, &c.

HAVING read in the *Public Advertiser*, on Saturday, the 7th of August, 1790, that *Milton's* coffin had been dug up in the parish church of St. Giles, Cripplegate, and was there to be seen, I went immediately to the church, and found the latter part of the information to be untrue; but, from conversations on that day, on Monday, the 9th, and on Tuesday, the 10th of August, with Mr. Thomas *Strong*, Solicitor and F.A.S., Red Cross Street, *Vestry-Clerk*; Mr. John *Cole*, Barbican, Silversmith, *Churchwarden*; Mr. John *Laming*, Barbican, *Pawnbroker*; and Mr. *Fountain*, Beech Lane, Publican, *Overseers*; Mr. *Taylor*, of Stanton, Derbyshire, *Surgeon*; a friend of Mr. *Laming*, and a visitor in his house; Mr. William *Ascough*, Coffin-maker, Fore Street, *Parish Clerk*; Benjamin *Holmes* and Thomas

Hawkesworth, journeymen to Mr. Ascough; Mrs. *Hoppey*, Fore Street, *Sexton;* Mr. *Ellis*, No. 9, Lamb's Chapel, comedian of the Royalty-theatre; and John *Poole* (son of Rowland Poole), Watch-spring maker, Jacob's Passage, Barbican, the following facts are established:

It being in the contemplation of some persons to bestow a considerable sum of money in erecting a monument, in the parish church of *St. Giles*, Cripplegate, to the memory of *Milton*, and the particular spot of his interment in that church having for many years past been ascertained only by tradition, several of the principal parishioners have, at their meetings, frequently expressed a wish that his coffin should be dug for, that incontestable evidence of its exact situation might be established, before the said monument should be erected. The entry, among the burials, in the register-book, 12th of November, 1674, is '*John Milton*, Gentleman, consumption, *chancell*.' The church of St. Giles, Cripplegate, was built in 1030, was burnt down (except the steeple) and rebuilt in 1545; was repaired in 1682; and again in 1710. In the repair of 1782, an alteration took place in the disposition of the inside of the church; the pulpit was removed from the second pillar, against which it stood, north of the chancel, to the south side of the present chancel, which was then formed, and pews were built over the old chancel. The tradition has always been that *Milton* was buried in the chancel, under the clerk's desk; but the circumstance of the alteration in the church, not having, of late years, been attended to, the clerk, sexton, and other officers of the parish have misguided inquirers, by showing the spot under the clerk's desk, in the present chancel, as the place of *Milton's* interment. I have twice, at different periods, been shown that spot as the place where *Milton* lay. Even Mr. *Baskerville*, who died a few years ago, and who had requested, in his will, to be buried by *Milton*, was deposited in the above-mentioned spot of the present chancel, in pious intention of compliance with his request. The church is now, August, 1790, under a general repair, by contract, for £1,350, and Mr. *Strong*, Mr. *Cole*, and other parishioners, having very prudently judged that the search would be made with much less inconvenience to the parish at this time, when the church is under repair, than at any period after the said repair should be completed, Mr. *Cole*, in the last days of July, ordered the workmen to dig in search of the coffin. Mr. *Ascough*, his father, and grandfather, have been parish clerks of *St. Giles* for upwards of ninety years past. His grandfather, who died in February, 1759-60, aged eighty-four, used often to say that *Milton* had been buried under the clerk's desk in the chancel. John *Poole*, aged seventy, used to hear his father talk of Milton's person, from those who had seen him; and also, that he lay under the common-councilmen's pew. The common-councilmen's pew is built over that very part of the old chancel, where the former clerk's desk stood. These traditions in the parish reported to Mr. *Strong* and Mr. *Cole* readily directed them to dig from the present chancel, northwards, towards the pillar, against which the former pulpit and desk had stood. On Tuesday afternoon, August 3rd, notice was brought to Messrs. *Strong* and *Cole* that the coffin was discovered. They went immediately to the church, and, by help of a candle, proceeded under the common-councilmen's pew to the place where the coffin lay. It was in a chalky soil, and directly over a wooden coffin, supposed to be that of *Milton's* father; tradition having always reported that *Milton* was buried next to his father. The registry of the father of *Milton*, among the burials, in the parish-book, is '*John Melton*, Gentleman, 15th of March, 1646-7.' In digging through the whole space from the present chancel, where the ground was opened, to the situation of the former clerk's desk, there was not found any other coffin, which could raise the smallest doubt of this being *Milton's*. The two oldest found in the ground had inscriptions, which Mr. *Strong* copied; they were of as late dates as 1727 and 1739. When he and Mr. *Cole* had examined the coffin, they ordered water and a brush to be brought, that they might wash it, in search of an inscription, or initials, or date; but, upon its being carefully cleansed, none was found.

The following particulars were given me in writing by Mr. *Strong*, and they contain the admeasurement of the coffin, as taken by him, with a rule. 'A leaden coffin, found under the common-councilmen's pew, on the north side of the chancel, nearly under the place where the old pulpit and clerk's desk stood. The coffin appeared to be old, much corroded, and without any inscription or plate upon it. It was, in length, five feet ten inches, and in width, at the broadest part, over the shoulders, one foot four inches.' Conjecture naturally pointed out, both to Mr. *Strong* and Mr. *Cole*, that, by moving the leaden coffin, there would be a great chance of finding some inscription on the wooden one underneath; but, with a just and laudable piety, they disdained to disturb the sacred ashes, after a requiem of one hundred and sixteen years; and having satisfied their curiosity, and ascertained the fact, which was the subject of it, Mr. *Cole* ordered the ground to be closed. This was on the afternoon of Tuesday, August the 3rd; and, when I waited on Mr. *Strong*, on Saturday morning, the 7th, he informed me that the coffin had been found on the Tuesday, had been examined, washed, and measured by him and Mr. *Cole;* but that the ground had been immediately closed, when they left the church;—not doubting that Mr. *Cole's* order had been punctually obeyed. But the direct contrary appears to have been the fact.

On Tuesday evening, the 3rd, Mr. *Cole*, Messrs. *Laming* and *Taylor, Holmes*, &c., had a *merry meeting*, as Mr. *Cole* expresses himself, at Fountain's house; the conversation there turned upon *Milton's* coffin having been discovered; and, in the course of the evening, several of those present expressing a desire to see it, Mr. *Cole* assented that, if the ground was not already closed, the closing of it should be deferred until they should have satisfied their curiosity. Between eight and nine on Wednesday morning, the 4th, the two overseers (*Laming* and *Fountain*) and Mr. *Taylor*, went to the house of *Ascough*, the clerk, which leads into the church-yard, and asked for *Holmes;* they then went with *Holmes* into the church, and pulled the coffin, which lay deep in the ground, from its original station to the edge of the excavation, into day-light. Mr. *Laming* told me that, to assist in thus removing it, he put his hand into a corroded hole, which he saw in the lead, at the coffin foot. When they had thus removed it, the overseers asked *Holmes* if he could open it, that they might see the body. *Holmes* immediately fetched a mallet and a chisel, and cut open the top of the coffin, slantwise from the head, as low as the breast; so that the top, being doubled backward, they could see the corpse; he cut it open also at the foot. Upon first view of the body, it appeared perfect, and completely enveloped in the shroud, which was of many folds; the ribs standing up regularly. When they disturbed the shroud, the ribs fell. Mr. *Fountain* told me that he pulled hard at the teeth, which resisted, until some one hit them a knock with a stone, when they easily came out. There were but five in the upper jaw, which were all perfectly sound and white, and all taken by Mr. *Fountain;* he gave one of them to Mr. *Laming;* Mr. *Laming* also took one from the lower jaw; and Mr. *Taylor* took two from it. Mr. *Laming* told me that he had, at one time, a mind to bring away the whole under-jaw, with the teeth in it; he had it in his hand, but tossed it back again. Also that he lifted up the head, and saw a great quantity of hair, which lay straight and even behind the head, and in the state of hair which had been combed and tied together before interment; but it was wet, the coffin having considerable corroded holes, both at the head and foot, and a great part of the water with which it had been washed on the Tuesday afternoon having run into it. The overseers and Mr. *Taylor* went away soon afterwards, and Messrs. *Laming* and *Taylor* went home to get scissors to cut off some of the hair: they returned about ten, when Mr. *Laming* poked his stick against the head, and brought some of the hair over the forehead; but, as they saw the scissors were not necessary, Mr. *Taylor* took up the hair, as it lay on the forehead, and carried it home. The water, which had got into the coffin on the Tuesday afternoon, had made a sludge at the bottom of it, emitting a nauseous smell, and which occasioned Mr. *Laming* to use his stick to procure the hair, and not to lift up the head a second time. Mr. *Laming* also took out one of the leg-bones, but threw it in again. *Holmes* went out of church, whilst Messrs. *Laming, Taylor,* and *Fountain* were there the first time, and he returned when the two former were come the second time. When Messrs. *Laming* and *Taylor* had finally quitted the church, the coffin was removed from the edge of the excavation back to its original station; but was no otherwise closed than by the lid, where it had been cut and reversed, being bent down again. Mr. *Ascough,* the clerk, was from home the greater part of that day, and Mrs. *Hoppey,* the sexton, was from home the whole day. Elizabeth *Grant,* the grave-digger, who is servant to Mrs. *Hoppey,* therefore now took possession of the coffin; and, as its situation under the common-councilmen's pew would not admit of its being seen without the help of a candle, she kept a tinder-box in the excavation, and, when any persons came, struck a light, and conducted them under the pew, where, by reversing the part of the lid which had been cut, she exhibited the body, at first for sixpence, and afterwards for threepence and twopence each person. The workers in the church kept the doors locked to all those who would not pay the price of a pot of beer for entrance, and many, to avoid that payment, got in at a window at the west end of the church, near to Mr. *Ascough's* counting-house.

I went on Saturday, the 7th, to Mr. *Laming's* house, to request a lock of the hair; but, not meeting with Mr. *Taylor* at home, went again on Monday, the 9th, when Mr. *Taylor* gave me part of what hair he had reserved for himself. *Hawkesworth* having informed me, on the Saturday, that Mr. *Ellis*, the player, had taken some hair, and that he had seen him take a rib-bone, and carry it away in paper under his coat, I went from Mr. *Laming's* on Monday to Mr. *Ellis*, who told me that he had paid 6^d to Elizabeth *Grant* for seeing the body; and that he had lifted up the head, and taken from the sludge under it a small quantity of hair, with which was a piece of the shroud, and, adhering to the hair, a bit of the skin of the skull, of about the size of a shilling. He then put them all into my hands, with the rib-bone, which appeared to be one of the upper ribs. The piece of the shroud was of coarse linen. The hair which he had taken was short; a small part of it he had washed, and the remainder was in the clotted state in which he had taken it. He told me that he had tried to reach down as low as the hands of the corpse, but had not been able to effect it. The washed hair corresponded exactly with that in my possession, and which I had just received from Mr. *Taylor*. *Ellis* is a very ingenious worker in hair, and he said that, thinking it would be of great advantage to him to possess a quantity of Milton's hair, he had returned to the church on Thursday, and had made his endeavours to get access a second time to the body; but had been refused admittance. *Hawkesworth* took a tooth, and broke a bit off the coffin; of which I was informed by Mr. *Ascough*. I purchased them both of *Hawkesworth*, on Saturday the 7th, for 2^s.; and he told me that, when he took the tooth out, there were but two more remaining; one of which was afterwards taken by another of Mr. *Ascough's* men. And *Ellis* informed me that, at the time when he was there, on Wednesday, the teeth were all gone; but the overseers say they think that all the teeth were not taken out of the coffin, though displaced from the jaws, but that some of them must have fallen among the other bones, as they very readily came out, after the first were drawn. *Haslib*, son of William *Haslib*, of Jewin Street, undertaker, took one of the small bones, which I purchased of him, on Monday, the 9th, for 2ˢ·

With respect to the identity of the person; anyone must be a skeptic against violent presumptions to entertain a doubt of its being that of *Milton*. The parish traditions of the spot; the age of the coffin— none other found in the ground which can at all contest with it, or render it suspicious—*Poole's* tradition that those who had conversed with his father about *Milton's* person always described him to have been thin, with long hair; the entry in the register-book that *Milton* died of consumption, are all strong confirmations, with the size of the coffin, of the identity of the person. If it be objected that, against the pillar where the pulpit formerly stood, and immediately over the common-councilmen's pew, is a monument to the family of *Smith*, which shows that 'near that place' were buried, in 1653, *Richard Smith*, aged 17; in 1655, *John Smith*, aged 32; and in 1664, *Elizabeth Smith*, the mother, aged 64; and in 1675, *Richard Smith*, the father, aged 85; it may be answered that, if the coffin in question be one of these, the others should be there also. The corpse is certainly not that of a man of 85; and, if it be supposed one of the first named males of the *Smith* family, certainly the two later coffins should appear; but none such were found, nor could that monument have been erected until many years after the death of the last person mentioned in the inscription; and it was then placed there, as it expresses, not by any of the family, but at the expense of friends. The flatness of the pillar, after the pulpit had been removed, offered an advantageous situation for it; and '*near this place,*' upon a mural monument, will always admit of a liberal construction. *Holmes,* who is much respected in that parish, and very ingenious and intelligent in his business, says that a leaden coffin, when the inner wooden-case is perished, must, from pressure and its own weight, shrink in breadth, and that, therefore, more than the present admeasurement of this coffin across the shoulders must have been its original breadth. There is evidence, also, that it was incurvated, both on the top and at the sides, at the time when it was discovered. But the strongest of all confirmations is the hair, both in its length and colour. Behold *Faithorne's* quarto-print of *Milton* taken *ad vivum* in 1760, five years before *Milton's* death. Observe the short locks growing towards the forehead, and the long ones flowing from the same place down the sides of the face. The whole quantity of hair which Mr. *Taylor* took was from the forehead, and all taken at one grasp. I measured on Monday morning, the 9th, that lock of it which he had given to Mr. *Laming,* six inches and a half by a rule; and the lock of it which he gave to me, taken at the same time, and from the same place, measures only two inches and a half. In the reign of *Charles* II. how few, besides *Milton,* wore their own hair! *Wood* says *Milton* had light-brown hair, the very description of that which we possess; and, what may seem extraordinary, it is yet so strong that Mr. *Laming*, to cleanse it from its clotted state, let the cistern-cock run on it for near a minute, and then rubbed it between his fingers without injury.

Milton's coffin lay open from Wednesday morning, the 4th, at 9 o'clock until 4 o'clock in the afternoon of the following day, when the ground was closed.

With respect to there being no inscriptions on the coffin, *Holmes* says that inscription-plates were not used, nor invented at the time when *Milton* was buried; that the practice then was to paint the inscription on the outside wooden coffin, which in this case was entirely perished.

It has never been pretended that any hair was taken except by Mr. *Taylor*, and by *Ellis* the player; and all which the latter took would, when cleansed, easily lie in a small locket. Mr. *Taylor* has divided his share into many small parcels; and the lock which I saw in Mr. *Laming's* hands on Saturday morning, the 7th, and which then measured six inches and a half, had been so cut and reduced by divisions among Mr. *Laming's* friends, at noon, on Monday, the 9th, that he thus possessed only a small bit, from two to three inches in length.

All the teeth are remarkably short, below the gums. The five which were in the upper jaw, and the middle teeth of the lower, are perfect and white. Mr. *Fountain* took the five upper jaw teeth; Mr. *Laming* one from the lower jaw; Mr. *Taylor* two from it; *Hawkesworth* one; and another of Mr. *Ascough's* men one; besides these, I have not been able to trace any, nor have I heard that any more were taken. It is not probable that more than ten should have been brought away, if the conjecture of the overseers, that some dropped among the other bones, be founded.

In recording a transaction which will strike every liberal mind with horror and disgust, I cannot omit to declare that I have procured those relics which I possess, only in hope of bearing part in a pious and honourable restitution of all that has been taken; the sole atonement which can now be made to the violated rights of the dead; to the insulted parishioners at large; and to the feelings of all good men. During the present repair of the church, the mode is obvious and easy. Unless that be done, in vain will the parish hereafter boast a sumptuous monument to the memory of *Milton;* it will but display their shame in proportion to its magnificence.

I collected this account from the mouths of those who were immediate actors in this most sacrilegious scene; and before the voice of charity had reproached them with their impiety. By it those are exculpated whose just and liberal sentiments restrained their hands from an act of violation, and the blood of the lamb is dashed against the door-posts of the perpetrators, not to save, but to mark them to posterity.

PHILIP NEVE.

Furnival's Inn,
14th of August, 1790.

This Mr. Neve, whose pious horror at the sacrilegious desecration of the poet's tomb seems only to have been awakened at the eleventh hour, and whose restitution of the relics he obtained does not appear, was probably the P.N. who was the author, in 1789, of 'Cursory Remarks on some of the Ancient English

Poets, particularly Milton.' It is a work of some erudition, but the hero of the book, as its title plainly shows, was Milton. Neve places him in the first rank, and can hardly find words with which to extol his genius and intellect, so that, probably, some hero-worship was interwoven in the foregoing relation of the discovery of Milton's body; and it may be as well if the other side were heard, although the attempt at refutation is by no means as well authenticated as Neve's narrative. It is anonymous, and appeared in the *St. James's Chronicle*, September 4-7th, 1790, and in the *European Magazine*, vol. xviii, pp. 206-7, for September, 1790, and is as follows:

MILTON.

Reasons why it is impossible that the Coffin lately dug up in the Parish Church of St. Giles, Cripplegate, should contain the reliques of MILTON.

First. BECAUSE *Milton* was buried in 1674, and this coffin was found in a situation previously allotted to a wealthy family, unconnected with his own.—See the mural monument of the *Smiths*, dated 1653, &c., immediately over the place of the supposed MILTON'S interment.—In the time that the fragments of several other sarcophagi were found; together with two skulls, many bones, and a leaden coffin, which was left untouched because it lay further to the north, and (for some reason, or no reason at all) was unsuspected of being the *Miltonic* reservoir.

Secondly. The hair of MILTON is uniformly described and represented as of a light hue; but far the greater part of the ornament of his pretended skull is of the darkest brown, without any mixture of gray.[1]

---

[1] The few hairs of a lighter colour, are supposed to have been such as had grown on the sides of the cheeks after the corpse had been interred.

This difference is irreconcileable to probability. Our hair, after childhood, is rarely found to undergo a total change of colour, and MILTON was 66 years old when he died, a period at which human locks, in a greater or less degree, are interspersed with white. Why did the Overseers, &c., bring away only such hair as corresponded with the description of *Milton's?* Of the light hair there was little; of the dark a considerable quantity. But this circumstance would have been wholly suppressed, had not a second scrutiny taken place.

Thirdly. Because the skull in question is remarkably flat and small, and with the lowest of all possible foreheads; whereas the head of MILTON was large, and his brow conspicuously high. See his portrait so often engraved by the accurate *Vertue*, who was completely satisfied with the authenticity of his original. We are assured that the surgeon who attended at the second disinterment of the corpse only remarked, 'that the little forehead there was, was prominent.'

Fourthly. Because the hands of MILTON were full of chalk stones. Now it chances that his substitute's left hand had been undisturbed, and therefore was in a condition to be properly examined. No vestige, however, of cretaceous substances was visible in it, although they are of a lasting nature, and have been found on the fingers of a dead person almost coeval with MILTON.

Fifthly. Because there is reason to believe that the aforesaid remains are those of a young female (one of the three Miss *Smiths*); for the bones are delicate, the teeth small, slightly inserted in the jaw, and perfectly white, even, and sound. From the corroded state of the pelvis, nothing could, with certainty, be inferred; nor would the surgeon already mentioned pronounce *absolutely* on the sex of the deceased. Admitting, however, that the body was a male one, its very situation points it out to be a male of the *Smith* family; perhaps the favourite son *John*, whom *Richard Smith*, Esq., his father, so feelingly laments. (See Peck's '*Desiderata Curiosa*,' p. 536).[1] To this darling child a receptacle of lead might have been allotted, though many other relatives of the same house were left to putrefy in wood.

Sixthly. Because MILTON was not in affluence[2]—expired in an emaciated state, in a cold month, and was interred by direction of his widow. An expensive outward coffin of lead, therefore, was needless, and unlikely to have been provided by a rapacious woman who oppressed her husband's children while he was living, and cheated them after he was dead.

Seventhly. Because it is improbable that the circumstance of MILTON's having been deposited under the desk should, if true, have been so effectually concealed from the whole train of his biographers.

---

[1] 'MDCLV. May vi, died my (now) only and eldest son, John Smith (*Proh Dolor*, beloved of all men!) at Mitcham in Surrey. Buried May ix in St. Giles, Cripplegate.'

[2] Edward Philips or Phillips, in his life of Milton, attached to 'Letters of State, written by Mr. John Milton,' &c., London, 1694, (p. 43), says: 'He is said to have dyed worth £1,500 in Money (a considerable Estate, all things considered), besides Houshold Goods; for he sustained such losses as might well have broke any person less frugal and temperate than himself; no less than £2,000 which he had put for Security and Improvement into the Excise Office, but, neglecting to recal it in time, could never after get it out, with all the Power and Interest he had in the Great ones of those Times; besides another great Sum by mismanagement and for want of good advice.'

It was, nevertheless, produced as an ancient and well-known tradition, as soon as the parishioners of Cripplegate were aware that such an incident was gaped for by antiquarian appetence, and would be swallowed by antiquarian credulity. How happened it that Bishop *Newton*, who urged similar inquiries concerning MILTON above forty years ago in the same parish, could obtain no such information ?[1]

[1] Thomas Newton, Bishop of Bristol, thus writes in his life of Milton, prefixed to his edition of 'Paradise Lost,' London, 1749: 'His body was decently interred near that of his father (who had died very aged about the year 1647) in the chancel of the church of St. Giles, Cripplegate; and all his great and learned friends in London, not without a friendly concourse of the common people, paid their last respects in attending it to the grave. Mr. Fenton, in his short but elegant account of the life of Milton, speaking of our author's having no monument, says that "he desired a friend to inquire at St. Giles's Church, where the sexton showed him a small monument, which he said was supposed to be Milton's; but the inscription had never been legible since he was employed in that office, which he has possessed about forty years. This sure could never have happened in so short a space of time, unless the epitaph had been industriously erased; and that supposition, says Mr. Fenton, carries with it so much inhumanity that I think we ought to believe it was not erected to his memory." It is evident that it was not erected to his memory, and that the sexton was mistaken. For Mr. Toland, in his account of the life of Milton, says that he was buried in the chancel of St. Giles's Church, "where the piety of his admirers will shortly erect a monument becoming his worth, and the encouragement of letters in King William's reign." This plainly implies that no monument was erected to him at that time, and this was written in 1698, and Mr. Fenton's account was first published, I think, in 1725; so that not above twenty-seven years intervened from the one account to the other; and consequently the sexton, who it is said was possessed of his office about forty years, must have been mistaken, and the monument must have been designed for some other person, and not for Milton.'

Eighthly. Because Mr. *Laming* (see Mr. *Neve's* pamphlet, second edition, p. 19) observes that the 'sludge' at the bottom of the coffin 'emitted a nauseous smell.' But, had this corpse been as old as that of MILTON, it must have been disarmed of its power to offend, nor would have supplied the least effluvium to disgust the nostrils of our delicate inquirer into the secrets of the grave. The last remark will seem to militate against a foregoing one. The whole difficulty, however, may be solved by a resolution not to believe a single word said on such an occasion by any of those who invaded the presumptive sepulchre of MILTON. The man who can handle pawned stays, breeches, and petticoats without disgust may be supposed to have his organs of smelling in no very high state of perfection.

Ninthly. Because we have not been told by *Wood, Philips, Richardson, Toland,* etc., that Nature, among her other partialities to MILTON, had indulged him with an uncommon share of teeth. And yet above a hundred have been sold as the furniture of his mouth by the conscientious worthies who assisted in the plunder of his supposed carcase, and finally submitted it to every insult that brutal vulgarity could devise and express. Thanks to fortune, however, his corpse has hitherto been violated but by proxy! May his genuine reliques (if aught of him remains unmingled with common earth) continue to elude research, at least while the present overseers of the poor of Cripplegate are in office. Hard, indeed, would have been the fate of the author of 'Paradise Lost' to have received shelter in a chancel, that a hundred and sixteen years after his interment his *domus ultima* might be ransacked by two of the lowest human beings, a retailer of spirituous liquors, and a man who lends sixpences to beggars on such despicable securities as tattered bed-gowns, cankered porridge-pots, and rusty gridirons.¹ *Cape saxa manu, cape robora, pastor!* But an Ecclesiastical Court may yet have cognisance of this more than savage transaction. It will then be determined whether our tombs are our own, or may be robbed with impunity by the little tyrants of a workhouse.

> 'If charnel-houses, and our graves, must send
> Those that we bury back, our monuments
> Shall be the maws of kites.'

It should be added that our Pawnbroker, Gin-seller, and Company, by deranging the contents of their ideal MILTON'S coffin, by carrying away his lower jaw, ribs, and right hand—and by employing one bone as an instrument to batter the rest—by tearing the shroud and winding-sheet to pieces, &c., &c., had annihilated all such further evidence as might have been collected from a skilful and complete examination of these nameless fragments of mortality. So far, indeed, were they mutilated that, had they been genuine, we could not have said with Horace,

> 'Invenies etiam disjecti membra Poetæ.'

Who, after a perusal of the foregoing remarks (which are founded on circumstantial truth), will congratulate the parishioners of St. Giles, Cripplegate, on their discovery and treatment of the imaginary dust

---

¹ Between the creditable trades of pawnbroker and dram-seller there is a strict alliance. As Hogarth observes, the money lent by Mr. Gripe is immediately conveyed to the shop of Mr. Killman, who, in return for the produce of rags, distributes poison under the specious name of cordials. See Hogarth's celebrated print called Gin Lane.

of MILTON? His favourite, *Shakespeare*, most fortunately reposes at a secure distance from the paws of Messieurs *Laming* and *Fountain*, who, otherwise, might have provoked the vengeance imprecated by our great dramatic poet on the remover of his bones.

From the preceding censures, however, Mr. *Cole* (Churchwarden), and Messrs. *Strong* and *Ascough* (Vestry and Parish Clerks), should, in the most distinguished manner, be exempted. Throughout the whole of this extraordinary business, they conducted themselves with the strictest decency and propriety. It should also be confessed, by those whom curiosity has since attracted to the place of MILTON'S supposed disinterment, that the politeness of the same parish officers could only be exceeded by their respect for our illustrious author's memory, and their concern at the complicated indignity which his nominal ashes have sustained.'

Now it was hardly likely that Mr. Neve, with the extremely plausible case that he had, would sit still and see his pet theory knocked on the head, so he issued a second edition of his pamphlet with this

POSTSCRIPT.

As some reports have been circulated, and some anonymous papers have appeared, since the publication of this pamphlet, with intent to induce a belief that the corpse mentioned in it is that of a woman, and as the curiosity of the public now calls for a second impression of it, an opportunity is offered of relating a few circumstances which have happened since the 14th of August, and which, in some degree, may confirm the opinion that the corpse is that of *Milton*.

On Monday, the 16th, I called upon the overseer,

Mr. *Fountain,* when he told me that the parish officers had then seen a surgeon who, on Wednesday the 4th, had got through a window into the church, and who had, upon inspection, pronounced the corpse to be that of a woman. I thought it very improbable that a surgeon should creep through a window, who could go through a door for a few half-pence; but I no otherwise expressed my doubts of the truth of the information than by asking for the surgeon's address. I was answered 'that the gentleman begged not to have it known, that he might not be interrupted by enquiries.' A trifling relic was, nevertheless, at the same time withholden, which I had expected to receive through Mr. *Fountain's* hands; by which it appeared that those in possession of them were still tenacious of the spoils of the coffin, although they affected to be convinced they were not those of *Milton.* These contradictions, however, I reserved for the test of an inquiry elsewhere.

In the course of that week I was informed that some gentlemen had, on Tuesday, the 17th, prevailed on the churchwardens to suffer a second disinterment of the coffin, which had taken place on that day. On Saturday, the 21st, I waited on Mr. *Strong,* who told me that he had been present at such second disinterment, and that he had then sent for an experienced surgeon of the neighbourhood, who, upon inspection and examination of the corpse, had pronounced it to be that of a man. I was also informed, on that day, the 21st, by a principal person of the parish, whose information cannot be suspected, that the parish officers had agreed among themselves that, from my frequent visits and inquiries, I must have an intention of delivering some account of the transaction to the world; and that, therefore, to stop the narrative from going forth, they must invent some story of a surgeon's inspection on the 4th, and of his declaration that the corpse was that of a woman. From this information it was easy to judge what would be the fate of any personal application to the parish officers, with intent to obtain a restitution of what had been taken from the coffin I, therefore, on Wednesday, the 25th, addressed the following letter to Mr. *Strong* :—

'DEAR SIR,

'The reflection of a few moments, after I left you on Saturday, clearly showed me that the probability of the coffin in question being *Milton's* was not at all weakened, either by the dates, or the number of persons on the *Smiths'* monument; but that it was rather confirmed by the latter circumstance. By the evidence which you told me was given by the surgeon, called in on Tuesday, the 17th, the corpse is that of a male; it is certainly not that of a man of eighty-five; if, therefore, it be one of the earlier buried *Smiths*, all the later coffins of that family should appear, but not one of them is found. I, then, suppose the monument to have been put there because the flat pillar, after the pulpit was removed, offered a convenient situation for it, and "*near this place*" to be open, as it is in almost every case where it appears, to very liberal interpretation.

'It is, therefore, to be believed that the unworthy treatment, on the 4th, was offered to the corpse of *Milton*. Knowing what I know, I must not be silent. It is a very unpleasant story to relate; but, as it has fallen to my task, I will not shrink from it. I respect nothing in this world more than truth, and the memory of *Milton;* and to swerve in a tittle from the first would offend the latter. I shall give the plain and simple narrative, as delivered by the parties themselves. If it sit heavy on any of their shoulders, it is a burthen of their own taking up, and their own backs must bear it. They are all, as I find, very fond of deriving honour to themselves from *Milton,* as their parishioner; perhaps the mode, which I have hinted, is the only one which they have now left themselves of proving an equal desire to do honour to him. If I had thought that, in personally proposing to the parish officers a general search for, and collection of, all the spoils, and to put them, together with the mangled corpse and old coffin, into a new leaden one, I should have been attended to, I would have taken that method; but, when I found such impertinent inventions as setting up a fabulous surgeon to creep in at a window practised, I felt that so low an attempt at derision would ensure that, whatever I should afterwards propose, would be equally derided, and I had then left no other means than to call in the public opinion in aid of my own, and to hope that we should, at length, see the bones of an honest man, and the first scholar and poet our country can boast, restored to their sepulchre.

'The narrative will appear, I believe, either to-morrow or on Friday; whenever it does, your withers are unwrung, and Mr. *Cole* has shown himself an upright churchwarden.

'I cannot conclude without returning you many thanks for your great civilities, and am, &c.'

The corpse was found entirely mutilated by those who disinterred it on the 17th; almost all the ribs, the lower jaw, and one of the hands gone. Of all those who saw the body on Wednesday, the 4th, and on Thursday, the 5th, there is not one person who discovered a single hair of any other colour than light brown, although both Mr. *Laming* and Mr. *Ellis* lifted up the head, and although the considerable quantity of hair which Mr. *Taylor* took was from the top of the head, and that which *Ellis* took was from behind it; yet, from the accounts of those who saw it on the 17th, it appears that the hair on the back of the head was found of dark brown, nearly approaching to black, although all the front hair remaining was of the same light brown as that taken on the 4th. It does not belong to me either to account for or to prove the fact.

On Wednesday, September the 1st, I waited on Mr. *Dyson*, who was the gentleman sent for on the 17th, to examine the corpse. I asked him simply, whether, from what had then appeared before him, he judged it to be male or female? His answer was that, having examined the pelvis and the skull, he judged the corpse to be that of a man. I asked what was the shape of the head? He said that the forehead was high and erect, though the top of the head was flat; and added that the skull was of that shape and flatness at the top which, differing from those of blacks, is observed to be common and almost peculiar to persons of very comprehensive intellects. I am a stranger to this sort of knowledge, but the opinion is a strong confirmation that, from all the premises before him, he judged the head to be that of *Milton*. On a paper, which he showed me, enclosing a bit of the hair, he had written '*Milton's hair.*'

Mr. *Dyson* is a surgeon, who received his professional education under the late Dr. *Hunter*, is in partnership with Mr. *Price*, in Fore Street, where the church stands, is of easy access, and his affability can be exceeded only by his skill in an extensive line of practice.

Mr. *Taylor*, too, who is a surgeon of considerable practice and eminence in his county, judged the corpse, on the 4th, to be that of a male.

A man, also, who has for many years acted as gravedigger in that parish, and who was present on the 17th, decided, upon first sight of the skull, that it was male; with as little hesitation, he pronounced another, which had been thrown out of the ground in digging, to be that of a woman. Decisions obviously the result of practical, rather than of scientific knowledge; for, being asked his reasons, he could give none, but that observation had taught him to distinguish such subjects. Yet this latter sort of evidence is not to be too hastily rejected; it may not be understood by everybody, but to anyone acquainted with those who are eminently skilled in judging of the genuineness of ancient coins, it will be perfectly intelligible. In that difficult and useful art, the eye of a proficent decides at once; a novice, however, who should inquire for the reasons of such decision, would seldom receive a further answer than that the decision itself is the result of experience and observation, and that the eye can be instructed only by long familiarity with the subject; yet all numismatic knowledge rests upon this sort of judgment.

G

After these evidences, what proofs are there, or what probable presumptions, that the corpse is that of a woman?

It was necessary to relate these facts, not only as they belonged to the subject, but lest, from the reports and papers above mentioned, I might, otherwise, seem to have given either an unfaithful or a partial statement of the evidences before me; whereas now it will clearly be seen what facts appeared on the first disinterment, which preceded, and what are to be attributed to the second, which succeeded the date of the narrative.

I have now added every circumstance which has hitherto come to my knowledge relative to this extraordinary transaction, and conclude with this declaration, that I should be very glad if any person would, from facts, give me reason to believe that the corpse in question is rather that of *Elizabeth Smith,* whose name I know only from her monument, than that of *John Milton.*

P. N.'

'8th of September, 1790.'

THE TRUE STORY OF EUGENE ARAM.

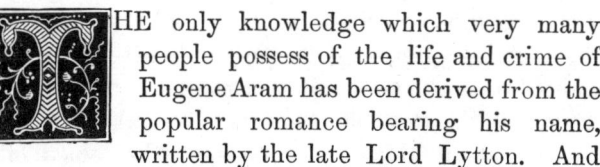HE only knowledge which very many people possess of the life and crime of Eugene Aram has been derived from the popular romance bearing his name, written by the late Lord Lytton. And this nobleman, influenced by his individual bias, has so woven fiction with a small modicum of fact, as to render the story, as a history of a celebrated crime, totally unreliable. Stripped of the gloss Lord Lytton has given it, and revealed in its bare nakedness, it shows Eugene Aram in a very different light from the solitary scholar, surrounded by books, with high, romantic aspirations and noble thoughts, winning the love of a pure and lovely girl; it shows us instead a poor country school-master, clever, but self-taught, married to a common woman, whose very faith he doubted, struggling with poverty, and heavily weighed down with several children; it paints him as a man whose companions were sordid and dishonest, whilst he himself was a liar, a thief, and a murderer, a selfish man who scrupled not to leave wife and children to shift for themselves, a man untrustworthy in his relations of life.

Eugenius, or Eugene Aram was born in the year

1704,[1] at Ramsgill, a little village in Netherdale, Yorkshire, and his father was a gardener, as he says, of great abilities in botany, and an excellent draughtsman, who served Dr. Compton, Bishop of London, and, afterwards, Sir Edward Blackett, of Newby, and Sir John Ingilby, of Ripley. When he was five or six years of age, the family removed to Bondgate, near Ripon, his father having purchased a little property there. Here he was sent to school, and was taught in a purely elementary manner to be capable of reading the New Testament, and this was all the education his parents gave him, with the exception of about a month's schooling some long time afterwards with the Rev. Mr. Alcock of Burnsal.

When about thirteen or fourteen, he joined his father at Newby, till the death of Sir Edward Blackett, and, his father having several books on mathematics, and the boy being of a studious turn of mind, he mastered their contents, and laid the foundation of his future scholarship. When about sixteen years of age, he went to London to be in the counting-house of Mr. Christopher Blackett as bookkeeper; but he had not been there more than a year or two when he caught the small-pox, and, on his recovery, went home into Yorkshire. His native air soon restored him to health, and he studied hard at poetry, history, and antiquities. He thus fitted himself for keeping a school, which he opened in Netherdale, and continued there for many years teaching and studying. There he married, as he says, 'un-

---

[1] Probably in the month of September, as the entry of his baptism in the registry of the chapelry of Middlesmoor, in Netherdale, says 'Eugenius Aram, son of Peter Aram, baptized the 2nd of October.'

fortunately enough for me, for the misconduct of the wife which that place afforded me has procured for me this place, this prosecution, this infamy, and this sentence.'

During these years he read the Latin and Greek authors, and obtained such a name for scholarship that he was invited to Knaresborough to keep a school there. He removed thither in the year 1734, and continued there until about six weeks after the murder of Daniel Clark. In the meantime he had mastered Hebrew, and when he went to London he got a situation to teach Latin, and writing, at a school in Piccadilly, kept by a Monsieur Painblanc, who not only gave him a salary, but taught him French. There he remained over two years, then went to Hays as a writing-master, after which he wandered from situation to situation, at one time earning his living by copying for a law-stationer. At last, somehow, he found himself an usher at the Free School at Lynn, where he lived until he was arrested for the murder of Daniel Clark.

This man was a shoemaker at Knaresborough, and was an intimate visitor at Aram's house—too intimate, indeed, Aram thought, with his wife, hence the reference to his wife previously quoted. He was a man of bad character, and was more than suspected of having, in company of another vagabond named Houseman, murdered a Jew boy, who travelled the country for one Levi as a pedlar, carrying a box containing watches and jewellery. The poor lad was decoyed to a place called Thistle Hill, where he was robbed, murdered, and buried. This was about the year 1744, and his bones were not found until 1758.

Richard Houseman, who was born the same year

as Aram, was a near neighbour of the latter's—in fact, he lived next door, and his occupation was that of a heckler of flax, when he gave out to the women of the village to spin for him. But, according to his own statement, he was a most unscrupulous blackguard.

Another intimate of Aram's was a publican, named Terry, but he only played a subsidiary part in the drama, and nothing was ever brought home to him.

In January, 1745, Clark married a woman with a small fortune of about two hundred pounds, and, immediately afterwards, this little nest of rogues contrived and carried out the following swindle. Clark, as he was known to have married a woman of some little money, was to obtain goods of any description from whomsoever would part with them on credit; these goods were to be deposited with, and hidden by, Aram and Houseman, and, after plundering all that was possible, Clark was to decamp, and leave his young wife to do the best she could. This was the scheme in which the noble and refined Eugene Aram of Lord Lytton was to, and did, bear his full part.

Velvet from one man, leather from another, whips from a third, table and bed linen from a fourth, money lent by a fifth—all was fish that came to their net; and, when obtained, they were hidden on the premises either of Aram or Houseman, or else in a place called St. Robert's Cave, which was situated in a field adjoining the Nid, a river near Knaresborough. When this source was thoroughly exploited, a new scheme was hit on by this 'long firm.' Clark should pretend to be about to give a great wedding-feast, and he went about gaily, borrowing silver tankards, salvers, salts, spoons, &c., from whoever would lend them. Indeed, so multifarious were his perquisitions, that, according to one contemporary account, he got, among other goods, the following: 'three silver tankards, four silver pints, one silver milk-pot, one ring set with an emerald, and two brilliant diamonds, another with three rose diamonds, a third with an amethyst in the shape of a heart, and six plain rings, eight watches, two snuff-boxes, Chambers' Dictionary, two vols. folio, Pope's "Homer," six vols., bound.'

Having got all that could be got, it was now high time that Clark should disappear. He was last seen on the early morning of the 8th February, 1745, and from that time until August 1, 1758, nothing was heard of him. He was supposed to have gone away with all his booty—and yet not all of it, for suspicion was aroused that both Aram and Houseman, from their intimacy with Clark, were accomplices in his frauds. And so it clearly proved, for, on Aram's house being searched, several articles were found the produce of their joint roguery, and in his garden were found buried, cambric and other goods, wrapped in coarse canvas. Still, neither he, nor Houseman, nor Terry were prosecuted,[1] but Aram thought it prudent to change his residence; so one fine day he left his wife and family, and wandered forth. We have seen the roving life he led, restless, and always changing his abode; yet, during those thirteen years of shifting exile, it must be said, to his credit, that no breath of scandal attached to him; he was studious,

[1] Though no warrants were issued against them, Aram was arrested for debt, in order to keep him; yet he immediately discharged this debt—not only so, he paid off a mortgage on his property at Bondgate. Suspicious facts, considering he was, notably, a poor man.

somewhat morose, yet he was so liked by the boys at the grammar-school at Lynn, that, when he was taken thence by the officers of justice, they cried at losing him.

Whilst at Lynn, he was recognised in June, 1758, by a horse-dealer, and this recognition eventually led to his apprehension; for, during that summer, a labourer, digging for stone or gravel at a place called Thistle Hill, near Knaresborough, found, at the depth of two feet, a skeleton, which appeared to have been buried doubled up. The remembrance of Clark's disappearance was at once awakened, and the body was set down as being his.

A country town has a keen recollection of anything which has occurred disturbing its equal pace, and the connection of Aram and Houseman with Clark was duly remembered. Aram was away, but Houseman still lived among them, and he was ordered by the coroner to attend the inquest. The principal witness was Anna Aram, Eugene's wife, and she had frequently, since her husband's departure, dropped hints of her suspicion that Clark had been murdered. Her evidence is clear. She said that Daniel Clark was an intimate acquaintance of her husband's, and that they had frequent transactions together before the 8th of February, 1744—5, and that Richard Houseman was often with them; particularly that, on the 7th of February, 1744—5, about six o'clock in the evening, Aram came home when she was washing in the kitchen, upon which he directed her to put out the fire, and make one above stairs; she accordingly did so. About two o'clock in the morning of the 8th of February, Aram, Clark, and Houseman came to Aram's house, and went upstairs to the room where she was. They stayed about an hour. Her husband asked her for a handkerchief for Dickey (meaning Richard Houseman) to tie about his head; she accordingly lent him one. Then Clark said, 'It will soon be morning, and we must get off.' After which Aram, Houseman, and Clark all went out together; that, upon Clark's going out, she observed him take a sack or wallet upon his back, which he carried along with him; whither they went she could not tell. That about five o'clock the same morning her husband and Houseman returned, but Clark did not come with them. Her husband came upstairs, and desired to have a candle that he might make a fire below. To which she objected, and said, 'There was no occasion for two fires, as there was a good one in the room above, where she then was.' To which Aram, her husband, answered, 'Dickey' (meaning Richard Houseman) 'was below, and did not choose to come upstairs.' Upon which she asked (Clark not returning with them), 'What had they done with Daniel?' To this her husband gave her no answer, but desired her to go to bed, which she refused to do, and told him, 'They had been doing something bad.' Then Aram went down with the candle.

She, being desirous to know what her husband and Houseman were doing, and being about to go downstairs, she heard Houseman say to Aram,

'She is coming.'

Her husband replied, 'We'll not let her.'

Houseman then said, 'If she does, she'll tell.'

'What can she tell?' replied Aram. 'Poor simple thing! she knows nothing.'

To which Houseman said, 'If she tells that I am here, 'twill be enough.'

Her husband then said, 'I will hold the door to prevent her from coming.'

Whereupon Houseman said, 'Something must be done to prevent her telling,' and pressed him to it very much, and said, 'If she does not tell now, she may at some other time.'

'No,' said her husband, 'we will coax her a little until her passion be off, and then take an opportunity to shoot her.'

Upon which Houseman appeared satisfied and said, 'What must be done with her clothes?' Whereupon they both agreed that they would let her lie where she was shot in her clothes.

She, hearing this discourse, was much terrified, but remained quiet, until near seven o'clock in the same morning, when Aram and Houseman went out of the house. Upon which Mrs. Aram, coming down-stairs, and seeing there had been a fire below and all the ashes taken out of the grate, she went and examined the dung-hill; and, perceiving ashes of a different kind to lie upon it, she searched amongst them, and found several pieces of linen and woollen cloth, very near burnt, which had the appearance of belonging to wearing apparel. When she returned into the house from the dung-hill, she found the handkerchief she had lent Houseman the night before; and, looking at it, she found some blood upon it, about the size of a shilling. Upon which she immediately went to Houseman, and showed him the pieces of cloth she had found, and said 'she was afraid they had done something bad to Clark.' But Houseman then pretended he was a stranger to her accusation, and said 'he knew nothing what she meant.'

From the above circumstances she believed Daniel Clark to have been murdered by Richard Houseman and Eugene Aram, on the 8th of February, 1744—5.

Several witnesses gave evidence that the last persons seen with Clark were Aram and Houseman, and two surgeons gave it as their opinion that the body might have lain in the ground about thirteen or fourteen years.

During the inquiry Houseman seemed very uneasy: he trembled, turned pale, and faltered in his speech; and when, at the instigation of the coroner, in accordance with the superstitious practice of the time, he went to touch the bones, he was very averse so to do. At last he mustered up courage enough to take up one of the bones in his hand; but, immediately throwing it down again, he exclaimed: 'This is no more Dan Clark's bone than it is mine!' He further said he could produce a witness who had seen Clark after the 8th of February; and he called on Parkinson, who deposed that, personally, he had not seen Clark after that time, but a friend of his (Parkinson's) had told him that he had met a person like Daniel Clark, but as it was a snowy day, and the person had the cape of his great-coat up, he could not say with the least degree of certainty who he was.

Of course, this witness did not help Houseman a bit, and then the suspicion increased that he was either the principal, or an accomplice in Clark's murder. Application was made to a magistrate, who granted a warrant for his apprehension. At his examination he made a statement, which he would not sign, saying, 'He chose to waive it for the present; for he might have something to add, and therefore desired to have time to consider of it.' This confirmed former suspicions, and he was committed to York Castle.

On his way thither he was very uneasy, and, hearing that the magistrate who committed him was at that time in York, he asked him to be sent for, and he made the following statement:

The examination of Richard Houseman, of Knaresbrough, flax-dresser.

'This examinant saies that true it is that Daniel Clark was murdered by Eugene Aram, late of Knaresbrough, schoolmaster, and, as he believes, it was on Friday morning, the 8th of February, 1744, as set forth by other informations, as to matter of time; for that he, and Eugene Aram and Daniel Clark were together at Aram's house early in the morning, when there was snow on the ground, and moonlight, and went out of Aram's house a little before them, and went up the street a little before them, and they called to him to go a little way with them; and he accordingly went with them to a place called St. Robert's Cave, near Grimble Bridge, where Aram and Clark stopt a little; and then he saw Aram strike him several times over the breast and head, and saw him fall, as if he was dead, and he, the examinant, came away and left them together, but whether Aram used any weapon or not to kill him with, he can't tell, nor does he know what he did with the body afterwards, but believes Aram left it at the Cave's mouth; for this examinant, seeing Aram do this, to which, he declares, he was no way abetting, or privy to, nor knew of his design to kill him at all. This made the examinant make the best of his way from him, lest he might share the same fate; and got to the bridge-end, and then lookt back, and saw him coming from the Cave-side, which is in a private rock adjoining the river; and he could discern some bundle in his hand, but does not know what it was. On which he, this informant, made the best of his way to the town, without joining Aram again, or seeing him again till the next day, and from that time to this, he has never had any private discourse with him.'

After signing this statement, Houseman said that Clark's body would be found in St. Robert's Cave, in the turn at the entrance of the cave, its head lying to the right; and, sure enough, in the spot described, and in that position, was a skeleton found, with two holes in its skull, made apparently with a pickaxe or hammer.

A warrant was at once issued for the apprehension of Aram, and duly executed at Lynn. When first questioned, he denied ever having been at Knaresborough, or that he had ever known Daniel Clark; but when he was confronted with the constable from Knaresborough, he was obliged to retract his words. On the journey to York, Aram was restless, inquiring after his old neighbours, and what they said of him. He was told that they were much enraged against him for the loss of their goods. Whereupon he asked if it would not be possible to make up the matter? and the answer was, perhaps it might be, if he restored what they had lost. He then said that was impossible, but he might, perhaps, find them an equivalent.

On his arrival at York, he was taken before a magistrate, to whom he made a statement, which was a parcel of lies. He was committed to York

Castle, but had not gone more than a mile on his way thither when he wished to return and make a second statement, which was as follows :

'That he was at his own house on the 7th of February, 1744—5, at night, when Richard Houseman and Daniel Clark came to him with some plate; and both of them went for more, several times, and came back with several pieces of plate, of which Clark was endeavouring to defraud his neighbours; that he could not but observe that Houseman was all night very diligent to assist him to the utmost of his power, and insisted that this was Houseman's business that night, and not the signing any note or instrument, as is pretended by Houseman; that Henry Terry, then of Knaresborough, ale-keeper, was as much concerned in abetting the said frauds as either Houseman or Clark; but was not now at Aram's house, because as it was market-day—his absence from his guests might have occasioned some suspicion; that Terry, notwithstanding, brought two silver tankards that night, upon Clark's account, which had been fraudulently obtained; and that Clark, so far from having borrowed twenty pounds of Houseman, to his knowledge never borrowed more than nine pounds, which he paid again before that night.

'That all the leather Clark had—which amounted to a considerable value—he well knows was concealed under flax in Houseman's house, with intent to be disposed of by little and little, in order to prevent suspicion of his being concerned in Clark's fraudulent practices.

'That Terry took the plate in a bag, as Clark and Houseman did the watches, rings, and several small things of value, and carried them into the flat, where they and he' (Aram) 'went together to St. Robert's Cave, and beat most of the plate flat. It was thought too late in the morning, being about four o'clock, on the 8th of February, 1744—5, for Clark to go off, so as to get to any distance; it was therefore agreed he should stay there till the night following, and Clark, accordingly, stayed there all that day, as he believes, they having agreed to send him victuals, which were carried to him by Henry Terry, he being judged the most likely person to do it without suspicion; for, as he was a shooter, he might go thither under the pretence of sporting; that the next night, in order to give Clark more time to get off, Henry Terry, Richard Houseman, and himself went down to the cave very early; but he' (Aram) 'did not go in, or see Clark at all; that Richard Houseman and Henry Terry only went into the cave, he staying to watch at a little distance on the outside, lest anybody should surprise them.

'That he believes they were beating some plate, for he heard them make a noise. They stayed there about an hour, and then came out of the cave, and told him that Clark was gone off. Observing a bag they had along with them, he took it in his hand, and saw that it contained plate. On asking why Daniel did not take the plate along with him, Terry and Houseman replied that they had bought it of him, as well as the watches, and had given him money for it, that being more convenient for him to go off with, as less cumbersome and dangerous. After which they all three went into Houseman's warehouse, and concealed the watches, with the small plate, there; but that Terry carried away with him the great plate; that, afterwards, Terry told him he carried it to How Hill, and hid it there, and then went into Scotland and disposed of it; but as to Clark, he could not tell whether he was murdered or not, he knew nothing of him, only they told him he was gone off.'

Terry, being thus implicated, was arrested and committed to gaol; but the prosecutors for the crown, after the bills of indictment were preferred against all three, finding their proof insufficient to obtain a conviction at the coming assizes, prevailed on the judge to hold the case over until the Lammas Assizes. There was not enough outside evidence to convict them all; evidence, if any, could only be furnished by the criminals themselves. There was sufficient to convict either Aram or Houseman singly, if one or other would tell the truth, and all he knew; so after many consultations as to the person whom it was most advisable and just to punish, it was unanimously agreed that Aram, who from his education and position was the worst of the lot, should be punished, and in order to do so it was necessary to try to acquit Houseman, who would then be available as evidence against Aram. The case against Terry was so slight, that he was, perforce, let go.

On Friday, 3rd of August, 1759, the trials took place, and Houseman was first arraigned, but there being no evidence against him he was acquitted, to the great surprise and regret of everyone who was not behind the scenes.

Then Aram was put in the dock to stand his trial, and deep, indeed, must have been his disgust, when he found his accomplice, Houseman, step into the witness-box and tell his version (undoubtedly perjured) of the murder. His evidence was, except in a few minor particulars, similar to his previous statement. Sweet innocent! When he saw Aram strike Clark, he made haste home, and knew nothing of the disposal of the body until the next morning, when Aram called on him, and told him he had left it in the cave, and dire were his threats of vengeance should Houseman ever disclose the dread secret of that eventful night.

After this sensational evidence the other witnesses must have seemed very tame. Clark's servant proved that his master had just received his wife's little portion, and that Aram was perfectly cognizant thereof. Another witness deposed to seeing Houseman come out of Aram's house about one o'clock in the morning of the 8th of February. A third deposed to the recovery of some of his own goods of which Clark had defrauded him, and which were found buried in Aram's garden. The constable who arrested him had a few words to say, and the skull was produced in Court, when a surgical expert declared that the fractures must have been produced by blows from some blunt instrument, and could not possibly proceed from natural decay.

Aram was then called upon for his defence, and he produced a manuscript of which the following is a copy. It is, as will be perceived, a laboured and casuistical defence, not having a true ring about it, and not at all like the utterance of a perfectly innocent man.

My Lord,
    I know not whether it is of right or through some indulgence of your Lordship that I am

allowed the liberty at this Bar and at this time to attempt a defence, incapable, and uninstructed as I am to speak. Since, while I see so many eyes upon me, so numerous and awful a concourse, fixed with attention, and filled with I know not what expectancy, I labour, not with guilt, my Lord, but with perplexity. For having never seen a Court but this, being wholly unacquainted with law, the customs of the Bar, and all judiciary proceedings, I fear I shall be so little capable of speaking with propriety in this place, that it exceeds my hope, if I shall be able to speak at all.

I have heard, my Lord, the indictment read, wherein I find myself charged with the highest crime, with an enormity I am altogether incapable of, a fact to the commission of which there goes far more insensibility of heart, more profligacy of morals, than ever fell to my lot. And nothing, possibly, could have admitted a presumption of this nature, but a depravity not inferior to that imputed to me. However, as I stand indicted at your Lordship's Bar, and have heard what is called evidence induced in support of such a charge, I very humbly solicit your Lordship's patience, and beg the hearing of this respectable audience, while I, single and unskilful, destitute of friends, and unassisted by counsel, say something, perhaps like an argument, in my defence. I shall consume but little of your Lordship's time; what I have to say will be short, and this brevity, probably, will be the best part of it. However, it is offered with all possible regard, and the greatest submission to your Lordship's consideration, and that of this honourable Court.

First. My Lord, the whole tenor of my conduct in

life contradicts every particular of this indictment. Yet I had never said this, did not my present circumstances extort it from me, and seem to make it necessary. Permit me here, my Lord, to call upon malignity itself, so long and cruelly busied in this prosecution, to charge upon me any immorality, of which prejudice was not the author. No, my Lord, I concerted not schemes of fraud, projected no violence, injured no man's person or property. My days were honestly laborious, my nights intensely studious. And I humbly conceive my notice of this, especially at this time, will not be thought impertinent or unreasonable, but, at least, deserving some attention. Because, my Lord, that any person, after a temperate use of life, a series of thinking and acting regularly, and without one single deviation from sobriety, should plunge into the very depth of profligacy, precipitately, and at once, is altogether improbable and unprecedented, and absolutely inconsistent with the course of things. Mankind is never corrupted at once; villainy is always progressive, and declines from right, step after step, till every regard of probity is lost, and all moral obligation totally perishes.

Again, my Lord, a suspicion of this kind, which nothing but malevolence could entertain, and ignorance propagate, is violently opposed by my very situation at that time, with respect to health. For, but a little space before, I had been confined to my bed, and suffered under a very long and severe disorder, and was not able, for half a year together, so much as to walk. The distemper left me, indeed, yet slowly, and in part; but so macerated, so enfeebled, that I was reduced to crutches, and was so far from being well about the time I am charged with this fact, that I never to this day perfectly recovered. Could, then, a person in this condition take anything into his head so unlikely, so extravagant? I, past the vigour of my age, feeble and valetudinary, with no inducement to engage, no ability to accomplish, no weapon wherewith to perpetrate such a fact; without interest, without power, without motive, without means.

Besides, it must needs occur to everyone that an action of this atrocious nature is never heard of, but, when its springs are laid open, it appears that it was to support some indolence or supply some luxury, to satisfy some avarice or oblige some malice, to prevent some real, or some imaginary want; yet I lay not under the influence of any one of these. Surely, my Lord, I may, consistent with both truth and modesty, affirm thus much; and none who have any veracity, and knew me, will ever question this.

In the second plea, the disappearance of Clark is suggested as an argument of his being dead; but the uncertainty of such an inference from that, and the fallibility of all conclusions of such a sort, from such a circumstance, are too obvious and too notorious to require instances; yet, superceding many, permit me to produce a very recent one, and that afforded by this castle.

In June, 1757, William Thompson, for all the vigilance of this place, in open daylight, and double-ironed, made his escape, and, notwithstanding an immediate inquiry set on foot, the strictest search, and all advertisements, was never seen or heard of since. If, then, Thompson got off unseen, through all these difficulties, how very easy was it for Clark, when none of them opposed him? But what would be thought of a prosecution commenced against any one seen last with Thompson?

Permit me next, my Lord, to observe a little upon the bones which have been discovered. It is said, which, perhaps, is saying very far, that these are the skeleton of a man. It is possible, indeed it may; but is there any certain known criterion which incontestibly distinguishes the sex in human bones? Let it be considered, my Lord, whether the ascertaining of this point ought not to precede any attempt to identify them.

The place of their deposition, too, claims much more attention than is commonly bestowed upon it. For, of all places in the world, none could have mentioned anyone wherein there was greater certainty of finding human bones than an hermitage, except he should point out a churchyard. Hermitages, in times past, being not only places of religious retirement, but of burial, too, and it has scarce or never been heard of, but that every cell now known, contains, or contained, these relics of humanity, some mutilated and some entire. I do not inform, but give me leave to remind, your Lordship, that here sat solitary sanctity, and here the hermit, or the anchoress, hoped that repose for their bones, when dead, they here enjoyed when living.

All this while, my Lord, I am sensible this is known to your Lordship, and many in this Court, better than I. But it seems necessary to my case, that others, who have not at all, perhaps, adverted to things of this nature, and may have concern in my trial, should be made acquainted with it. Suffer me, then, my Lord, to produce a few of many evidences that these cells were used as repositories of the dead, and to enumerate a few, in which human bones have been found, as it happened in this in question, lest, to some, that accident might seem extraordinary, and, consequently, occasion prejudice.

1. The bones, as was supposed, of the Saxon, St. Dubritius, were discovered buried in his cell at Guy's Cliff near Warwick, as appears from the authority of Sir William Dugdale.

2. The bones, thought to be those of the anchoress Rosia, were but lately discovered in a cell at Royston, entire, fair, and undecayed, though they must have lain interred for several centuries, as is proved by Dr. Stukeley.

3. But our own country, nay, almost this neighbourhood, supplies another instance; for in January, 1747, was found by Mr. Stovin, accompanied by a reverend gentleman, the bones in part of some recluse, in the cell at Lindholm, near Hatfield. They were believed to be those of William of Lindholm, a hermit, who had long made this cave his habitation.

4. In February, 1744, part of Woburn Abbey being pulled down, a large portion of a corpse appeared, even with the flesh on, and which bore cutting with a knife, though it is certain this had lain above two hundred years, and how much longer is doubtful, for this abbey was founded in 1145, and dissolved in 1558 or 1559.

What would have been said, what believed, if this had been an accident to the bones in question?

Further, my Lord, it is not yet out of living memory that a little distance from Knaresborough, in a field, part of the manor of the worthy and patriotic baronet who does that borough the honour to represent it in Parliament, were found, in digging for gravel, not one human skeleton alone, but five or six, deposited side by side, with each an urn placed at its head, as your Lordship knows was usual in ancient interments.

About the same time, and in another field, almost close to this borough, was discovered also, in searching for gravel, another human skeleton; but the piety of the same worthy gentleman ordered both pits to be filled up again, commendably unwilling to disturb the dead.

Is the invention[1] of these bones forgotten, then, or industriously concealed, that the discovery of those in question may appear the more singular and extraordinary? whereas, in fact, there is nothing extraordinary in it. My Lord, almost every place conceals such remains. In fields, in hills, in highway sides, and in commons lie frequent and unsuspected bones. And our present allotments for rest for the departed, is but of some centuries.

Another particular seems not to claim a little of your Lordship's notice, and that of the gentlemen of the jury; which is, that perhaps no example occurs of more than *one* skeleton being found in *one* cell, and in the cell in question was found but *one*; agreeable, in this, to the peculiarity of every other known cell in Britain. Not the invention of one skeleton, then, but of two, would have appeared suspicious and uncommon.

But then, my Lord, to attempt to identify these, when even to identify living men sometimes has proved so difficult—as in the case of Perkin Warbeck and Lambert Symnel at home, and of Don Sebastian abroad—will be looked upon, perhaps, as an attempt to determine what is indeterminable. And I hope,

[1] Finding.

too, it will not pass unconsidered here, where gentlemen believe with caution, think with reason, and decide with humanity, what interest the endeavour to do this is calculated to serve, in assigning proper personality to those bones, whose particular appropriation can only appear to eternal omniscience.

Permit me, my Lord, also, very humbly to remonstrate that, as human bones appear to have been the inseparable adjuncts of every cell, even any person's naming such a place at random as containing them, in this case, shows him rather unfortunate, than conscious prescient, and that these attendants on every hermitage only accidentally concurred with this conjecture. A mere casual coincidence of *words* and *things*.

But it seems another skeleton has been discovered by some labourer, which was full as confidently averred to be Clark's as this. My Lord, must some of the living, if it promotes some interest, be made answerable for all the bones that earth has concealed, and chance exposed? and might not a place where bones lay, be mentioned by a person by chance, as well as found by a labourer by chance? Or, is it more criminal accidentally to *name* where bones lie, than accidentally to *find* where they lie?

Here, too, is a human skull produced, which is fractured; but was this the *cause* or was it the consequence of death—was it owing to violence, or was it the effect of natural decay? If it was violence, was that violence before or after death? My Lord, in May, 1732, the remains of William, Lord Archbishop of this province, were taken up by permission, in this cathedral, and the bones of the skull were found broken; yet certainly he died by no violence offered to him alive, that could occasion that fracture there.

Let it be considered, my Lord, that upon the dissolution of religious houses, and the commencement of the Reformation, the ravages of those times affected the living and the dead. In search after imaginary treasures, coffins were broken up, graves and vaults broken open, monuments ransacked, and shrines demolished; your Lordship knows that these violations proceeded so far, as to occasion parliamentary authority to restrain them; and it did, about the beginning of the reign of Queen Elizabeth. I entreat your Lordship, suffer not the violence, the depredations, and the iniquities of these times to be imputed to this.

Moreover, what gentleman here is ignorant that Knaresborough had a castle, which, though now a ruin, was once considerable, both for its strength and garrison. All know it was vigorously besieged by the arms of the Parliament. At which siege, in sallies, conflicts, flights, pursuits, many fell in all the places around it; and where they fell were buried. For every place, my Lord, is burial-earth in war; and many, questionless, of these yet rest unknown, whose bones futurity shall discover.

I hope, with all imaginable submission, that what has been said will not be thought impertinent to this indictment, and that it will be far from the wisdom, the learning, and the integrity of this place to impute to the living what zeal, in its fury, may have done; what nature may have taken off, and piety interred; or what war alone may have destroyed, alone deposited.

As to the circumstances that have been raked together, I have nothing to observe; but that all circumstances whatsoever are precarious, and have been but too frequently found lamentably fallible; even the strongest have failed. They may rise to the utmost degree of probability, yet they are but probability still. Why should I name to your Lordship the two Harrisons, recorded in Dr. Howel, who both suffered upon circumstances, because of the sudden disappearance of their lodger, who was in credit, had contracted debts, borrowed money, and went off unseen, and returned again a great many years after their execution. Why name the intricate affair of Jaques du Moulin under King Charles II., related by a gentleman who was counsel for the Crown. And why the unhappy Coleman, who suffered innocent, though convicted upon positive evidence, and whose children perished for want, because the world uncharitably believed the father guilty. Why mention the perjury of Smith, incautiously admitted king's evidence; who, to screen himself, equally accused Fainlotte and Loveday of the murder of Dunn; the first of whom, in 1749, was executed at Winchester; and Loveday was about to suffer at Reading, had not Smith been proved perjured, to the satisfaction of the court, by the surgeon of Gosport Hospital.

Now, my Lord, having endeavoured to show that the whole of this process is altogether repugnant to every part of my life; that it is inconsistent with my condition of health about that time; that no rational inference can be drawn that a person is dead who suddenly disappears; that hermitages were the constant repositories of the bones of the recluse; that the proofs of this are well authenticated; that the revolution in religion, or the fortunes of war, has mangled, or buried, the dead; the conclusion remains, perhaps no less reasonably, than impatiently, wished for. I, last, after a year's confinement, equal to either fortune. put myself upon the candour, the justice, and the humanity of your Lordship, and upon yours, my countrymen, gentlemen of the jury.'

It will be seen from this elaborate defence that it must have been written long before his trial, and before his hopes of acquittal were crushed by the appearance of Houseman in the witness-box to give evidence against him; for he did not attempt to discredit his evidence, nor did he attempt to shake his testimony by cross-examination, and he must have anticipated the result. The judge summed up carefully; he recapitulated the evidence, and showed how Houseman's testimony was confirmed by the other witnesses; and, taking Aram's defence, he pointed out that he had alleged nothing that could invalidate the positive evidence against him. The jury, without leaving the court, returned a verdict of 'Guilty,' and the judge pronounced the awful sentence of the law. Aram had behaved with great firmness and dignity during the whole of his trial, and he heard his conviction, and his doom, with profound composure, leaving the bar with a smile upon his countenance.

In those days the law allowed but little time for appeal. Aram was tried, convicted, and sentenced on Friday, the 3rd of August, 1759, and he had to die on the following Monday—only two whole days of life being allowed him. Those days must have been days of exquisite torture to him, when he thought of the upturned faces of the mob, all fixing their gaze upon him, yelling at, and execrating him, and we can scarcely wonder at his attempting to commit suicide. On the Monday morning, when the clergyman came to visit him, and at his request to administer the Sacrament to him, he was astonished to find Aram stretched on the floor of his cell in a pool of blood. He had managed to secrete a razor, and had cut the veins of his arms in two places. Surgeons were sent for, and they brought him back to life, when he was put into the cart and led to execution. Arrived at the gallows, he was asked if he had any speech to make, and he replied in the negative. He was then hanged, and, when dead, his body was cut down, put in a cart, taken to Knaresborough, and there suspended in chains, on a gibbet which was erected on Knaresborough forest, south or south-east of the Low Bridge, on the right hand side going thence to Plumpton. It was taken down in 1778, when the forest was enclosed.

He left his latest thoughts in writing, for, on the table in his cell, was found a paper on which was written,

'What am I better than my fathers? To die is natural and necessary. Perfectly sensible of this, I fear no more to die than I did to be born. But the manner of it is something which should, in my opinion, be decent and manly. I think I have regarded both these points. Certainly nobody has a better right to dispose of man's life than himself; and he, not others, should determine how. As for any indignities offered to anybody, or silly reflections on my faith and morals, they are (as they were) things indifferent to me. I think, though, contrary to the common way of thinking; I wrong no man by this, and I hope it is not offensive to that eternal being who formed me and the world; and as by this I injure no man, no man can be reasonably offended.

I solicitously recommend myself to the eternal and almighty Being, the God of Nature, if I have done amiss. But perhaps I have not, and I hope this thing will never be imputed to me. Though I am now stained by malevolence, and suffer by prejudice, I hope to rise fair and unblemished. My life was not polluted, my morals irreproachable, and my opinions orthodox.

'I slept soundly till three o'clock, awak'd, and then writ these lines.

> ' " Come, pleasing Rest, eternal Slumber fall;
> Seal mine, that once must seal the eyes of all;
> Calm and compos'd my soul her journey takes,
> No guilt that troubles, and no heart that aches.
> Adieu! thou sun, all bright like her arise;
> Adieu! fair friends, and all that's good and wise."'

Aram never made any regular confession of his guilt—but in a letter he wrote to the vicar of Knaresborough, in which he gives his autobiography, he says, 'Something is expected as to the affair upon which I was committed, to which I say, as I mentioned in my examination, that all the plate of Knaresborough, except the watches and rings, were in Houseman's possession; as for me, I had nothing at all. My wife knows that Terry had the large plate, and that Houseman himself took both that and the watches, at my house, from Clark's own hands; and, if she will not give this in evidence for the town, she wrongs both that and her own conscience; and, if it is not done soon, Houseman will prevent her. She likewise knows that Terry's wife had some velvet, and, if she will, can testify it. She deserves not the regard of the town, if she will not. That part of Houseman's evidence, wherein he said I threatened him, was absolutely false; for what hindered him, when I was so long absent and far distant? I must need observe another thing to be perjury in Houseman's evidence, in which he said he went home from Clark; whereas he went straight to my house, as my wife can also testify, if I be not believed.'

The contemporary accounts of his trial, whether published in York or London, have the following:

'Aram's sentence was a just one, and he submitted to it with that stoicism he so much affected; and the morning after he was condemned, he confessed the justness of it to two clergymen (who had a licence from the judge to attend him), by declaring that he murdered Clark. Being asked by one of them what his motive was for doing that abominable action, he told them, 'he suspected Clark of having an unlawful commerce with his wife; that he was persuaded at the time, when he committed the murder, he did right, but, since, he had thought it wrong.'

'After this, pray,' said Aram, 'what became of Clark's body, if Houseman went home (as he said upon my trial) immediately on seeing him fall?'

One of the clergymen replied, 'I'll tell you what became of it. You and Houseman dragged it into the cave, stripped and buried it there; brought away his clothes, and burnt them at your own house.'

To which he assented. He was asked whether Houseman did not earnestly press him to murder his wife, for fear she should discover the business they had been about. He hastily replied,

'He did, and pressed me several times to do it.'

Aram's wife lived some years after his execution; indeed, she did not die until 1774. She lived in a small house near Low Bridge, within sight of her husband's gibbet; and here she sold pies, sausages, &c. It is said that she used to search under the gibbet for any of her husband's bones that might have fallen, and then bury them.

Aram, by his wife, had six children, who survived their childhood—three sons and three daughters. All these children, save one, Sally, took after their mother; but Sally resembled her father, both physically and mentally. She was well read in the classics, and Aram would sometimes put his scholars to the blush, by having Sally in their class. Her father was very fond of her, and she was living with him at Lynn when he was arrested, and she clung to him when in prison at York. On his death, she went to London, and, after a time, she married, and, with her husband, kept a public-house on the Surrey side of Westminster Bridge.

Houseman went back to Knaresborough, where he abode until his death. He was naturally mobbed, and never dared stir out in the day time, but sometimes slunk out at night. Despised and detested by all, his life must have been a burden to him, and his punishment in this world far heavier than Aram was called upon to bear.

REDEMPTIONERS.

SLAVERY, properly so called, appears to have been from the earliest ages, and in almost every country, the condition of a large portion of the human race; the weakest had ever to serve the strong—whether the slave was a captive in battle, or an impecunious debtor unable to satisfy the claims of his creditor, save with his body. Climate made no difference. Slavery existed in Europe, Asia, and Africa, and in our own 'right little, tight little island,' our early annals show that a large proportion of the Anglo-Saxon population was in a state of slavery. These unfortunate bondsmen, who were called theows, throels, and esnes,[1] were bought and sold with land, and were classed in the inventory of their lord's wealth, with his sheep, swine, and oxen, and were bequeathed by will, precisely as we now dispose of our money, or furniture.

The condition of the Anglo-Saxon slaves was very degraded indeed; their master might put them in bonds, might whip them, nay, might even brand them, like cattle, with his own distinguishing mark, a

[1] The esne was a man of the servile class, a poor mercenary, serving for hire, or for his land, but was not of so low a rank as the other classes.

state of things which existed until Alfred the Great enacted some laws, whereby the time of the servitude of these unhappy people was limited to six years, and the institution of slavery received such a blow, that it speedily became a thing of the past. They were no longer slaves, but redemptioners, *i.e.*, they had the hope of redemption from servitude, and the law gave them the power to enforce their freedom.

We have only to turn to the pages of holy writ to find slavery flourishing in rank luxuriance in the time of the patriarchs, and before the birth of Moses. Euphemistically described in Scripture history as servants, they were mostly unconditional and perpetual slaves. They were strangers, either taken prisoners in war or purchased from the neighbouring nations; but the Jews also had a class of servants who only were in compulsory bondage for a limited time, and they were men of their own nation.

These were men who, by reason of their poverty, were obliged to give their bodies in exchange for the wherewithal to support them, or they were insolvent debtors, and thus sought to liquidate their indebtedness, or men who had committed a theft, and had not the means of making the double, or fourfold, restitution that the law required. Their thraldom was not perpetual, they might be redeemed, and, if not redeemed, they became free on the completion of their seventh year of servitude.

Exodus, chap. 21, vv. 2—6. 'If thou buy an Hebrew servant, six years shall he serve : and in the seventh he shall go out free for nothing. If he came in by himself, he shall go out by himself; if he were married, then his wife shall go out with him. If his master have given him a wife, and she have borne him sons or daughters, the wife and her children shall be her master's, and he shall go out by himself. And if the servant shall plainly say, I love my master, my wife, and my children : I will not go out free: then his master shall bring him unto the judges; he shall also bring him to the door, or unto the doorpost; and his master shall bore his ear through with an awl, and he shall serve for ever.'

Here, then, we have a redemptioner, one whose servitude was not a hopeless one, and we find this limited bondage again referred to in Leviticus, chap. 25, vv. 39, 40, 41.

' And if thy brother that dwelleth by thee be waxen poor, and be sold unto thee, thou shalt not compel him to serve as a bond servant : but as an hired servant, and as a sojourner, he shall be with thee, and shall serve thee unto the year of jubilee. And then shall he depart from thee, both he and his children with him, and shall return unto his own family, and unto the possession of his fathers shall he return.'

Here in England we are accustomed to look upon the slave from one point of view only, as an unhappy being of a different race and colour to ourselves, few of us knowing that there has been a time (and that not so very long ago) when members of our own nation, so utterly forlorn and miserable from the rude buffetings Fortune had given them in their way through the world, have been glad to sell their bodies for a time, to enable them to commence afresh the struggle for existence, in another land, and, perchance, under more favourable circumstances.

In 'his Majesty's plantations' of Virginia, Maryland, and New England, and in the West Indies, these unfortunates were first called servants, and as such are officially described; but in America in later times they received the appellation of redemptioners, a name by which they were certainly called in the middle of this century, for in Dorsey's 'Laws of Maryland,' published in 1840, we find an Act[1] (cap. 226) was passed in 1817 to alleviate the condition of these poor people. The preamble sets forth, 'Whereas it has been found that German and Swiss emigrants, who for the discharge of the debt contracted for their passage to this country are often obliged to subject themselves to temporary servitude, are frequently exposed to cruel and oppressive impositions by the masters of the vessels in which they arrive, and likewise by those to whom they become servants,' &c.

It is impossible to fix any date when this iniquitous traffic first began. It arose, probably, from the want of labourers in the plantations of our colonies in their early days, and the employment of unscrupulous agents on this side to supply their needs in this respect. A man in pecuniary difficulties in the seventeenth and eighteen centuries was indeed in woeful plight: a gaol was his certain destination, and there he might rot his life away, cut off from all hope of release, unless death came mercifully to his relief. All knew of the horrors of a debtor's prison, and, to escape them, an able-bodied man had recourse to the dreadful expedient of selling himself into bondage, for a term of years, in one of the plantations, either in America or the West Indies, or he would believe the specious tales of the 'kidnappers,' as they were called, who would promise anything, a free passage, and a glorious life of ease and prosperity in a new land.

[1] An Act relative to German and Swiss redemptioners.

Thoroughly broken down, wretched, and miserable, his thoughts would naturally turn towards a new country, wherein he might rehabilitate himself, and, in an evil hour, he would apply to some (as we should term it) emigration agent, who would even kindly advance him a trifle for an outfit. The voyage out would be an unhappy experience, as the emigrants would be huddled together, with scant food, and, on his arrival at his destination, he would early discover the further miseries in store for him; for, immediately on landing, or even before he left the ship, his body would be seized as security for passage money, which had, in all probability, been promised him free, and for money lent for his outfit; and, having no means of paying either, utterly friendless, and in a strange country, he would be sold to slavery for a term of years to some planter who would pay the debt for him.

Having obtained his flesh and blood at such a cheap rate, his owner would not part with him lightly, and it was an easy thing to arrange matters so that he was always kept in debt for clothes and tobacco, &c., in order that he never should free himself. It was a far cry to England, and with no one to help him, or to draw public attention to his case, the poor wretch had to linger until death mercifully released him from his bondage; his condition being truly deplorable, as he would be under the same regulations as the convicts, and one may be very sure that *their* lot was not enviable in those harsh and merciless times. It was not for many years, until the beginning of this century, that the American laws took a beneficial turn in favour of these unhappy people; and it was then too late, for the institution of redemptioners died a speedy death, owing to the influx of free emigration.

One of the earliest notices of these unfortunates is in a collection of Old Black letter ballads, in the British Museum, where there is one entitled, 'The Trappan'd Maiden, or the Distressed Damsel,' $\frac{\text{c. 22, e. 2}}{186}$, in which are depicted some of the sorrows which were undergone by these unwilling emigrants, at that time. The date, as nearly as can be assigned to it, is about 1670.

> The Girl was cunningly trapan'd,
> Sent to Virginny from England;
> Where she doth Hardship undergo,
> There is no cure, it must be so;
> But if she lives to cross the main,
> She vows she'll ne'er go there again.
>
> Give ear unto a Maid
> That lately was betray'd,
> And sent into Virginny, O :
> In brief I shall declare,
> What I have suffered there,
> When that I was weary, O.
>
> When that first I came
> To this Land of Fame,
> Which is called Virginny, O :
> The Axe and the Hoe
> Have wrought my overthrow,
> When that I was weary, O.
>
> Five years served I
> Under Master Guy,
> In the land of Virginny, O :
> Which made me for to know
> Sorrow, Grief, and Woe,
> When that I was weary, O.

When my Dame says, Go,
Then must I do so,
In the land of Virginny, O :
When she sits at meat
Then I have none to eat,
When that I was weary, O.

The cloathes that I brought in,
They are worn very thin,
In the land of Virginny, O :
Which makes me for to say
Alas! and well-a-day,
When that I was weary, O.

Instead of Beds of Ease,
To lye down when I please,
In the land of Virginny, O :
Upon a bed of straw,
I lay down full of woe,
When that I was weary, O.

Then the Spider, she
Daily waits on me,
In the land of Virginny, O :
Round about my bed
She spins her tender web,
When that I was weary, O.

So soon as it is day,
To work I must away,
In the land of Virginny, O :
Then my Dame she knocks
With her tinder-box,
When that I was weary, O.

I have played my part
Both at Plow and Cart,
In the land of Virginny, O ;
Billats from the Wood,
Upon my back they load,
When that I was weary, O.

Instead of drinking Beer,
I drink the waters clear,
In the land of Virginny, O;
Which makes me pale and wan,
Do all that e'er I can,
When that I was weary, O.

If my Dame says, Go,
I dare not say no,
In the land of Virginny, O;
The water from the spring
Upon my head I bring,
When that I was weary, O.

When the Mill doth stand,
I'm ready at command,
In the land of Virginny, O;
The Morter for to make,
Which made my heart to ake,
When that I was weary, O.

When the child doth cry,
I must sing, By-a-by,
In the land of Virginny, O;
No rest that I can have
Whilst I am here a slave,
When that I was weary, O.

A thousand Woes beside,
That I do here abide,
In the land of Virginny, O;
In misery I spend
My time that hath no end,
When that I was weary, O.

Then let Maids beware,
All by my ill-fare,
In the land of Virginny, O:
Be sure thou stay at home,
For if you do here come,
You will all be weary, O.

> But if it be my chance,
> Homeward to advance,
> From the land of Virginny, O :
> If that I once more
> Land on English shore,
> I'll no more be weary, O.

Some of these complaints would seem to us to be rather of the 'crumpled rose-leaf' order, but probably there was enough humanity left in their owners to treat their female 'servants' more tenderly than the male, whose sorrows were genuine enough.

Ned Ward, in his 'London Spy,' 1703, gives a most graphic account of the sort of men who enticed these human chattels to the plantations. He was pursuing his perambulations about the City, exercising those sharp eyes of his, which saw everything, and was in the neighbourhood of the Custom-house, when he turned down a place called Pig Hill (so called, he says, from its resembling the steep descent down which the Devil drove his Hogs to a Bad Market).

'As we walked up the Hill, as Lazily as an Artillery Captain before his Company upon a Lord Mayor's Day, or a Paul's Labourer up a Ladder, with a Hod of Mortar, we peeped in at a Gateway, where we saw two or three Blades, well drest, but with Hawkes' Countenances, attended with half-a-dozen Ragamuffingly Fellows, showing Poverty in their Rags and Despair in their Faces, mixt with a parcel of young, wild striplings, like runaway 'Prentices. I could not forbear enquiring of my Friend about the ill-favoured multitude, patched up of such awkward Figures, that it would have puzzled a Moor-

Fields Artist,[1] well-read in physiognomy, to have discovered their Dispositions by their Looks.

'"That House," says my Friend, "which they there are entering is an Office where Servants for the Plantations bind themselves to be miserable as long as they live, without a special Providence prevents it. Those fine Fellows, who look like Footmen upon a Holy day, crept into cast suits of their Masters, that want Gentility in their Deportments answerable to their Apparel, are Kidnappers, who walk the 'Change and other parts of the Town, in order to seduce People who want services and young Fools crost in Love, and under an uneasiness of mind, to go beyond the seas, getting so much a head of Masters of Ships and Merchants who go over, for every Wretch they trepan into this Misery. These young Rakes and Tatterdemallions you see so lovingly hearded are drawn by their fair promises to sell themselves into Slavery, and the Kidnappers are the Rogues that run away with the Money."'

And again, when he goes on 'Change, he further attacks these villains.

'"Now," says my Friend, "we are got amongst the Plantation Traders. This may be call'd Kidnapper's Walk; for a great many of these Jamaicans and Barbadians, with their Kitchen-stuff Countenances, are looking as sharp for servants as a Gang of Pick-pockets for Booty .... Within that Entry is an Office of Intelligence, pretending to help Servants to Places, and Masters to Servants. They have a knack of Bubbling silly wenches out of their Money; who loiter hereabouts upon the expectancy,

---

[1] Bedlam was then in Moorfields.

till they are pick'd up by the Plantation Kidnappers, and spirited away into a state of misery."'

And yet once more Ward, in his 'Trip to America,' says,

'We had on board an Irishman going over as Servant, who, I suppose, was Kidnapped. I asked him whose Servant he was, "By my Fait," said he, "I cannot tell. I was upon 'Change, looking for a good Master, and a brave Gentleman came to me, and asked me who I was, and I told him I was myn own self; and he gave me some good Wine and good Ale, and brought me on Board, and I have not seen him since."'

Then, as since, the emigration from Great Britain was mostly fed by the poorer classes of Ireland; and, in the latter part of William III.'s reign, such was the numbers that were sent over to the plantations as 'servants,' or in other words, slaves, that it was found necessary to enact special laws, in Maryland, to check the excessive importation, it being considered a source of danger to the State, as tending to introduce Popery. Accordingly, several acts were passed, placing a duty of twenty shillings per head on each Irish person landed; which, proving insufficient for the purpose, was further increased to forty shillings a few years afterwards.

In 1743, there was a *cause célèbre*, in which James Annesley, Esq., appeared as the plaintiff, and claimed the earldom of Anglesey from his uncle Richard, who, he maintained (and he got a verdict in his favour), had caused him to be kidnapped when a lad of thirteen years of age, and sent to America, there to be sold as a slave. That this was absolutely the fact, no one who has read the evidence can

possibly doubt, and the hardships endured by the
'servants' at that time are plaintively alluded to
in a little book, called, 'The Adventure of an Unfortunate Young Nobleman,' published 1743. 'Here
the Captain repeating his former Assurances, he was
sold to a rich Planter in Newcastle County called
Drummond, who immediately took him home, and
entered him in the Number of his Slaves.

'A new World now opened to him, and, being
set to the felling of Timber, a Work no way pro-
portioned to his Strength, he did it so awkwardly,
that he was severely corrected. Drummond was a
hard, inexorable Master, who, like too many of the
Planters, consider their Slaves, or Servants, as a
different Species, and use them accordingly. Our
American Planters are not famous for Humanity,
being often Persons of no Education, and, having
been formerly Slaves themselves, they revenge the
ill-usage they received on those who fall into their
Hands. The Condition of European Servants in
that Climate is very wretched; their Work is hard,
and for the most part abroad, exposed to an unwholesome Air, their Diet coarse, being either Poul
or bread made of Indian Corn, or Homine or Mush,
which is Meal made of the same kind, moistened
with the Fat of Bacon, and their Drink Water sweetened with a little Ginger and Molasses.'

Although, as before stated, Mr. Annesley won his
case with regard to his legitimacy and property, for
some reason or other he never contested the title with
his usurping uncle, who continued to be recognized
as Earl of Anglesey until his death.

Defoe, writing in 1738 in his 'History of Colonel
Jack,' makes his hero to be kidnapped by the master

of a vessel at Leith, and carried to Virginia, where he was consigned to a merchant, and disposed of as he saw fit—in fact, treated with the same *nonchalance* as an ordinary bale of goods would be. He was sold to a planter for five years, and had three hard things to endure, viz., hard work, hard fare, and hard lodging. He describes the arrival of a ship from London with several 'servants,' and amongst the rest were seventeen transported felons, some burnt in the hand, and some not, eight of whom his master purchased for the time specified in the warrant for their transportation, so that the unfortunate men were in no better position than, and were under the same severe laws as, the convict. Their ranks were recruited by many gentlemen concerned in the Rebellion, and taken prisoners at Preston, who were spared from execution and sold into slavery at the plantations, a condition which must often have made them dissatisfied with the clemency extended to them. In many cases, with kind masters, their lot was not so hard, and when their time of bondage was expired they had encouragement given them to plant for themselves, a certain number of acres being allotted to them by the State; and, if they could get the necessary credit for clothes, tools, &c., they were in time enabled to put by money, and, in some rare instances, became men of renown in the colony.

The usage these poor people endured on their passage to the plantations was frequently abominable, and a writer in 1796 describes the arrival, at Baltimore, of a vessel containing three hundred Irish 'passengers' who had been nearly starved by the captain, the ship's water being sold by him at so much a pint, and this treatment, combined with other cruelties too shocking to relate, caused a contagious disorder to break out on board, which carried off great numbers, whilst most of these unhappy folk who were spared at that time, subsequently died whilst performing quarantine in the Delaware.

The redemptioners mainly sailed from the northern ports of Ireland, Belfast or Londonderry, though this country by no means enjoyed the unenviable monopoly of this traffic: Holland and Germany sending their wretched quota of white slaves. The particular class of vessels employed in this iniquitous trade were known by the name of 'White Guineamen,' and belonged to the 'free and enlightened' citizens of the sea-ports in America, who had their kidnappers stationed at certain parts of Scotland, Ireland, Wales, and also in Holland, to provide them with human cargoes. Seduced by the glowing descriptions of a trans-Atlantic paradise, with bright and alluring visions of American happiness and liberty, the miserable, the idle, and the unwary among the lower classes of Europe were entrapped into the voyage, the offer of gratuitous conveyance being an additional bait, which was eagerly accepted; but we have seen how, on their arrival at the promised land, they were speedily disillusioned. The difficulty of hiring tolerable servants was so great, that many persons were obliged to deal with their fellow-creatures in this way, who would otherwise have utterly abhorred the thought of being slave-dealers.

Some of the laws for their regulation in the colonies are curious. For instance, in Virginia, after they had served their time, they were obliged to have a certificate from their master to say that they had done so, and if any person should entertain any hired servant running away without such a certificate, he had to pay the master of such servant thirty pounds weight of tobacco for every day and night he should so harbour him.

Pursuit after runaway servants was made at the public expense, and, if caught, they had to serve for the time of their absence, and the charge disbursed. In case the master refused to pay the charge, the servant was sold, or hired out, until by their services they had reimbursed the amount expended in capturing them, after which they were returned to their master to serve out their time. Whoever apprehended them was to have as reward two hundred pounds weight of tobacco, if the capture took place about ten miles from the master's house, or one hundred pounds weight if above five miles, and under ten. This reward was to be paid by the public, and the servant had to serve some one four months for every two hundred pounds weight of tobacco paid for him.

'Every Master that hath a Servant that hath run away twice, shall keep his Hair close cut, and not so doing, shall be fined one hundred pounds weight of Tobacco for every time the said Fugitive shall, after the second time, be taken up.'

If they ran away in company with any negro, then they had to serve the master of that negro as long as the negro was at large. If any servant laid violent hands on his master, mistress, or overseer, and was convicted of the same in any court, he had to serve one year longer at the expiration of his term.

'A Woman-servant got with Child by her Master, shall, after her time of indenture or custom is expired, be, by the Church-wardens of the Parish where she lived, sold for two Years, and the Tobacco employed for the use of the Parish.'

'No Minister shall publish the Banns, or celebrate the Contract of Marriage between any Servants, unless he hath a Certificate from both their Masters that it is with their consent, under the Penalty of 10,000 lbs. of Tobacco. And the Servants that procure themselves to be married without their Masters' consent, shall each of them serve their respective Master a year longer than their time; and if any person, being free, shall marry with a Servant without the Master's Licence, he or she so marrying shall pay the Master 1500 lbs. of Tobacco, or one year's service.'

In Maryland, the laws respecting servants were somewhat milder, but, if they ran away, they had to serve ten days for every one day's absence. In this colony, however, 'Every Man-Servant shall have given him at the time of the expiration of his Service, one new Hat, a good Cloath Suit, a new Shift of White Linnen, a pair of new French full Shooes and Stockings, two Hoes, and one Axe, and one gun of 20s. price, not above four foot Barrel, nor less than three and a half. And every Woman-Servant shall have given her, at the expiration of her Servitude, the like Provision of Cloaths, and three Barrels of Indian Corn.'

In New England they dealt still more tenderly and fairly by their servants. If a servant fled from the cruelty of his or her master, he or she was to be protected and harboured, provided that they fled to the house of some free man of the same town, and ' If any Man or Woman Hurt, Maim, or Disfigure a Servant, unless it be by meer Casualty, the Servant shall go free, and the Master or Mistress shall make such recompense as the Court shall award. Servants that have serv'd diligently, and faithfully, to the end of their Times, shall not be sent away empty; and such as have been unfaithful, negligent, or unprofitable shall not be sent away unpunished, but shall make such satisfaction as Authority shall direct.'

In Jamaica the laws were pretty fair, and in Barbadoes there was a very just enactment. 'Whatever Master or Mistress shall turn off a Sick Servant, or not use, or endeavour, all lawful means for the recovery of such servant, during the time of Servitude, he or she shall forfeit 2,200 lbs of Sugar. To be levyed by Warrant of a Justice of Peace, and disposed towards the maintenance of such Servant, and the said Servant so neglected, or turned off, shall be Free.'

In the last few years of the eighteenth century, it was no uncommon thing to meet with advertisements in the American papers, couched in the following strain: 'To be disposed of, the indentures of a strong, healthy Irishwoman; who has two years to serve, and is fit for all kinds of house work. Enquire of the Printer.'

'STOP THE VILLAIN!

'Ran away this morning, an Irish Servant, named Michael Day, by trade a Tailor, about five feet eight inches high, fair complexion, has a down look when spoken to, light bushy hair, speaks much in the Irish dialect, &c. Whoever secures the above-described in any gaol, shall receive thirty dollars reward, and all reasonable charges paid. N.B.—All masters of Vessels are forbid harbouring or carrying off the said Servant at their peril.'

The laws which regulated them were originally

framed for the English convicts before the Revolution, and were not repealed. They were, of necessity, harsh and severe, so much so that, towards the end of the eighteenth century, several societies sprang up, both Irish and German, whose members did all in their power to mitigate the severity of these laws, and render their countrymen, during their servitude, as comfortable as circumstances would permit. These societies were in all the large towns south of Connecticut.

When the yellow fever was raging in Baltimore in the year 1793, but few vessels would venture near the city, and every one that could do so fled from the doomed place. But a 'White Guinea-man,' from Germany, arrived in the river, and, hearing that such was the fatal nature of the infection that for no sum of money could a sufficient number of nurses be procured to attend the sick, conceived the philanthropic idea of supplying this deficiency from his redemption passengers, and, sailing boldly up to the city, he advertised his cargo for sale thus: 'A few healthy Servants, generally between seventeen and twenty-one years of age; their times will be disposed of by applying on board the brig.' It was a truly generous thought to thus nobly sacrifice his own countrywomen *pro bono publico!*

As the eighteenth century drew to a close a more humane state of things came into existence; and in Maryland, in 1817, as before stated, a law was passed for the relief of the German and Swiss redemptioners. It was enacted that there should be, in every port, a person to register the apprenticeship, or servitude, of these emigrants, and, unless drawn up or approved by him, no agreement to service was binding. Minors, under twenty-one, were not allowed to be sold, unless by their parents or next-of-kin, and the indentures covenanted that at least two months schooling must be given, annually, to them by their masters. No emigrant was bound to serve more than four years, except males under seventeen, and females under fourteen, who were to serve, respectively, till twenty-one and eighteen. There were many other clauses that related both to their better treatment on board the vessels and on land, and, if this law had been strictly acted up to, the condition of these poor people would have been much ameliorated.

But, happily, in course of years, as the prosperity of the United States of America grew by 'leaps and bounds,' attracting labour in abundance from all parts of Europe, there was no longer any need for the traffic in human flesh and blood, and the redemptioner became a thing of the past.

A TRIP TO RICHMOND IN SURREY.

HE following *morceau* gives so quaint an account of a day's outing in the last century that I have thought it a pity to let it remain buried. It is by J. West, and was published in 1787:

From London to Richmond I took an excursion,
For the sake of my health and in hopes of diversion:
Thus, walking without any cumbersome load,
I mark'd ev'ry singular sight on the road.

In Hyde Park I met a hump-back'd macarony
Who was pleased I should see how he manag'd his pony.
The Cockney was dresst in true blue and in buff,
In buckskin elastic, but all in the rough;
He wore patent spurs on his boots, with light soles,
And buttons as big as some halfpenny rolls;
His hair out of curls, with a tail like a rat,
And sideways he clapt on his head a round hat;
His cravat was tied up in a monstrous large bunch,
No wonder the ladies should smile at his hunch.

The next figure I saw, 'twas a milliner's maid,
A high cap and pink ribbons adorning her head,
Which was made to sit well, but a little fantastic,
With a hundred black pins and a cushion elastic.
She stalked like a peacock when waving her fan,
And us'd an umbrella upon a new plan;
Her elbows she lean'd on her hoop as on crutches,
And wagg'd her silk gown with the air of a duchess.

Now forward I stept to behold her sweet face;
She ogled and smil'd with a seeming good grace;
However, there was no dependence upon it,
Although her eyes sparkled from under her bonnet,
I question'd her love, so I wished her farewel;
But something more clever I'm ready to tell.

From yon spot in the Park, just where the Parade is,
Approach'd a grand sportsman, attended by ladies
On bay horses mounted; they swift tore the ground,
Escorted by servants and terriers around;
I guess'd that my Lord went to sport with his Graces
To Windsor's wide forest or Maidenhead races.

Through Kensington passing I saw a fine show
Of chaises, gigs, coaches, there all in a row!
When I came to a well where a girl stood close by,
Who ask'd to what place do these folk go? and why?
I, smiling, replied, 'They, my dear, go to Windsor,
To see king and queen,'—but could not convince her.
On tiptoe the titt'ring girl ran off the stand,
And broke half the pitcher she had in her hand.

In Hammersmith's parish I stopp'd for a minute;
A stage-coach here halted—I saw who was in it,
A grave-looking man with a long nose and chin,
Two sparks and three damsels were laughing within;
The outside was crowded, good Lord! what a rabble!
Some Cits from Fleet Market, some Jews from Whitechapel,
Some sailors from Wapping, and other such crew;
But now in the basket[1] I took a short view,
Two wenches, one jolly, the other but lean,
With barrels of oysters and shrimp-sacks between.
The spirited coachman, o'ercharg'd with stout ale,
When he started, drove faster than Palmer's[2] new mail;

[1] A large wickerwork receptacle behind the mail-coach.
[2] Palmer invented the mail-coach, and supplied horses to the Post-Office.

He smack'd his long whip—and zounds! what a flight!
His six horses running were soon out of sight;
A lad standing by, cried (as if in a swoon),
'By Jove! they fly up like Lunardi's[1] balloon.'
Much pleas'd with my path when I march'd on apace,
I reach'd Turnham Green; on that sweet rural place
I stopp'd at an inn near a lane down to Chiswick,
I call'd for some ale, but it tasted like physick.
As good luck would have it, I could not drink more,
When, seeing Jack Tar and his wife at the door,
Join'd close arm-in-arm like a hook on a link,
I reach'd him my mug and invited to drink;
Jack, pleased with the draught, gave me thanks with an echo,
And cramm'd in his jaw a large quid of tobacco.

Again I set off on my way to Kew Bridge,
Some boys and some girls came from under a hedge;
They jump'd and they tumbled headforemost around,
Each vied with the other to measure the ground;
For halfpence they begg'd, and I gave 'em a penny,
When I found that I'd left myself without any
To pay toll at the bridge and to buy a few plumbs;
My silver I chang'd for a handful of Brums.[2]

But, my sight being struck with the beauty of Kew,
I forgot my expenses, when, having in view
The new Royal Bridge[3] and its elegant Arches
There o'er the bright Thames, where the people in barges
And pleasure-boats sail!—how delightful the scene!
'Twixt the shades of Old Brentford and smiling Kew Green.

Now forward for Richmond, and happy my lot!
I soon reach'd that lofty and beautiful spot

[1] Lunardi made the first balloon ascent in England, Sept. 21, 1784.
[2] Birmingham halfpence, struck by Boulton and Watts at their works at Soho, Birmingham.
[3] Kew Bridge was opened to the public, September, 1789.

Which is called Richmond Hill—what a prospect amazing!
Extensive and pleasant; I could not help gazing
On yonder fine landscape of Twick'nam's sweet plains,
Where kind Nature its thousandfold beauty maintains.
To trace all its pleasures too short was the day;
The dinner-bell ringing, I hasten'd away
To a cheerful repast at a Gentleman's seat,
Whose friendship vouchsaf'd me a happy retreat.

GEORGE ROBERT FITZGERALD,

COMMONLY CALLED 'FIGHTING FITZGERALD.'

SHOULD anyone wish for a graphic account of Irish life in the later portion of the eighteenth century, he should read Sir Jonah Barrington's 'Personal Sketches of Ireland,' and he will find afterwards that Lever's novels afford but a faint reflection of the manners and customs existing in the west and south of Ireland. Ignorance, idleness, and dissipation were the characteristic of the wealthier classes, and a meeting of the 'gentry' could seldom take place without quarrelling and bloodshed. At races, fairs, and elections, the lower class enjoyed themselves likewise, after their kind, in breaking of heads and drunkenness. It was a singular state of things, but it must be borne in mind, whilst reading the following memoirs, as, otherwise, the facts therein related would scarcely be credited.[1]

The Fitzgeralds of County Mayo come of an ancient stock, from no less than the great Geraldine

---

[1] Some idea of the duelling that went on in Ireland in the latter part of last century may be gathered from the following extract from Sir Jonah's book (vol. ii, p. 3): 'I think I may challenge any country in Europe to show such an assemblage of

family, through the Desmond branch, and George, the father of George Robert Fitzgerald, had a very good property at Turlough, near Castlebar. It probably had some influence in his future career that 'Fighting Fitzgerald' should have had for his mother Lady Mary Hervey, who had been maid-of-honour to the Princess Amelia, and who was the daughter of one, and the sister of two, Earls of Bristol. The family from which she sprang was noted for eccentricity, so much so, that it passed into a saying that 'God made Men, Women, and Herveys.' She did not live long with her husband, his lax morality and dissipated manners could not be borne, and she left him to his own devices and returned to England. By him she had two sons, George Robert (born 1749), and Charles Lionel. The elder, in due time, was

gallant *judicial* and *official* antagonists at fire and sword as is exhibited even in the following list:

The Lord Chancellor of Ireland, Earl Clare, fought the Master of the Rolls, Curran.

The Chief Justice, K.B.. Lord Clonmell, fought Lord Tyrawley (a privy counsellor), Lord Llandaff, and two others.

The judge of the county of Dublin, Egan, fought the Master of the Rolls, Roger Barrett, and three others.

The Chancellor of the Exchequer, the Right Hon. Isaac Corry, fought the Right Hon. Henry Grattan (a privy counsellor), and another.

A Baron of the Exchequer, Baron Medge, fought his brother-in-law and two others.

The Chief Justice, C. P. Lord Norbury, fought Fire-eater Fitzgerald and two other gentlemen, and frightened Napper Tandy, and several besides: one hit only.

The judge of the Prerogative Court, Dr. Dingenan, fought one barrister and frightened another on the ground. N.B.— The latter case a curious one.

The Chief Counsel to the Revenue, Henry Deane Grady,

sent to Eton, where he seems to have learnt as much Latin and Greek as was requisite for a gentleman of those days, and he used occasionally in after life to write a little poetry now and again, of which one piece, 'The Riddle,' was printed after his execution.

From Eton he, in 1766, being then in his seventeenth year, was gazetted to a lieutenancy in the 69th regiment, and was quartered at Galway, a nice place for a newly-emancipated schoolboy, and a red-hot, wild Irishman to boot. Here he soon got into a scrape, owing to his conduct with a shop-girl, which ended in a duel, in which neither the combatants were hurt. He next managed to pick a quarrel with a young officer of his own regiment, named Thomp-

---

fought Counsellor O'Mahon, Counsellor Campbell, and others: all hits.

The Master of the Rolls fought Lord Buckinghamshire, the Chief Secretary, &c.

The provost of the University of Dublin, the Right Hon. Hely Hutchinson, fought Mr. Doyle, Master in Chancery, and some others.

The Chief Justice C. P. Patterson, fought three country gentlemen, one of them with swords, another with guns, and wounded all of them.

The Right Hon. George Ogle (a privy counsellor) fought Barney Coyle, a distiller, because he was a Papist. They fired eight shots, and no hit; but the second broke his own arm.

Thomas Wallace, K.C., fought Mr. O'Gorman, the Catholic Secretary.

Counsellor O'Connell fought the Orange chieftain; fatal to the champion of Protestant ascendency.

The collector of the customs of Dublin, the Hon. Francis Hutchinson, fought the Right Hon. Lord Mountmorris.

Two hundred and twenty-seven memorable and official duels have actually been fought during my grand climacteric.

son, who was a quiet and inoffensive man, and they met. The first round was fired by both without injury, but Lieutenant Thompson's second bullet struck Fitzgerald's forehead, and he fell. The surgeons, after examination, came to the conclusion that the only way to save his life was by performing upon him the operation of trepanning, or cutting a round piece out of the skull in order to relieve the pressure on the brain. It was an operation that was very risky, but in this case it was successful. Still, one cannot help thinking, judging by his after career, that his brain then received some permanent injury which deprived him of the power of reasoning, and of control over his actions.

He now left the army, and went home to live with his father. Here he lived the regular Irishman's life of the period : hunting, shooting, cock-fighting, &c., until he fell in love with a lady of good family, a Miss Conolly of Castletown; but even here he could not act as other men do. He could not be married quietly, but ran away with his bride, and an incident in their elopement is amusingly told, it being put in the mouth of his servant.

'But hoo did the Captain mak' it up again wi' the Square? Ye omadhaun, it was with the young misthress he med it up; and she took Frinch lave with him, wan fine moonlight night soon afther. It was mysel' that had the chaise an' four waitin' for them; an' a divilish good thing happened at the first inn we stopt at. The Captain in coorse ordhered the best dhrawin'-room for the misthress ; an' sure, if it was goold, she was worthy ov it. But the beggarly-lookin' waither sed it was taken up with some grand Englishmen.

' "Request thim," sis the Captain, " to accommodate a lady that's fatigued, with the apartment."

' Well an' good, the waither delivered the message, when one of the Englishers roars out, " Damn the fellow's cursed insolence, we shan't give up the room to any rascal."

' " Here," sis one of thim, " show Paddy this watch, an' ax him to tell what o'clock it is."

' So the waither brings the watch with the message in to where the Captain and mysel' was—the misthress had gone with her maid to another room to change her dhress.

' " Very well," sis the Captain, " I think I can show them what o'clock it is." So he dhraws his soord, and puts the point through his chain; "Channor," thin says he to me, " attend me."

' With that we went in among them, an' the Captain sthretched over the watch at the sword's point to ache of them, beggin', with a polite bow, to know to which o' thim it belonged. But little notions, ye may swair, they had ov ownin' it *theirs*. Every wan o' the cowardly rascals swore it did not belong to himsel'!

' " Oh, I was thinkin', jintlemen, it was all a bit ov a mistake," sis the Captain, " so I think you must have it, Channor, for want of a betther owner." So with that he hands it over to mysel'. It was a fine goold watch, an' here I have it still.'

Not only was young Mrs. Fitzgerald reconciled to her relations, but an arrangement was made with old Fitzgerald that, on payment of a certain sum of money down, he would give his son a rent charge of £1,000 a year on his estate, and he had a very handsome fortune with his wife besides.

The young couple thereupon went to France, and, having introductions to the best society in Paris, enjoyed themselves immensely. He dressed splendidly, and he astonished the Parisians, who asked each other, 'Qui est ce seigneur? d'où vient il? Il n'est pas Français,—Quelle magnificence! Quelle politesse! Est-il possible qu'il soit étranger?' In his hat he wore diamonds, and the same precious stones adorned his buckles and his sword-knot; indeed, all through his life he was fond of such gewgaws, and when his house at Turlough was wrecked by the mob—no one preventing—he estimated his loss in jewellery, &c., at £20,000. They must have been costly, for he enumerates among the stolen collection: 'A casquet containing a complete set of diamond vest buttons, two large emeralds, a hat-band with five or six rows of Oriental pearls, worth £1,500, a large engraved amethyst, a gold watch and chain studded with diamonds, several other gold watches and seals, a great number of antique and modern rings, gold shoe and knee buckles, silver shaving apparatus, several pairs of silver shoe and knee buckles, with £6,300 worth of other jewels.'

He joined eagerly in the dissipations of the gay French capital, especially in gaming, and the twenty thousand pounds he had with his wife soon came to an end; and among other people to whom he was in debt was the Comte d'Artois, afterwards Charles X., to whom he owed three thousand pounds. One evening afterwards he offered a bet of one thousand pounds on the prince's hand of cards, which the Comte d'Artois overhearing, he asked Fitzgerald for payment, and, being told that it was not then convenient, the prince took the Irishman by the arm, led him to the top of the stairs, and then, giving him one kick, left him to get downstairs as quickly as he could. This indignity was one which it was very hard on the hot-blooded Irishman to be obliged to endure, for he might not challenge with impunity a prince of the blood, and from the public nature of the insult he naturally lost his place in society. It was certain he must leave France; but before he left he must somehow distinguish himself. And he did it in this wise. The king was hunting at Fontainebleau, and Fitzgerald, regardless of the etiquette which always allowed the foremost place to the king and royal family, took the hunting of the pack upon himself, riding close to the hounds, cheering and encouraging them. But for some time the stag kept well in the open, and gave Fitzgerald no opportunity of showing off his horsemanship, until it suddenly turned off towards the river Seine, on the banks of which a wall had been built. This it leaped, and, to use a hunting phrase, 'took soil' in the river. Over streamed the hounds, and over flew Fitzgerald, reckless of a drop of fourteen feet on the other side, going plump into the river. The hunt stopped at that wall, none daring to take it, and watched with amazement Fitzgerald emerge, his feet still in the stirrups, and, swimming the river, climb the opposite bank and ride away.

He went to London, where he was well received in society, notwithstanding that his fame as a duellist was well known, he having fought eleven duels by the time he was twenty-four years of age. Whether it was then that he forced his way into Brookes' Club I know not, but it is certain that he did, and as I cannot tell the story as well as it is told in that most amusing but anonymously written book, 'The Clubs of London,' I extract it.

'Fitzgerald having once applied to Admiral Keith Stewart to propose him as a candidate for "Brookes's," the worthy admiral, well knowing that he must either fight or comply with his request, chose the latter alternative. Accordingly, on the night in which the balloting was to take place (which was only a mere form in this case, for even Keith Stewart himself had resolved to *black-ball* him), the duellist accompanied the gallant admiral to St. James's Street, and waited in the room below, whilst the suffrages were taken, in order to know the issue.

'The ballot was soon over, for without hesitation every member threw in a *black ball*, and, when the scrutiny took place, the company were not a little amazed to find not even *one* white one among the number. However, the point of rejection being carried *nem. con.*, the grand affair now was as to which of the members had the hardihood to announce the same to the expectant candidate. No one would undertake the office, for the announcement was sure to produce a challenge, and a duel with Fighting Fitzgerald had in almost every case been fatal to his opponent. The general opinion, however, was that the proposer, Admiral Stewart, should convey the intelligence, and that in as polite terms as possible; but the admiral, who was certainly on all proper occasions a very gallant officer, was not inclined to go on any such embassy.

'"No, gentlemen,' said he; "I proposed the fellow because I knew you would not admit him; but, by G—d, I have no inclination to risk my life against that of a madman."

'" But, admiral," replied the Duke of Devonshire, " there being no *white ball* in the box, he must know that *you* have black-balled him as well as the rest, and he is sure to call you out, at all events."

'This was a poser for the poor admiral, who sat silent for a few seconds amidst the half-suppressed titter of the members. At length, joining in the laugh against himself, he exclaimed,

'" Upon my soul, a pleasant job I've got into! D——n the fellow! No matter! I won't go. Let the waiter tell him that there was *one* black ball, and that his name must be put up again if he wishes it."

' This plan appeared so judicious that all concurred in its propriety. Accordingly the waiter was a few minutes after despatched on the mission.

'In the meantime Mr. Fitzgerald showed evident symptoms of impatience at being kept so long from his " dear friends " above stairs, and frequently rang the bell to know *the state of the poll*. On the first occasion he thus addressed the waiter who answered his summons:

'" Come here, my tight little fellow. Do you know if I am *chose* yet?"

'" I really can't say, sir," replied the young man, " but I'll see."

'" There's a nice little man; be quick, d'ye see, and I'll give ye sixpence when ye come with the good news."

'Away went the *little man;* but he was in no hurry to come back, for he as well as his fellows was sufficiently aware of Fitzgerald's violent temper, and wished to come in contact with him as seldom as possible.

'The bell rang again, and to another waiter the impatient candidate put the same question:

'"Am I chose yet, waither?"

'"The balloting is not over yet, sir," replied the man.

'"Not over yet!" exclaimed Fitzgerald. "But, sure, there is no use of balloting at all when my dear friends are all unanimous for me to come in. Run, my man, and let me know how they are getting on."

'After the lapse of another quarter-of-an-hour, the bell was rung so violently as to produce a contest among the poor servants, as to whose turn it was to visit the lion in his den! and Mr. Brookes, seeing no alternative but resolution, took the message from the waiter, who was descending the staircase, and boldly entered the room with a coffee equipage in his hand.

'"Did you call for coffee, sir?"

'"D—n your coffee, sur! and you too," answered Mr. Fitzgerald, in a voice which made the host's blood curdle in his veins—"I want to know, sur, and that without a moment's delay, sur, if I am *chose* yet."

'"Oh, sir!" replied Mr. Brookes, who trembled from head to foot, but attempted to smile away the appearance of fear, "I beg your pardon, sir; but I was just coming to announce to you, sir, with Admiral Stewart's compliments, sir, that unfortunately there was one black ball in the box, sir; and, consequently, by the rules of the club, sir, no candidate can be admitted without a new election, sir; which cannot take place, by the standing regulations of the club, sir, until one month from this time, sir!"

'During this address Fitzgerald's irascibility appeared to undergo considerable mollification; and, at its conclusion, the terrified landlord was not a little surprised and pleased to find his guest shake him by the hand, which he squeezed heartily between his own two, saying,

'"My dear Mr. Brookes, *I'm chose*; and I give ye much joy: for I'll warrant ye'll find me the best customer in your house! But there must be a small matter of mistake in my election; and, as I should not wish to be so ungenteel as to take my sate among my dear friends above-stairs, until that mistake is duly rectified, you'll just step up and make my compliments to the gentlemen, and say, as it is only a mistake of *one* black ball, they will be so good as to waive all ceremony on my account, and proceed to re-elect their humble servant without any more delay at all; so now, my dear Mr. Brookes, you may put down the coffee, and I'll be drinking it whilst the new election is going on!"

'Away went Mr. Brookes, glad enough to escape with whole bones, for this time at least. On announcing the purport of his errand to the assembly above-stairs, many of the members were panic-struck, for they clearly foresaw that some disagreeable circumstance was likely to be the finale of the farce they had been playing. Mr. Brookes stood silent for some minutes, waiting for an answer, whilst several of the members whispered, and laughed, in groups, at the ludicrous figure which they all cut. At length the Earl of March (afterwards Duke of Queensbury) said aloud,

'"Try the effect of *two* black balls; d——n his Irish impudence; if two balls don't take effect upon him, I don't know what will." This proposition met with unanimous approbation, and Mr. Brookes was ordered to communicate accordingly.

'On re-entering the waiting-room, Mr. Fitzgerald rose hastily from his chair, and, seizing him by the hand, eagerly inquired,

'"Have they elected me right now, Mr. Brookes?"

'"I hope no offence, Mr. Fitzgerald," said the landlord, "but I am sorry to inform you that the result of the second balloting is—that *two* black balls were dropped in, sir."

'"By J——s, then," exclaimed Fitzgerald, "there's now *two* mistakes instead of one. Go back, my dear friend, and tell the honourable members that it is a very uncivil thing to keep a gentleman waiting below-stairs, with no one to keep him company but himself, whilst they are enjoying themselves with their champagne, and their cards, and their Tokay, up above. Tell them to try again, and I hope they will have better luck this time, and make no more mistakes, because it's getting late, and I won't be chose to-night at all. So now, Mr. Brookes, be off with yourself, and lave the door open till I see what despatch you make.'

Away went Mr. Brookes for the last time. On announcing his unwelcome errand, everyone saw that palliative measures only prolonged the dilemma: and General Fitzpatrick proposed that Brookes should tell him: "His cause was hopeless, for that he was *black-balled all over* from head to foot, and it was hoped by all the members that Mr. Fitzgerald would not persist in thrusting himself into society where his company was declined."

'This message, it was generally believed, would prove a sickener, as it certainly would have done to any other candidate under similar circumstances. Not so, however, to Fitzgerald, who no sooner heard the purport of it, than he exclaimed,

'" Oh, I perceive it is *a mistake altogether*, Mr. Brookes, and I must see to the rectifying of it myself; there's nothing like dealing with principals, and so I'll step up at once, and put the thing to rights, without any more unnecessary delay."

'In spite of Mr. Brookes's remonstrance that his entrance into the club-room was against all rule and etiquette, Fitzgerald found his way up-stairs, threatening to throw the landlord over the bannisters for endeavouring to stop him. He entered the room without any further ceremony than a bow, saying to the members, who indignantly rose up at this most unexpected intrusion,

'" Your servant, gentlemen! I beg ye will be sated." Walking up to the fire-place, he thus addressed Admiral Stewart: " So, my dear admiral, Mr. Brookes informs me that I have been *elected* three times."

'" You have been balloted for, Mr. Fitzgerald, but I am sorry to say you have not been chosen,' said Stewart.

'" Well, then," replied the duellist, " did you black-ball me?'

'" My good sir," answered the admiral, " how could you suppose such a thing?"

'" Oh, I *supposed* no such thing, my dear fellow, I only want to know who it was dropped the black balls in by accident, as it were."

'Fitzgerald now went up to each individual member, and put the same question *seriatim*, " Did you black-ball me, sir?" until he made the round of the whole club; and it may well be supposed that in every case he obtained similar answers to that of the admiral. When he had finished his inquisition, he thus addressed the whole body, who preserved as dread and dead a silence as the urchins at a parish school do on a Saturday when the pedagogue orders half-a-score of them to be *horsed* for neglecting their catechism, which they have to repeat to the parson on Sunday:

'" You see, gentlemen, that as none of ye have black-balled me, *I must be chose;* and it is Misthur Brookes that has made the mistake. But I was convinced of it from the beginning, and I am only sorry that so much time has been lost as to prevent honourable gentlemen from enjoying each other's good company sooner. Waither! Come here, you rascal, and bring me a bottle of champagne, till I drink long life to the club, and wish them joy of their unanimous election of a raal gentleman by father and mother, and—" this part of Fitzgerald's address excited the risible muscles of everyone present; but he soon restored them to their former lugubrious position by casting around him a ferocious look, and saying, in a voice of thunder—' *and who never missed his man!* Go for the champagne, waithur; and, dy'e hear, sur, tell your masthur—Misthur Brookes, that is —not to make any more mistakes about black balls, for, though it is below a gentleman to call him out, I will find other means of giving him a bagful of broken bones."

'The members now saw that there was nothing for it but to send the intruder to Coventry, which they appeared to do by tacit agreement; for when Admiral Stewart departed, which he did almost immediately,

Mr. Fitgerald found himself completely cut by all
"his dear friends." The gentlemen now found themselves in groups at the several whist-tables, and no
one chose to reply to his observations, nor to return
even a nod to the toasts and healths which he drank
whilst discussing three bottles of the sparkling liquor
which the terrified waiter placed before him in succession. At length, finding that no one would communicate with him in either kind, either for drinking
or for fighting, he arose, and, making a low bow, took
his leave as follows:

'" Gentlemen, I bid you all good night; I am glad
to find ye so *sociable*. I'll take care to come earlier
next night, and we'll have a little more of it, please
G—d."

' The departure of this bully was a great relief to
everyone present, for the restraint caused by his
vapouring and insolent behaviour was intolerable.
The conversation immediately became general, and
it was unanimously agreed that half-a-dozen stout
constables should be in waiting the next evening to
lay him by the heels and bear him off to the watchhouse if he attempted again to intrude. Of some
such measure Fitzgerald seemed to be aware, for he
never showed himself at "Brookes's" again, though
he boasted everywhere that he had been unanimously
chosen a member of the club.'

He lived the life of a man about town, and not a
very reputable one, either a bully whom everyone
feared and no one liked, until the summer of 1773,
when he appeared before the public in a dispute of
which there is a long account in a contemporary
pamphlet, 'The Vauxhall Affray, or Macaronies
defeated.' The Rev. Henry Bate (afterwards Sir H.

B. Dudley), the proprietor and editor of the *Morning Post*, was at Vauxhall in company with Mrs. Hartley, the actress, her husband, Mr. Colman, and a friend, when Fitzgerald, accompanied by the Hon. Thomas Lyttleton, Captain Croftes, and some others, all more or less intoxicated, behaved so rudely to Mrs. Hartley that she could stand it no longer, and complained. Parson Bate was a notable 'bruiser,' and he took her part, and struck Croftes a blow. Cards were exchanged, and next morning an interview was arranged, at which the clergyman and officer were reconciled, when in bounced Fitzgerald, and declared, in a most insolent manner, that Mr. Bate should give immediate satisfaction to his friend, Captain Miles, whom, he said, the former had grossly insulted the evening before. Miles was introduced, and declared that he had been affronted by the clergyman, and if he did not immediately strip and fight with him, he (Miles) would post him as a coward, and cane him wherever he met him.

Mindful of his cloth, Mr. Bate hesitated; but Miles, saying something about cowardice, the parson threw all consideration of his calling to the winds, a ring was formed, and Captain Miles received the handsomest thrashing he ever had. Soon afterwards it transpired that Captain Miles was Fitzgerald's own servant, who had been compelled by his master so to behave. Mr. Bate very properly exposed the affair in the *Morning Post*.

We next hear of him engaged in a duel with Captain Scawen of the Guards, which was fought at Lille, and twice he fired before his adversary. Luckily he missed him, and the second time the captain, having fired in the air, the affair ended.

He was concerned in another duel, which made some stir at the time (1775). There was a young fellow named Walker, the son of a plumber and painter, whose father left him a large fortune, and Daisy Walker, as he was called, became a cornet in Burgoyne's Light Dragoons. His fortune soon went in gambling, and he had to retire from the service, whilst his guardians looked into his affairs. At that time Fitzgerald held a bill of his for three thousand pounds, and pressed for payment. It was ultimately compromised, and, on receipt of five hundred pounds, he gave up the bill. Subsequently Daisy Walker made some lucky bets, and Fitzgerald at once became clamourous for payment of two thousand five hundred pounds. Walker denied his liability, saying the matter was settled by the payment of five hundred pounds and the return of the bill; but this was not Fitzgerald's view of the matter, and he dunned young Walker whenever he met him, and at last, at Ascot races, he cut him across the face with his cane.

Of course, in those days, there could be but one course to be taken, and a challenge was sent, and accepted. Walker, as being the insulted party, should fire first. They duly met, and the distance was fixed at ten paces, but the second who measured the ground took such strides that it was virtually twelve paces. Walker fired, and his antagonist was unhurt. Fitzgerald, who had the whole etiquette of the duello at his finger's ends, then stepped forward and apologised for having struck Walker—which apology was accepted. But, as soon as this ceremony was finished, Fitzgerald again began dunning for his £2,500, and, when he was told that it was not owing, he prepared to take his shot, offering to bet £1,000 that he hit his adversary. The pistol missed fire, and he calmly chipped the flint, reiterating his offer to bet. He fired, and the ball grazed Walker in the arm just below the shoulder, but did not wound him, and they left the field. Subsequently, however, Fitzgerald declared that Walker was 'papered,' *i.e.*, protected in some way, and published an account of the duel in a pamphlet, addressed to the Jockey Club. To this Walker replied, and Fitzgerald followed up with another pamphlet, in which he says:—

'I should most certainly have fixed it at *six* instead of *ten* paces. My predilection for that admeasurement of ground is founded upon the strictest principles of humanity. For 1 know, from trials successively repeated, twenty times one after the other, I can, at that distance, hit any part of the human body to a *line*, which, possibly you may know, is only the *twelfth part of an inch.*'

And he again refers to his pistol-practice. 'So, then, you had one Surtout on; are you certain you had not half-a-dozen? If no more than one Surtout, pray how many coats and waistcoats? You give us no account of your under-garments. I ask these questions, Sir, because, after reading your pamphlet, I took the same pistol, charged it with the same quantity of powder, used a bullet cast in the same mould, measured out twelve good paces with a yard wand, and then fired at a thick stick, which I had previously covered over with two waistcoats lined, one coat lined, and one double-milled drab Surtout. What think you, Sir, was the result? Why, Sir, the ball penetrated through the Surtout, the coat, two waistcoats, and lodged itself an inch deep in the stick. There is nothing like experimental philosophy for a fair proof, it beats your *ipse dixits* all halloo. You see how ingeniously I pass away my private hours—I am always hard at study.'

This affair made London too hot for him, and he went over to France with an old brother officer named Baggs, and they picked up a living by horse-racing and gambling—which led to a duel between the two, for Baggs had fleeced a young Englishman named Sandford, and there was a quarrel as to the division of the spoil, which ended in Fitzgerald drawing his gloves across Baggs' face, and Baggs returning the compliment by dashing his hat in his partner's face. Of course the outcome of this was a duel, which is graphically described by Hamilton Rowan in his 'Autobiography.'

'They fired together, and were in the act of levelling their second pistols, when Baggs fell on his side, saying,

'" Sir, I am wounded."

'" But you are not dead !" said Fitzgerald.

'At the same moment he discharged his second pistol at his fallen antagonist.

'Baggs immediately started on his legs and advanced on Fitzgerald, who, throwing the empty pistol at him, quitted his station, and kept a zig-zag course across the field, Baggs following. I saw the flash of Bagg's second pistol, and, at the same moment, Fitzgerald lay stretched on the ground. I was just in time to catch Baggs as he fell, after firing his second shot. He swooned from intense pain, the small bone of his leg being broken. Mr. Fitzgerald now came up, saying,

'"We are both wounded; let us go back to our ground."'

But this could not be allowed, and the wounded were carried home. Fitzgerald's wound was in the thigh, and rendered him slightly lame ever after.

When he got well, he returned to Ireland, and, thanks to his uncle, the Earl of Bristol and Bishop of Derry, he lived in very fair style, either in Merrion Street, Dublin, or at Rockfield, near Turlough. While living in Dublin he fought a duel with John Toler (afterwards Lord Norbury), fired a pistol at Denis Browne, Lord Altamont's brother, in Sackville Street, in broad daylight, and insulted and struck John Fitzgibbon, afterwards Lord Chancellor Clare.

Death now took away his guardian-angel, his amiable and patient wife, leaving him a little daughter. His grief for her loss was extravagant, and amounted to little short of frenzy. After the funeral he behaved more than ever like a madman. He took to hunting by night, and hunted anything that was about after dark. In this wild chase he was always accompanied by a band of mounted servants, carrying torches, and, when the peasants were roused from their slumbers by the noise of hounds, and the cries of men, they knew that Mad Fitzgerald was abroad.

When he hunted by day, he would peremptorily order home anyone to whom he had even a fancied dislike. He would tell one man to go home for he was more fitted to follow the plough than the hounds; another would be bidden to go and mind his sheep, and a third would be told to quit the field, as he was too fat for the sport. And they had to go, for their monitor would not have scrupled to have used his whip, and, if that had been objected to, there was always the *ultima ratio* of a duel, and men were rather shy of meeting 'Fighting Fitzgerald.'

He had a particular dislike to the family of Lord Altamont, and behaved in a most high-handed and outrageous manner towards them. For instance, he heard that a relation of my lord's, a Mr. Browne, was out shooting on a bog near Westport, so he got together his men and dogs, and went in quest of him. When Mr. Browne saw him enter on the scene, he retired; Fitzgerald pursued, Mr. Browne increased his pace, so did Fitzgerald, until he literally hunted the offending sportsman home. Another time he rode over to Lord Altamont's house, and asked to see the wolf-dog, which, for its size and fierceness, was the admiration and terror of the neighbourhood. No sooner was he shown the dog than he shot it, charging the servants to tell their master that, until he became more charitable to the poor, who only came to his door to be barked at and bitten, he should not allow such a beast to be kept, but that he had no objection to the three ladies of the family each keeping a lap-dog.

After a time, his grief at the loss of his wife subsided, and he fell in love with the only child and heiress of a Mr. Vaughan, of Carrowmore, County Mayo, and singularly, although she well knew his reckless character, she returned his affection. We know how he ran away with his first wife; the story of his wedding with his second is yet more romantic.

Mr. Vaughan was, not unnaturally, averse to Fitzgerald marrying his daughter, but, at the same time, he did not forbid him the house. So one night Fitzgerald was suddenly attacked by a very acute illness, writhing about in great agony, and at last begged

to be allowed to remain there that night. In the
morning he was much worse, and at death's door,
lamenting the iniquity of his past life, and begging
that a priest should be sent for. Of course one soon
came, but, in the midst of his spiritual exercises,
Fitzgerald sprang out of bed, and, presenting a
pistol to the head of the priest, swore he would blow
out his brains if he did not instantly marry him to
Miss Vaughan, and the terror-stricken priest had no
option but to comply. Mr. Vaughan had to bow to
the inevitable, and the new Mrs. Fitzgerald never
had reason to complain of her husband's treatment of
her, as he was uniformly kind and affectionate to her.

When Fitzgerald returned to Ireland, he found his
father, a weak, false, vicious old man, almost in his
dotage, and entirely under the control of his younger
son Lionel, a low woman whom he had taken as his
mistress, and an unscrupulous pettifogger named
Patrick Randal MacDonnell. Charles Lionel, the
younger son, was his brother's enemy, because he
saw nothing but poverty before him if his father
paid George Robert the £1,000 a year to which he
was entitled, for the old spendthrift was always in
debt. The mistress had every reason to keep things
as they were, and MacDonnell did not like to see his
pickings done away with. It is questionable whether
Fitzgerald had ever received any portion of his
settlement—at all events, it was £12,000 in arrear.
He saw the estate that was ultimately to come to
him being wasted, his father getting more hope-
lessly into debt, and spending his substance on an
immoral and greedy woman, and he was determined
to put a stop to it. He had a difficulty to get a
solicitor in Dublin to undertake his case, but at last

he found one, and arranged with him to accompany him in his carriage to Mayo. The story of that ride is told by Sir Jonah Barrington (vol. iii, p. 170, ed. 1832) as follows:

'Mr. Fitzgerald sent for the attorney, and told him that, if his going down was previously known, there would be several of the tenants and others, under the adverse influence of his father and brother, who would probably abscond, and that, therefore, since spies were watching him perpetually, to give notice in the county of his every movement, it was expedient that he should set out two or three hours before daybreak, so as to have the start of them. That his own travelling-carriage should be ready near the gate of the Phœnix Park to take up Mr. T——, who might bring his trunk of papers with him in a hack-carriage, so that there should be no suspicion.

'All this was reasonable and proper, and accordingly done. Mr. Fitzgerald's carriage was on the spot named, near the wall of the Phœnix Park. The attorney was punctual, the night pitch dark, and the trunk of papers put into the boot; the windows were all drawn up. Mr. T—— stepped into the carriage with as great satisfaction as ever he had felt in his whole lifetime, and away they drove cheerily, at a good round pace, for the county of Galway.

'Mr. T—— had no idea that anybody else was coming with them, Mr. Fitzgerald not having mentioned such a thing. He found, however, a third gentleman in a travelling-cloak sitting between himself and his client, who was dozing in the far corner. The stranger, too, he found not over-courteous; for, though the carriage was not very roomy, and the gentleman was bulky, he showed no disposition whatever to accommodate the attorney, who begged him, with great suavity and politeness, to "move a little." To this he received no reply, but a snoring both from the strange traveller and Mr. Fitzgerald. Mr. T—— now felt himself much crowded and pressed, and again earnestly requested "the gentleman" to allow him, if possible, a little more room; but he only received a snore in return. He now concluded that his companion was a low, vulgar fellow. His nerves became rather lax; he got alarmed, without well knowing why; he began to twitter—the twitter turned into a shake, and, as is generally the case, the shake ended with a cold sweat, and Mr. T—— found himself in a state of mind and body far more disagreeable than he had ever before experienced.

'The closeness and pressure had elicited a hot perspiration on the one side, while his fears produced a cold perspiration on the other, so that (quite unlike the ague he had not long recovered from) he had hot and cold fits at the same moment. All his apprehensions were now awakened; his memory opened her stores, and he began to recollect dreadful anecdotes of Mr. Fitzgerald, which he never before had credited, or indeed had any occasion to remember. The ruffians of Turlow passed as the ghosts in "Macbeth" before his imagination. Mr. Fitzgerald, he supposed, was in a fox's sleep, and his bravo in another, who, instead of receding at all, on the contrary, squeezed the attorney closer and closer. His respiration now grew impeded, and every fresh idea exaggerated his horror; his untaxed costs, he anticipated, would prove his certain death, and that a cruel one. Neither of his companions would answer him a single question, the one replying only by a rude snore, and the other by a still ruder.

'"Now," thought Mr. T——, "my fate is consummated. I have often heard how Mr. Fitzgerald cut a Jew's throat in Italy, and slaughtered numerous creditors while on the grand tour of Europe. God help me! unfortunate solicitor that I am, my last day, or rather night, has come!"

'He thought to let down the window and admit a little fresh air, but it was quite fast. The whole situation was insupportable, and at length he addressed Mr. Fitzgerald, most pathetically, thus:

'"Mr. Fitzgerald, I'll date the receipt the moment you choose, and whenever it's your convenience I have no doubt you'll pay it most honourably—no doubt, no doubt, Mr. Fitzgerald—but not necessary at all till perfectly convenient, or never, if more agreeable to you and this other gentleman."

'Fitzgerald could now contain himself no longer, but said, quite in good humour,

'"Oh, very well, Mr. T——, very well, quite time enough; make yourself easy on that head."

'The carriage now arrived at Maynooth, where the horses were instantly changed, and they proceeded rapidly on their journey, Mr. Fitzgerald declaring he would not alight till he reached Turlow, for fear of pursuit.

'The attorney now took courage, and, very truly surmising that the other gentleman was a foreigner, ventured to beg of Mr. Fitzgerald to ask "his friend" to sit over a little, as he was quite crushed.

'Mr. Fitzgerald replied, "That the party in question did not speak English, but when they arrived at Killcock the matter should be better arranged."

'The attorney was now compelled for some time longer to suffer the hot press, inflicted with as little compunction as if he were only a sheet of paper; but, on arriving at the inn at Killcock, dawn just appeared, and Mr. Fitzgerald, letting down a window, desired his servant, who was riding with a pair of large horse-pistols before him, to rouse the people at the inn, and get some cold provisions and a bottle of wine brought to the carriage. "And, Thomas," said he, " get five or six pounds of raw meat, if you can—no matter of what kind—for this foreign gentleman."

'The attorney was now petrified; a little twilight glanced into the carriage, and nearly turned him into stone. The stranger was wrapped up in a blue travelling cloak with a scarlet cape, and had a great white cloth tied round his head and under his chin; but when Mr. Solicitor saw the face of his companion he uttered a piteous cry, and involuntarily ejaculated, "Murder! murder!" On hearing this cry, the servant rode back to the carriage window and pointed to his pistols. Mr. T—— now offered up his soul to God, the stranger grumbled, and Mr. Fitzgerald, leaning across, put his hand to the attorney's mouth, and said he should direct his servant to give him reason for that cry, if he attempted to alarm the people of the house. Thomas went into the inn, and immediately returned with a bottle of wine and some bread, but reported that there was no raw meat to be had; on hearing which, Mr. Fitzgerald ordered him to seek some at another house.

'The attorney now exclaimed again, "God protect me!" Streaming with perspiration, his eye every now and then glancing towards his mysterious companion, and then, starting aside with horror, he at length shook as if he were relapsing into his old ague; and the stranger, finding so much unusual motion beside him, turned his countenance upon the attorney. Their cheeks came in contact, and the reader must imagine—because it is impossible adequately to describe—the scene that followed. The stranger's profile was of uncommon prominence; his mouth stretched from ear to ear, he had enormous grinders, with a small twinkling eye, and his visage was all be-whiskered and mustachioed—more, even, than Count Platoff's of the Cossacks.

'Mr. T———'s optic nerves were paralysed as he gazed instinctively at his horrid companion, in whom, when he recovered his sense of vision sufficiently to scrutinize him, he could trace no similitude to any being on earth save a bear!

'And the attorney was quite correct in this comparison. It was actually a Russian bear, which Mr. Fitzgerald had educated from a cub, and which generally accompanied his master on his travels. He now gave Bruin a rap upon the nose with a stick which he carried, and desired him to hold up his head. The brute obeyed. Fitzgerald then ordered him to "kiss his neighbour," and the bear did as he was told, but accompanied his salute with such a tremendous roar as roused the attorney (then almost swooning) to a full sense of his danger. Self-preservation is the first law of Nature, and at once gives courage, and suggests devices. On this occasion, every other kind of law—civil, criminal, or equitable—was set aside by the attorney. All his ideas, if any he had, were centred in one word—"escape"; and as a weasel, it is said, will attack a man if driven to desperation, so did the attorney spurn the menaces of Mr. Fitzgerald, who endeavoured to hold and detain him.

'The struggle was violent, but brief; Bruin roared loud, but interfered not. Horror strengthened the solicitor. Dashing against the carriage-door, he burst it open, and, tumbling out, reeled into the public-house—then rushing through a back-door, and up a narrow lane that led to the village of Summer Hill (Mr. Roly's demesne), about two miles distant, he stumbled over hillocks, tore through hedges and ditches, and never stopped till he came, breathless, to the little alehouse, completely covered with mud, and his clothes in rags. He there told so incoherent a story, that the people all took him for a man either bitten by a mad dog, or broken loose from his keepers, and considered it their duty to tie him, to prevent his biting, or other mischief. In that manner they led him to Squire Roly's, at the great house, where the hapless attorney was pinioned and confined in a stable for some hours, till the squire got up. They put plenty of milk, bread, butter, and cheese into the manger, from the cock-loft above, to prevent accidents, as they said.'

Fitzgerald, finding the estate going to the dogs —for his father was letting the lands at absurdly low prices to his favourites; as, for instance, he let his son Charles Lionel a valuable tract of land worth fifteen shillings an acre at one shilling and sixpence, and the deer park at the same price—took the necessary legal proceedings to protect himself; and, whilst they were pending, his father was arrested for a debt of £8,000, and taken to a Dublin sponging-house. Although his father had been trying to injure him by all the means in his power, yet Fitzgerald paid the debt, and became responsible for the other debts of his father, who, in return, ratified the settlement which had been in abeyance so long.

Fitzgerald then applied to the Lord Chancellor for possession of the estate, on the grounds that, under its present management, the property was deteriorating, and as security for the money his father owed him, which amounted to £20,000—£12,000 of which were arrears of his income of £1,000 per annum, and £8,000 lent to obtain his release; and, in 1780, the Chancellor made the order as prayed. Had Fitzgerald gone with bailiffs, and demanded possession, there would have been bloodshed, in all probability; for the King's writs did not run easily in that part of Ireland. So he waited until one day, when his father went over to Turlough, and he then made a forcible entry into Rockfield, with a troop of armed dependants, and dislodged the servants then in the house.

Naturally his father did not take this quietly, and possession was not held peacefully. There were many collisions; and old Fitzgerald indicted his son for having headed a riotous mob, one of whom, he alleged, had, at his son's instigation, attempted to take away his life, by firing a loaded musket at him. The charge could not be sufficiently proved, and Fitzgerald was acquitted.

He now turned his attention towards improving his estate, and imported some Scotch Presbyterians, a sober and industrious set of men, to whom he gave five hundred pounds towards building a meeting-house, and settled fifty pounds per annum on their minister; but his father's party were always annoying him, and, in consequence, he refused to give maintenance to his father, who, thereupon, had recourse to the law-courts in Dublin to compel him so to do; and a writ was issued empowering the father to secure the body of his son until a maintenance was granted him. It would have been perfectly useless to have served the writ upon him at Turlough: it is probable no man could have been found bold enough to attempt it. So they waited until the next assizes at Balinrobe; and then, when they thought they had him safe in the grand jury room, they made application to the judge to arrest him there. Leave was granted, but Fitzgerald got wind of it, and when they went to capture him, lo! he was not to be found.

He evidently thought two could play at that game, and he determined to get the old man into his power. In those days, in that part of Ireland, law was not much regarded, especially by men of Fighting Fitzgerald's stamp; and he speedily put his plan into execution. As his father was going from Balinrobe to Dublin, he was waylaid by his son and a party of armed men, and carried off *vi et armis* to George Robert's house at Turlough.

This open violation of the law could not be submitted to tamely, and his younger brother went to Dublin, and stated his case before the judges, who granted him a writ of *habeas corpus*. But no one would serve that at Turlough, so they waited, as of aforetime, until he was at the grand jury room, and, leave having been given, his brother, who was bigger

and stronger than he, went in, and, literally collaring
him, dragged him out, spite of all his protests that he
was a grand jury man, and could not be touched
while in the exercise of his functions. He was at
once put on his trial, and the grand jury found a
true bill against him, unanimously: nay, more, they
publicly addressed the judge in court, expressing
their abhorrence of the charge made against Fitzgerald. After the finding of a true bill, his trial at
once took place, in despite of all efforts to postpone
it to the next assizes, and it lasted from nine in the
morning until nearly twelve at night, when, the
judge having summed up, the jury found him guilty,
and he was fined £1,000, to be imprisoned for three
years, and until he should pay the fine.

What happens next in this man's extraordinary
career is almost difficult to believe, and shows the
lawless state of the country. Fitzgerald was committed to Castlebar prison, but he seems to have been
at large therein, for, four days after his committal, he
calmly walked out of gaol, armed with a brace of
pistols, and scattering a bag of silver to be scrambled
for by the gaolers. The doors were all open, a horse
was in readiness, and off he went, tantivy, for
Turlough, where he was welcomed by his people with
volleys of small arms and discharge of cannon. These
latter Fitzgerald had procured from a ship, under the
pretext that they would be useful for his volunteers,
of which he was the colonel. These he mounted as
a regular battery, and it was garrisoned in a perfectly
military manner by his volunteers.

But an escape from prison was, by the law of Ireland, deemed a capital felony, and the sheriff of the
county issued proclamations and rewards for his

apprehension, at which Fitzgerald only laughed, for he could rely on his men, and he had his father still in his custody, as the old man did not go away when his son was, as he thought, safely imprisoned. He was some fifteen months at large before the majesty of the law asserted itself. Then a little army, consisting of three companies of foot, a troop of horse, and a battery of artillery, under the command of Major Longford, was sent to reduce this rebel. But, when they got to Rockfield, they found the cannon spiked, and the birds flown to Killala, whither they were followed by Charles Lionel, at the head of the Castlebar volunteers. But many people gathered round Fitzgerald, and he soon had a party which was too strong for them to attack. But, a large reinforcement arriving, he had to flee, and, with his father, and two or three attendants, he put to sea in an open boat, landing on a small island in the bay of Sligo.

Here his father offered him terms, that if he would give him £3,000 to clear off his debts, and pay him a small annuity, he would give him up the estate, and completely exonerate him of all blame in his capture and detention. To these terms Fitzgerald assented, and set off with his father through bye, and unfrequented roads to Dublin. But no sooner had the old man got into his old lodging, than he refused to ratify his bargain, and set his son at defiance.

Fitzgerald, although there was a reward out of £300 for his apprehension, took no pains to conceal himself, and, consequently, had not been long in Dublin, before Town-Major Hall heard of his whereabouts, and, taking twelve soldiers of the Castle guard with him, arrested Fitzgerald, and safely lodged him in the Castle, where he was confined in the officer's room; and there he abode till the general election, when, through the influence of his powerful friends, he was released. During his incarceration he wrote an appeal to the public on his case, although some say the author was one Timothy Brecknock, a somewhat unscrupulous lawyer whom Fitzgerald employed.

The first use he made of his newly-acquired liberty was to revenge himself on a man who he fancied had done him some grievous injury, a somewhat eccentric gentleman named Dick Martin, and he determined to insult him in the most public manner. He met him at the theatre, struck him with his cane, calling him the bully of the Altamonts, and walked away. Of course, in those days a gentleman so insulted could but do one thing, and that was to send a challenge—and Martin did send Fitzgerald one by the hand of a cousin of the latter, a Mr. Lyster. While he was explaining the object of his visit, Fitzgerald rang the bell, and requested his footman to bring him his cudgel 'with the green ribbon.' This being brought, he walked up to his cousin, and ferociously asked how *he* dared to deliver such a message to *him*: then, not waiting for a reply, he belaboured him most unmercifully, with such violence indeed, as to break a diamond ring from off his finger. When he considered him sufficiently punished, he made him pick up his ring and present it to him—but he did not keep it, he wrapped it up in paper, and returned it, telling his cousin not to go about swearing that he had robbed him of it.

Martin could get no satisfaction out of Fitzgerald in Dublin, the object of the latter being to let his adversary have the reputation of being an insulted man. But, afterwards, they met at Castlebar, and a meeting was arranged. Martin was hit, and his bullet struck Fitzgerald, but glanced off: according to some it hit a button; according to others, Fitzgerald was *plastroné*, or armoured.

His behaviour was more like that of a lunatic than of a sane man. Take the following example, for instance. He had a house and grounds near Dublin, and his neighbours all fought shy of him—nay, one of them, a retired officer, Captain Boulton, would neither accept his invitations nor invite him to his mansion. This conduct galled Fitzgerald, and he devised a novel method of avenging himself of the insult. He would shoot on the captain's grounds without leave. So he went down with his man and dogs and began killing the game in fine style. This soon brought out the steward, who began to remonstrate with the trespasser. Fitzgerald's answer was a bullet, which whizzed close to the head of the poor steward, who turned, and ran for his life, Fitzgerald after him with a second gun, with the certain determination of shooting him. Luckily the man got safely into the mansion. Baffled of his victim, Fitzgerald began abusing Captain Boulton, calling on him to come out, and give him satisfaction for his man's behaviour. But the captain, not seeing the force of the argument, refrained, and Fitzgerald fired his gun at the dining-room window. As this, however, did not bring out the captain, he fired at the windows as fast as his man could load, and only left off when he had smashed everyone of them.

Another time he waged war against all the dogs in Castlebar, shooting them whenever he got a chance;

but the people did not stand it tamely; they rose, visited his kennels, and shot his dogs.

His father died; but his brother, his father's mistress, and MacDonnell, took advantage of every circumstance in their power to maliciously vex him. Law-suits were stirrred up against him, and had to be met with the assistance of Timothy Brecknock, who was Fitzgerald's legal adviser, and the followers of both parties were not particular in exchanging a shot or two, one with the other.

At length MacDonnell kidnapped one of Fitzgerald's servants, and kept him prisoner for twenty days. Then the man escaped, and Fitzgerald applied for, and obtained warrants against, MacDonnell and two other men, named Hipson and Gallagher. To execute these warrants personally must have been a congenial task to Fitzgerald, and he set out for that purpose, followed by a large body of men. On their approach, MacDonnell fled to the neighbouring village of Ballivary, and his friends did the best they could to defend themselves, firing on his party and wounding six or seven of them. They then went after MacDonnell, and, after more firing, succeeded in apprehending MacDonnell, Hipson, and Gallagher. These unfortunate men begged to be taken before the nearest magistrate; but Fitzgerald had them bound, and taken to his house, where they remained all night.

Early the next morning they were sent, guarded by a man of his, one Andrew Craig, and about eighteen or twenty more, all well armed, to be examined by the magistrates. Before their departure Fitzgerald gave the guard strict instructions to kill the prisoners should they attempt to escape. When they had gone about three-quarters of a mile a shot was fired, and one of the escort was laid low. But very little was wanted to rouse their wild blood, and it was at once considered that a rescue was intended. Remembering the instructions given them by Fitzgerald, they fired on their prisoners, killing Hipson, who fell into a ditch, dragging Gallagher with him, wounded with three bullets in his arm. MacDonnell, by the same volley, had both his arms broken, but he was soon afterwards despatched. Gallagher was then discovered, and they were about to kill him, only Fitzgerald ordered him to be taken to his house.

News was sent to Castlebar of what had taken place, and Fitzgerald calmly awaited the result. Fully aware of the dangerous character they had to deal with, the authorities sent a large body, both of regular troops, and volunteers, to Turlough, and these were accompanied by an immense mob of people. What happened is best related in the following graphic account:

'Brecknock was for remaining, as with the calmness of conscious innocence, and boldly demanding a warrant against Gallagher and others. This opinion, however, did not agree with Fitzgerald's own, who justly dreaded the fury of the volunteers and the populace, with whom MacDonnell had been so popular. Neither did it coincide with that of the Rev. Mr. Henry, the Presbyterian clergyman of Turlough, who had been latterly a resident in the house, and was now wringing his hands in wild alarm for what had occurred. This gentleman's horse was at the door, and he strongly urged George Robert to mount, and ride for his life out of the country altogether, till the powerful intercession he could command might be made for him. In compliance with this advice, which entirely coincided with his own opinion, it is stated that he made several attempts to mount; but that, splendid horseman as he was, whether through nervous excitement, guilty terror, or the restiveness of the animal, he was unable to attain the saddle, and, in consequence, obliged to fly into the house again, as the military were announced to be approaching near. It is also generally asserted that the Rev. Mr. Ellison, who headed the soldiers, sent them on to Gurth-na-fullagh, without halting them at Turlough, where he himself stopped.

'Were this circumstance even true, however, Fitzgerald gained but a short respite by it, as the volunteers, with many of the populace, came furiously up immediately after; and, some of them being placed about the house, the remainder entered to search and pillage it. Brecknock and Fulton were immediately captured, but, after ransacking every corner and crevice more than once without finding him, the volunteers were beginning to think that Fitzgerald must have effected his escape before their arrival, when one of them, forcing open a clothes-chest in a lower apartment, discovered him among a heap of bed-clothes in his place of concealment.

'"What do you want, you ruffian?" he said, on finding himself detected.

'"To dhrag ye, like a dog's head, to a bonfire," replied another volunteer, named Morran, a powerful man, who seized him at the same time by the breast, and drew him forth by main force.

'A pistol was now presented at him by a third to

take summary vengeance; but a comrade snapped it from his hands, asking if there was not murder enough already.

'"What mercy did himself or his murdherers show to those every way their betthers?"

'"Well, let them pay for that on the gallows, but let us be no murdherers; let us give him up to the law."

'He was, accordingly, hauled out to the front of the house, where, perceiving Mr. Ellison, he exclaimed,

'"Ellison, will you allow me to be handled thus by such rabble?"

'Mr. Ellison's response to this saved him from further molestation for a time, and exertions were then made to withdraw the pillagers from the wholesale plundering they were practising within. One fellow had girded his loins with linen almost as fine as Holland—so fine that he made some hundred yards fit round his body without being much observable. Another, among other valuables, made himself master of the duellist's diamond-buttoned coat; while a third contrived to appropriate to himself all the jewels, valued at a very high amount. In short, so entire were the spoliation and destruction that, before sunset, not a single pane of glass was left in the windows.

'The remainder of those implicated in the murders were speedily apprehended, except Craig, who escaped for the time, but was taken soon after near Dublin.

'We must now pause to sustain our character as an accurate chronicler to relate an act as unprecedented, as lawless, and as terrible as the most terrible of Fitzgerald's own. He was alone, on the night of his capture, in the room assigned to him in the gaol. It was not a felon's apartment, but was guarded on the outside by two armed soldiers, lest he should make any desperate attempt to escape. It was some hours after nightfall that Clarke, the then sub-sheriff, removed one of those sentinels to another portion of the prison, where he stated he required his presence. They had scarcely disappeared, when the remaining soldier, McBeth (according to his own account), was knocked down, and his musket taken from him, while the door was burst open, and a number of men, all armed with pistols, sword-canes, and the sentinel's musket, commenced a furious and deadly attack on Fitzgerald, who, though totally unarmed, made a most extraordinary defence. Several shots were discharged rapidly at him, one of which lodged in his thigh, while another broke a ring on the finger of one of his hands, which he put up to change the direction of the ball.

He was then secured by John Gallagher, one of the assailants, and a powerful man, and, whilst struggling in his grip, thrust at with blades and bayonets, one of the former of which broke in the fleshy part of his arm. The latter, too, in forcing out two of his teeth, had its point broken, and was thereby prevented from passing through his throat. After having freed himself, by great exertions, from Gallagher's grasp, he was next assaulted with musket-stock, pistol-butts, and the candlestick, which had been seized by one of the assailants, who gave the candle to a boy to hold. By one of the blows inflicted by these weapons he was prostrated under the table, and, while lying there, defending himself with unimpaired powers against other deadly-aimed blows, he exclaimed,

'Cowardly rascals, you may now desist; you have done for me, which was, of course, your object.'

The candle had by this time been quenched in the struggling, and the gaol and streets thoroughly alarmed, so that the assailants, fearing to injure one another, and deeming that their intended victim was really dispatched, retreated from the prison, leaving Fitzgerald, though wounded, once more in security.

In consequence of this outrage, his trial was postponed for two months, and the government ordered his assailants to be prosecuted, but on trial they were acquitted. Fitzgerald himself was tried the same day (June 8, 1786), the chief witnesses against him being his own man, Andrew Craig, and Andrew Callagher, the latter of whom deposed that when he, Hipson, and MacDonnell, were confined in Fitzgerald's house, there was a pane broken in the window, and 'At day he saw a number of men regularly drawn up, to the number of twenty or thirty. He saw Andrew Craig and James Foy settling them. Mr. Fitzgerald and Mr. Brecknock came to the flag of the hall-door; through the broken pane he heard them conversing; they spoke in French for some time, and afterwards in English, but he could not hear what they said, but the names of himself, MacDonnell, and Hipson were severally mentioned. He heard at that time nothing more than their names. Mr. Fitzgerald called over James Foy and Andrew Craig, who were settling the guard, and ordered them to move a little higher, about ten or twelve yards above the house. There was some other conversation which he did not hear. As soon as the guard were settled, Mr. Fitzgerald gave them —Foy and Craig—orders "If they saw any rescue, or colour of a rescue, be sure they shot the prisoners, and take care of them."

'When these orders were given, Mr. Fitzgerald said to Mr. Brecknock,

'"Ha! we shall soon get rid of them now."

'Mr. Brecknock replied: "Oh, then we shall be easy indeed."

'After the guard was settled, Mr. Fitzgerald called back Andrew Craig, and when Craig came within ten yards of him, he, Mr. Fitzgerald, said,

'"Andrew, be sure you kill them. Do not let one of the villains escape."

'Andrew answered: "Oh, never fear, please your honour."'

At his trial he had a bitter enemy both in the judge, Yelverton, and the prosecuting counsel, Fitzgibbon. Nor could he reckon the high sheriff, Denis Browne, among his friends, so that it was scarcely possible that it should have but one issue, and the jury returned a verdict of guilty against both him and Brecknock, and the judge sentenced them to immediate execution. Fitzgerald begged for a little delay, so that he might settle his worldly affairs; it was denied him, and, at six in the evening, he walked forth to his doom. Brecknock had already suffered. Fitzgerald dreaded the scene of the scaffold and the journey thither along the high road, in a cart, and asked, as a last favour from the sheriff, to be allowed to walk and go by a by-way. It was granted, and he went to his doom preceded by the hangman, who wore a large mask. He walked very fast, and was dressed in a ragged coat of the Castletown hunt, a dirty flannel waistcoat and drawers, both of which were without buttons, brown worsted or yarn stockings, a pair of coarse shoes without buckles, and an old round hat, tied round with a pack-thread band.

When he jumped off the ladder the rope broke, although he was but a slightly-built man and a light weight, and he had to wait until another, and a stronger, one was procured. After forty minutes' hanging his body was cut down, and was waked by the light of a few candles in a barn at Turlough; it was interred, the next morning, in the family tomb, situated in a ruined chapel adjoining a round tower, but his remains were disturbed some years afterwards at the burial of his brother in the same tomb. He was thirty-eight years of age.

His daughter had a portion of £10,000 left her by him, and she was a very gentle and interesting girl. She mostly resided with her uncle at Castletown, and was unaware, for a long time, of her father's fate. But it so happened that, being one day alone in the library, and looking over the upper shelves, she lit upon a copy of his trial. She read it, and from that time never lifted up her head, nor smiled—she could not bear her position as the daughter of a felon, and she gradually pined away, and died at an early age.

EIGHTEENTH-CENTURY AMAZONS.

PUGNACITY is not confined to the male sex, as everyone well knows, and none better than the police-force, but in these latter and, presumably, degenerate days, the efforts, in this direction, of the softer sex are confined to social exhibitions, there being, as far as is known, no woman serving in Her Majesty's force either by land or by sea. Indeed, with the present medical examination, it would be impossible; and so it would have been in the old days, only then all was fish that came to the net. His, or Her Majesty, as the case might be, never had enough men, and 'food for powder' was ever acceptable, and its quality never closely scrutinised. It is incredible, were it not true, that these women, whose stories I am about to relate, were not discovered to be such —they were wounded, they were flogged, and yet there was no suspicion as to their sex.

We get the particulars of the life of the first of that century's Amazons in a book of one hundred and eighty-one pages, published (second edition) in 1744, entitled, 'The British Heroine: or, an Abridgment of the Life and Adventures of Mrs. Christian Davis, commonly called Mother Ross.' She was born in Dublin, A.D. 1667, and was the daughter of a maltster and brewer, named Cavanagh, who occupied a small farm about two miles from Dublin. Here Miss Christian resided with her mother, and, although her education was not neglected, for she learned to read and sew, yet the charms of physical exertion were more attractive, and she took greater delight in using the flail, or following the plough, than in sedentary occupations. She was a regular tomboy, bestriding bare-backed horses and, without saddle or bridle, scampering about, taking hedges and ditches whenever they came in her way.

After the abdication of James II. her father sold all his standing corn, &c., and with the produce, and the money he had by him, he raised a troop of horse and joined the king's army. He was wounded at the battle of Aghrim, and soon afterwards died of fever. His wife had very prudently negotiated a pardon for him, but, as soon as he was dead, the government confiscated all his goods; yet still the mother and daughter managed to get along somehow or other.

She grew up to be a buxom and sprightly lass, when it was her misfortune to meet with her cousin, the Reverend Thomas Howell, a Fellow of Dublin University, who first seduced and then abandoned her. Her grief at this told upon her health, and her mother sent her for a change of air to Dublin, there to stop with an aunt, who kept a public-house. With her she lived for four years, when her aunt died and left her all she had, including the business. She afterwards married a servant of her aunt's, one Richard Welch, and lived very happily with him for four years, when her husband one day went out, with fifty pounds in his pocket, to pay his brewer, and never returned.

For nearly twelve months she heard no tidings of him, but one day came a letter, in which he told her he had met a friend, and with him had too much drink, went on board ship, and had more drink; and when he recovered from the effects of his debauch, found himself classed as a recruit for his Majesty's army, sailing for Helvoetsluys. The receipt of this letter completely upset his wife, but only for a short time, when she took the extraordinary resolution of entering the army as a recruit, in order that she might be sent to Flanders, and there might possibly meet with her husband. She let her house, left her furniture in charge of her neighbours, sent one child to her mother's, and put the other out to nurse. She then cut her hair short, put on a suit of her husband's clothes, hat and wig, and buckled on a silver-hilted sword. There was a law then in existence by which it was an offence to carry out of the kingdom any sum exceeding five pounds, but this she evaded by quilting fifty guineas in the waistband of her breeches.

She then enlisted in a foot regiment under the name of Christopher Welch, and was soon shipped, with other recruits, and sent to Holland. She was, with the others, put through some sort of drill, but much time could not then be wasted on drill, and then they were sent to the grand army, and incorporated in different regiments. Almost directly after joining, she was wounded by a musket-ball in the leg, at the battle of Landen, and had to quit the field. This wound laid her up for two months, and when she rejoined her regiment they were ordered into winter quarters. Here she, in common with the other British soldiers, helped the Dutch to repair their dykes.

In the following campaign she had the ill-luck to be taken prisoner by the French, and was sent to St. Germains en Laye, where Mary of Modena, the wife of James II. paid particular attention to the wants of the English prisoners, having them separated from the Dutch, and allowing each man five farthings for tobacco, a pound of bread, and a pint of wine daily. She was imprisoned for nine days, when an exchange of prisoners took place, and she was released.

Once more the troops went into winter quarters, and Mrs. Welch must needs ape the gallantry of her comrades. She made fierce love to the daughter of a rich burgher, and succeeded so well that the girl would fain have married her. Now it so happened that a sergeant of the same regiment loved the same girl, but with other than honourable intentions, and one day he endeavoured to gain her compliance by force. The girl resisted and in the scuffle got nearly all the clothes torn off her back. When Mrs. Welch heard of this affair she 'went for' that sergeant, and the result was a duel with swords. Mrs. Welch received two wounds in her right arm, but she nearly killed the sergeant, and afterwards, dreading his animosity when he should have recovered, she exchanged into a dragoon regiment (Lord John Hayes) and was present at the taking of Namur.

When the troops again went into winter quarters a curious adventure befell her, which goes to prove how completely masculine was her appearance. She resisted the advances of a woman, who thereby was so angered that she swore she would be revenged, and accordingly, when a child was born to her, she swore that the trooper, Christopher Welch, was its father. This, of course, could have been easily disproved, but then good-bye to her hopes of meeting with her husband; so, after mature deliberation, she accepted the paternity of the child, who, however, did not trouble her for long, as it died in a month.

After the peace of Ryswick in 1697, the army was partially disbanded, and Mrs. Welch returned home to Dublin. She found her mother, children, and friends all well, but finding that she was unrecognized, owing to her dress and the hardships of campaigning, she did not make herself known, but re-enlisted in 1701 in her old regiment of dragoons, on the breaking out of the War of Succession. She went through the campaigns of 1702 and 1703, and was present at many of the engagements therein, receiving a wound in the hip, at Donawert, and, although attended by three surgeons, her sex was not discovered. She never forgot her quest, but all her inquiries after her husband were in vain. Yet she unexpectedly came upon him, after the battle of Hochstadt in 1704, caressing and toying with a Dutch camp follower. A little time afterwards she discovered herself to him. Having seen what she had, she would not return to her husband as his wife, but passed as a long-lost brother, and they met frequently.

At the battle of Ramilies, in 1705, a piece of a shell struck the back of her head, and fractured her skull, for which she underwent the operation of trepanning, and then it was, whilst unconscious, that her sex was discovered, and her husband came forward and claimed her as his wife. Her pay went on until she was cured, when the officers of the regiment, who, naturally, were interested in this very romantic affair, made up a new wardrobe for her, and she was re-married to her husband with great solemnity, and many and valuable were her marriage-presents. She could not be idle, so she turned sutler, and, by the indulgence of the officers, she was allowed to pitch her tent in the front, whilst all the others were sent to the rear, but she was virtually unsexed by the rough ways of the camp, although a child was born to her amongst the din and confusion of the campaign.

Her husband was killed at the battle of Malplaquet, in 1709, and then this rough woman could not help showing that she possessed some of the softer feelings of her sex. Her grief was overpowering. She bit a great piece out of her arm, tore her hair, and then threw herself upon the corpse in an ecstasy of passion, and, had any weapon been handy, she would, undoubtedly, have killed herself. With her own hands she dug his grave, and with her own hands would she have scraped the earth away, in order to get one more glimpse of her husband's face, had she not been prevented. She refused food; she became absolutely ill from grief, and yet, within eleven weeks from her husband's death, she married a grenadier named Hugh Jones! Her second married life was brief—for her husband was mortally wounded at the siege of St. Venant.

After her husband's death, she got a living by cooking for the officers, and went through the whole campaign, till 1712, when she applied to the Duke of Ormond for a pass to England—which he not only gave her, but also money enough to defray her expenses on the way. On her arrival in England, she called on the Duke of Marlborough, to see whether he could not get some provision made for her; but he was not in power, and, however good his will towards her might have been, he had not the means. She then tried the Duke of Argyle, who advised her to have a petition to the Queen drawn up, and take it to the Duke of Hamilton, and he himself would back it up.

She did so, and took it to the duke, who, when he was assured she was no impostor, advised her to get a new petition drawn up, and present herself to the Queen. So, the next day, she dressed herself in her best, and went to Court, waiting patiently at the foot of the great staircase, and when Queen Anne, supported by the Duke of Argyle, came down, she dropped on one knee, and presented her petition to the Queen, who received it with a smile, and bade her rise and be of good cheer, for that she would provide for her; and, perceiving her to be with child, she added, 'If you are delivered of a boy, I will give him a commission as soon as he is born.' Her Majesty also ordered her fifty pounds, to defray the expenses of her lying-in. She lived some little time in London, being helped very materially by the officers to whom she was known; and it was during this time, on Saturday morning, the 15th of November, 1712, she was going through Hyde Park, and was an eye-witness of the historical duel between Lord Mohun and the Duke of Hamilton.

A natural longing came upon her to see her mother and her children, and she wrote to her to say she would be in Dublin by a certain date. The old woman, although over a hundred years of age, trudged the whole ten miles to Dublin, to see this daughter whom she had so long given up as dead; and the meeting was very affecting. When she came to inquire after her children, she found one had died at the age of eighteen, and the other was in the workhouse, where it had very speedily been placed by the nurse in whose charge it had been left. She went to look after the furniture and goods which she had housed with her neighbours; but there was only one who would give any account of them. A man had taken possession of her freehold house, and refused to give it up; and, having lost the title-deeds, she could not force him, besides which she had no money to carry on a lawsuit.

These misfortunes did not dishearten her; she always had been used to victualling. So she took a public-house, and stocked it, and made pies, and altogether was doing very well, when she must needs go and marry a soldier named Davies, whose discharge she bought, but he afterwards enlisted in the Guards.

Queen Anne, besides her gift of fifty pounds, ordered Mrs. Davies a shilling a day for life, which Harley, Earl of Oxford, for some reason or other, cut down to fivepence, with which she was fain to be content until a change of ministry took place. Then she applied to Mr. Craggs, and she got her original pension restored.

She did not do very well in her business, but she found plenty of friends in the officers of the Army who knew her. She once more bought her husband's discharge, and got him into Chelsea Hospital, with the rank of sergeant. She also was received into that institution; and there she died on the 7th of July, 1739, and was interred in the burying-ground attached to Chelsea Hospital, with military honours.

Hannah Snell's grandfather entered the Army in the reign of William III. as a volunteer, and, by his personal bravery, he earned a commission as lieutenant, with the rank of captain. He was wounded at Blenheim, and mortally wounded at Malplaquet. Her brother was also a soldier, and was killed at Fontenoy; so that she may be said to have come of a martial race. Her father was a hosier and dyer, and she was born at Worcester on St. George's Day, 23rd of April, 1723.

According to a contemporary biography of her,[1] 'Hannah, when she was scarce Ten Years of Age, had the seeds of Heroinism, as it were, implanted in her nature, and she used often to declare to her Companions that she would be a Soldier, if she lived; and, as a preceding Testimony of the Truth, she formed a Company of young Soldiers among her Playfellows, and of which she was chief Commander, at the Head of whom she often appeared, and was used to parade the whole City of Worcester. This Body of young Volunteers were admired all over the Town, and they were styled young "Amazon Snell's Company"; and this Martial Spirit grew up with her, until it carried her through the many Scenes and Vicissitudes she encountered for nigh five Years.'

Her father and mother being dead, she, in 1740, moved to London, where she arrived on Christmas Day, and took up her abode with one of her sisters, who had married a carpenter named Gray, and was living at Wapping. Two years afterwards she was

[1] 'The Female Soldier; or, The Surprising Life and Adventures of Hannah Snell,' &c. London, 1750.

married, at the Fleet, to a German or Dutch sailor named James Summs, on the 6th of January, 1743; but he was a worthless fellow, and as soon as he found she was with child by him, having spent all her money, he deserted her. She heard of his death subsequently; he was at Genoa, and, in a quarrel, he killed a Genoese. For this he was condemned to death, sewn up in a sack with a quantity of stones, and sunk in the sea. Her child survived its birth but seven months, and she was left a free woman.

Up to this time her story presents nothing of particular interest; but, like 'Long Meg of Westminster,' she was a *virago*, more man than woman, and, with the hope of some day meeting with her husband, she donned male attire, and set forth on her quest. She soon fell in with a recruiting party at Coventry, whither she had walked, and where she found her funds exhausted. A little drink, the acceptance of a shilling, a visit to a magistrate, were the slight preliminaries to her military career, and the 27th of November, 1743, found her a private in the army of King George II. The guinea, and five shillings, her little 'bounty money,' had to follow the fate of all similar sums, in treating her comrades. There was scant time for drills, and she was, after about three weeks' preparation, drafted off to Carlisle to join her regiment. There were no railway passes in those days, so the weary march northward took twenty-two days.

She had not been long in Carlisle before her sergeant, named Davis, requested her aid in an intrigue he was endeavouring to establish with a young woman of that town; but, instead of helping him, she warned the young person of his intentions, and absolutely won the girl's heart. Davis's jealousy was excited, and to punish Jemmy Gray (which was the name under which Hannah Snell had enlisted), he reported her for some neglect of duty, and, as commanding officers then were rather severe than lenient in their punishments, she was sentenced to receive six hundred lashes, five hundred of which she absolutely received, and would have taken the whole had not some officers interfered. It seems marvellous that her sex, when she was tied up and partially stripped, was not discovered, and in a romance it would be a weak spot; but, as a matter-of-fact, no one suspected she was a woman, and when her back was healed she returned to her duty. Flogging was common enough in those days.

But a worse danger of exposure threatened her, for a fellow-townsman from Worcester enlisted in the same regiment, and so she determined to desert. The female friend on whose account she had suffered such severe punishment, found some money, and Hannah Snell fled towards Portsmouth, surreptitiously changing coats in a field by the way. She stopped but little time in Portsmouth, and then she enlisted in the Marines, in which corps she was certain to be sent abroad on service, and might have greater opportunities of meeting with her husband.

Scarce three weeks after her enlistment had elapsed when a draft was made to join Admiral Boscawen's fleet for the East Indies, and she was sent on board the sloop of war, the *Swallow*. Here she soon became very popular with her mess-mates, her skill in cooking, washing, and mending their shirts made her a general favourite, and she did her duty with the best of her comrades, being especially noted for her smartness, so much so, indeed, that she was made an officer's servant.

Those old ships were not very good sailors in a gale. The French beat us hollow at ship-building, and we much improved by studying the make of the prizes we were constantly taking, so it is not to be wondered at if that rolling old tub, the *Swallow*, came to grief. The marvel would have been had it not occurred. Twice, before the Cape was made, they had to repair and refit. They were then ordered to the Mauritius, and eventually they went to the Coromandel coast, where they landed and laid siege to and took Areacopong. They then besieged Pondicherry (in September, 1748); but that town was not fated to fall into the hands of the British until 1760. In all the hardships of the siege Hannah Snell bore her full part, fording rivers breast high, sleeping in and working at the trenches, &c., until at last she was desperately wounded, receiving six shots in her right leg, five in her left, and a bullet in her groin. Anyone would think that thus wounded, and in hospital, her sex would have been discovered; but it was not. She managed to extract the ball from her groin, and with the connivance of an old black nurse, she always dressed the wound herself, so that the surgeons did not know of its existence.

Three months she lay in hospital, going back to her duty as a Marine on her discharge. But her comrades bantered her on her somewhat feminine appearance, her smooth cheeks not being in accordance with her age. Besides, she was somewhat quiet, and different from the rollicking Jack Tars by whom she was surrounded, and so she earned the name of Miss Molly Gray. A continuance of this quiet *rôle* might have led to discovery, so when they came to Lisbon, and the 'liberty men' went on shore, she was as racketty as any of them, and 'Miss Molly' was soon lost, and in her place was 'Hearty Jemmy.' From Lisbon they sailed for home, and on her arrival at Spithead, she was either discharged, or sent on furlough; at all events, there ended her military and naval career, for she went straight to her sister at Wapping, and was at once recognized.

Campaigning had made her restless, and, although many of the officers who had known her assisted her pecuniarily, it was light come, light go, and the money was soon spent. So her friends advised her to petition the Duke of Cumberland, pointing out her services, and also dilating upon her wounds. On the 16th of June, 1750, she found a very favourable opportunity of presenting her memorandum to the duke, and, after full inquiry, she was awarded a pension of a shilling a day. This, however, would not keep her, and finding that, as an Amazon, she had a market value, she engaged with the proprietor of the New Wells in Goodman's Fields (the Royalty Theatre, Wellclose Square) to appear on the stage as a soldier. In this character she sang several songs, and 'She appears regularly dress'd in her Regimentals from Top to Toe, with all the Accoutrements requisite for the due Performance of her Military Exercises. Here she and her Attendants fill up the Stage in a very agreeable Manner. The tabor and Drum give Life to her March, and she traverses the stage two or three times over, Step by Step, in the same Manner as our Soldiers march on the Parade in St. James's Park.

'After the Spectators have been sufficiently amused

with this formal Procession, she begins her Military
exercises, and goes through the whole Catechism (if I
may be allowed the Expression) with so much Dex-
terity and Address, and with so little Hesitation or
Default, that great Numbers even of Veteran Soldiers,
who have resorted to the Wells out of mere curiosity
only, have frankly acknowledged that she executes
what she undertakes to Admiration, and that the
universal Applause which she meets with is by no
means the Result of Partiality to her in Consideration
of her Sex, but is due to her, without Favour or Affection, as the Effect of her extraordinary Merit.

'As our Readers may be desirous of being informed
in what Dress she now appears, we think it proper to
inform them that she wears Men's Cloaths, being, as
she says, determined so to do, and having bought
new Cloathing for that Purpose.'

This theatrical performance, of course, could not
last long; so, with her savings, she took a public-
house at Wapping, which she christened 'The Widow
in Masquerade,' and on one side of the sign she was
delineated in her full regimentals, on the other in
plain clothes.

She afterwards married, for in the *Universal
Chronicle* (November $\frac{3}{10}$, 1759, p. 359, col. 3)
may be read: 'Marriages. At Newbury, in the
county of Berks, the famous Hannah Snell, who
served as a marine in the last war, and was wounded
at the siege of Pondicherry, to a carpenter of that
place.' His name was Eyles. In 1789 she became
insane, and was taken to Bethlehem, where she died
on the 8th of February, 1792, aged sixty-nine.

The examples quoted of women joining the army
are by no means singular, for in 1761 a lynx-eyed

sergeant detected a woman who wished to enlist under the name of Paul Daniel, in the hope that she might be sent to Germany, where her husband was then serving in the army. And in the same year a woman named Hannah Witney was masquerading at Plymouth in man's attire, and was laid hold of by a press-gang and lodged in Plymouth gaol. She was so disgusted at the treatment she received that she disclosed her sex, at the same time telling the astonished authorities that she had served as a marine for five years.

There is a curious little chap-book, now very rare, of the 'Life and Adventures of Maria Knowles . . . by William Fairbank, Sergeant-major of the 66th Regiment of Foot,' and, as it is very short, it may be as well to give its *ipsissima verba*.

'The heroine of the following story is the only daughter of Mr. John Knowles, a reputed farmer,[1] of the parish of Bridworth, in the county of Cheshire, where Maria was born, and was her father's only daughter. At an early age she lost her mother, and was brought up under the care of a mother-in-law, who treated her with more kindness than is usually done to motherless children. Her father having no other child, his house might have proved a comfortable home for one of a more sober disposition. At the age of nineteen she was so very tall that she was styled the 'Tall Girl.' She had a very handsome face, which gained her plenty of sweethearts. Many young men felt the weight of her fists for giving her offences. She refused many offers of marriage, and that from persons of fortune.

'Being one day at the market in Warrington, she

A farmer of repute.

saw one Cliff, a sergeant of the Guards on the recruiting service, with whom she fell deeply in love; he in a short time was called to join the regiment, and she, not being able to bear her love-sick passion, eloped from her father's house, immediately went up to London, disguised in man's apparel, and enlisted in the same regiment with her sweetheart, in which she made a most martial appearance in her regimentals; her height covered the deception. As a red coat captivates the fair sex, our female soldier made great advances, being a lover of mirth and a smart girl . . . .

'A part of the Guards were ordered to Holland, with whom sailed Maria and her sweetheart. The British troops were stationed at Dort, and a party was sent in gunboats to annoy the French, who were then besieging Williamstadt. From Holland they were ordered to French Flanders, where Maria was at several desperate battles and sieges. At Dunkirk she was wounded in three different parts, in her right shoulder, in her right arm, and thigh, which discovered her sex, and, of course, her secret.

'After being recovered from her wounds, and questioned by her commanding officer, she related to him the particulars of her life, and the reason of her being disguised, and entering for a soldier, which was to seek her fortune, and share the fate of the man on whom she had irrevocably fixed her affection.

'The news soon reached her lover, who flew to the arms of so faithful a girl, whom he embraced with the most ardent zeal, vowing an eternal constancy to her; and, in order to reward such faithful love, the officers raised a handsome subscription for them, after which they were married by the chaplain of the regiment, to their great joy . . . . . .

'But this was not all, for the adjutant of the 66th Regiment of Foot dying of his wounds, Sergeant Cliff was promoted to that berth, and Sergeant Fairbank to sergeant-major, as Cliff and him were always comrades together. In a little time the regiment was sent to Gibraltar, where they stayed most part of the year, during which Mrs. Cliff was delivered of a fine son, after which the regiment was sent to the West Indies, and, after a passage of twenty-eight days, landed safely on the island of St. Vincent, where they remained some time; but, the yellow fever raging among the troops, Mr. Cliff died, to the great grief of his disconsolate wife and her young son. She was still afraid of the raging distemper, but, happily for her and her son, neither of them took it.

'Great indulgence was given her, and also provisions allowed them both; but this did not suffice, for Mrs. Cliff, losing the man she had ventured her life so many times for, was now very unhappy, and made application to the commanding officer for her passage to England; and a great many men, unfit for duty, coming home, she was admitted a passenger. I, being unfit to act as sergeant-major, on account of a wound that I received in my left leg, the same day Mrs. Cliff was wounded, and although it was cured, as soon as I came into a hot country it broke out again, and I, being unfit for duty, was sent home, and recommended.[1] So I came home in the same ship, with this difference, that she was in the cabin, and I among the men. We sailed in the *Eleanor* on the 25th of January, 1798, and, after forty

[1] For a pension.

days' sail, we reached Spithead, and, after performing a short quarantine, we landed at Portsmouth on the 16th of March, where I left Mrs. Cliff to pursue her journey to her father's, and I came to London.'

I have been unable to trace the fate of this heroine any further.

There is yet another woman of the eighteenth century, who acted the part both of soldier and sailor; and we read of her in the *Times*, 4th of November, 1799.

'There is at present in the Middlesex Hospital a young and delicate female, who calls herself Miss T—lb—t, and who is said to be related to some families of distinction; her story is very singular:— At an early period of her life, having been deprived, by the villainy of a trustee, of a sum of money bequeathed to her by a deceased relation of high rank, she followed the fortunes of a young naval officer to whom she was attached, and personated a common sailor before the mast, during a cruise in the north seas. In consequence of a lover's quarrel she quitted the ship, and assumed, for a time, the military character; but her passion for the sea prevailing, she returned to her favourite element, did good service, and received a severe wound on board Earl St. Vincent's ship, on the glorious 14th of February,[1] and again bled in the cause of her country in the engagement off Camperdown. On this last occasion her knee was shattered, and an amputation is likely to ensue. This spirited female, we understand, receives

[1] The action off Cape St. Vincent, when Sir John Jervis, with fifteen sail of the line, attacked and defeated the Spanish fleet, consisting of twenty-seven sail of the line.

a pension of £20 from an illustrious lady, which is about to be doubled.'

Voilà comment on écrit l'histoire! This newspaper report is about as truthful as nine-tenths of the paragraphs now-a-days; there is a substratum of truth, but not 'the whole truth and nothing but the truth.' But this can be read in a little tractate entitled, 'The Life and Surprising Adventures of Mary Ann Talbot, in the name of John Taylor. Related by herself.' London, 1809. This pamphlet is extracted from 'Kirby's Wonderful Museum of Remarkable Characters, &c.,' and professes to be an autobiography. It is highly probable that it is so, as she was a domestic servant in Mr. Kirby's house for three years before her death.

According to this relation she was the youngest of sixteen natural children whom her mother had by Lord William Talbot, Baron of Hensol, steward of his Majesty's household, and colonel of the Glamorganshire Militia. She was born the 2nd of February, 1778, and her mother died on giving her birth. She was put out to nurse in the country, until she was five years of age, when she was placed in a boarding-school at Chester, where she remained nine years, being looked after by a married sister who lived at Trevalyn, county Denbigh. At her death a man named Sucker, living at Newport, county Salop, became her guardian, and he behaved to her with such severity that she cordially hated him. He introduced her to a Captain Bowen, of the 82nd Regiment of Foot, who took her to London in January, 1792, where, friendless and alone, she soon became his victim.

His regiment was ordered to embark for Santo Domingo, and he had so thoroughly subjugated her to his will, and she was so utterly helpless, that she accompanied him on board as his 'little foot page.' Captain Bowen made John Taylor (for such was the name Miss Talbot then took) thoroughly act up to her assumed character, and she had to live and mess with the lowest of the ship's company, and, what was more, had to do her turn of duty with the ship's crew.

After a stormy voyage, with short provisions, they arrived at Port-au-Prince, but stayed there a very short time, as orders came for them to return to Europe, and join the troops on the Continent, under the command of His Royal Highness the Duke of York. Then it was that Captain Bowen made her enrol herself as a drummer in his regiment, threatening her unless she did so he would sell her up-country for a slave. There was nothing for her but to comply, so she put on the clothes and learned the business of a drummer-boy, having, besides, still to be the drudge of her paramour.

At the siege of Valenciennes she received two wounds, neither of them severe enough to incapacitate her from serving, and she cured them, without going into hospital, with a little basilicon, lint, and Dutch drops. In this siege Captain Bowen was killed, and she, finding the key of his desk in his pocket, searched the desk and found several letters relating to her, from her quondam guardian, Sucker.

Being now released from her servitude, she began to think of quitting the service, and, having changed her military dress for one she had worn on ship-board, she deserted, and, after some wandering, reached Luxembourg, but, it being in the occupation of the French, she was not permitted to go further. Being thus foiled in her design of reaching England, and destitute of every necessary of life, she was compelled to engage on board a French lugger, a cruiser. In the course of their voyage, they fell in with the British fleet under the command of Lord Howe. The French vessel made a show of fighting, and John Taylor refused to fight against her countrymen, for which she received a severe thrashing from the French captain.

After a very faint resistance the lugger was captured, and she, as being English, was taken on board the *Queen Charlotte* to be interrogated by Lord Howe. Her story, being backed up by the French captain, gained her release, and she was allowed to join the navy, a berth being found for her on board the *Brunswick* as powder-monkey, her duty being to hand powder, &c., for the guns when in action. Captain Harvey, of the *Brunswick*, noticed the pseudo lad, and straightly examined her as to whether she had not run away from school, or if she had any friends; but she disarmed his suspicions by telling him her father and mother were dead, and she had not a friend in the world; yet the kindly captain took such a friendly interest in her that he made her principal cabin-boy.

In the memorable fight off Brest, on the 'Glorious First of June,' Captain Harvey was killed, and our heroine severely wounded both in the ankle by a grape-shot and in the thigh a little above the knee. She was, of course, taken to the cockpit; but the surgeon could not extract the ball in the ankle, and would not venture to cut it out; nor, when they arrived home, and she was taken to Haslar Hospital, could they extract the ball. Partially cured, she was discharged, and shipped on board the *Vesuvius* bomb, belonging to Sir Sydney Smith's squadron, where she acted as midshipman, although she did not receive the pay which should have accompanied the position; and, while thus serving, a little anecdote she tells give us a fair idea of what stuff she was made.

'It was necessary for some one on board to go to the jib-boom to catch the jib-sheet, which in the gale had got loose. The continual lungeing of the ship rendered this duty particularly hazardous, and there was not a seaman on board but rejected this office. I was acting in the capacity of midshipman, though I never received pay for my service in this ship but as a common man. The circumstance I mention only to show that it was not my particular duty to undertake the task, which, on the refusal of several who were asked, I voluntarily undertook. Indeed, the preservation of us all depended on this exertion. On reaching the jib-boom I was under the necessity of lashing myself fast to it, for the ship every minute making a fresh lunge, without such a precaution I should inevitably have been washed away. The surges continually breaking over me, I suffered an uninterrupted wash and fatigue for six hours before I could quit the post 1 occupied. When danger is over, a sailor has little thought or reflection, and my mess-mates, who had witnessed the perilous situation in which I was placed, passed it off with a joke observing, "that I had only been sipping sea broth"; but it was a broth of a quality that, though most seamen relish, yet few, I imagine, would like to take it in the quantity I was compelled to do.'

By the fortune of war the *Vesuvius* was captured,

and the crew were conveyed to Dunkirk, where they were lodged in the prison of St. Clair, and the rigour of their captivity seems to have been extreme, especially in the case of Mary Anne Talbot, who perhaps partially deserved it, as she attempted, in company with a mess-mate, to escape. 'We were both confined in separate dungeons, where it was so dark that I never saw daylight during the space of eleven weeks, and the only allowance I received was bread and water, let down to me from the top of the cell. My bed consisted only of a little straw, not more than half a truss, which was never changed. For two days I was so ill in this dreadful place that I was unable to stir from my wretched couch to reach the miserable pittance, which, in consequence, was drawn up in the same state. The next morning, a person—who, I suppose, was the keeper of the place—came into the dungeon without a light (which way he came I know not, but I suppose through a private door through which I afterwards passed to be released), and called to me, "Are you dead?" To this question I was only able to reply by requesting a little water, being parched almost to death by thirst, resulting from the fever which preyed on me. He told me he had none, and left me in a brutal manner, without offering the least relief. Nature quickly restored me to health, and I sought the bread and water with as eager an inclination as a glutton would seek a feast. About five weeks after my illness, an exchange of prisoners taking place, I obtained my liberty.'

She then shipped to America as steward, and from thence to England, and was going on a voyage to the Mediterranean, when she was seized by a press-gang, and sent on board a tender. But she had no wish to serve His Majesty at sea any more, and, discovering her sex, she was examined by a surgeon, and of course at once discharged.

Her little stock of money getting low, she applied at the Navy pay-office, in Somerset House, for the cash due to her whilst serving in the *Brunswick* and *Vesuvius*, as well as her share of prize-money, arising from her being present on the 'glorious 1st of June.' She was referred to a prize-agent, who directed her to call again; this not being to her taste, she returned to Somerset House, and indulged in very rough language, for which she was taken off to Bow Street. She told her story, and was ordered to appear again, when a subscription was got up in her behalf; and she was paid twelve shillings a week, until she received her money from the Government.

Her old wound in the leg became bad again, and she went into St. Bartholomew's Hospital, and on her discharge, partially cured, she petitioned the King and the Duke of York for relief. The latter gave her five pounds. Then she cast about for the means of earning a livelihood, and bethought her that, when she was a prisoner at Dunkirk, she had watched a German make little ornaments out of gold-wire, which he sold at a good profit; and she did the same, working at the shop of a jeweller in St. Giles's, and so expert was she that she made the chains for a gold bracelet worn by Queen Charlotte. But the old wound still broke out, and she went into St. George's Hospital for seven months. When she came out, she led a shiftless, loafing existence, always begging for money—of Mr. Dundas, of the Duke of York, or anyone else that might possibly be generous.

At last these kind friends got her case introduced in the very highest quarters, and she kissed the Queen's hand at Buckingham House, as it was then called; and soon afterwards she was directed to apply at the War Office, in her sailor's dress, to receive a half-year's payment of a pension the Queen had granted her, in the name of John Taylor. Still her wound kept breaking out, and twice she had to go into Middlesex Hospital. She had some idea of going on the stage, and performed several parts at the Thespian Society in Tottenham Court Road, but she gave it up, finding begging a more profitable business; but even then she had to go to Newgate for a small debt. She took in washing, but the people did not pay her, and misfortune pursued her everywhere.

One night, in September, 1804, she was thrown from a coach into a hole left by the carelessness of some firemen, in Church Lane, Whitechapel, and she broke her arm, besides bruising herself badly. The fire office would give her no compensation, but many people were interested in her case, among them a Mr. Kirby, a publisher in Paternoster Row, who employed her as a domestic servant. In 1807, she fell into a decline, doubtless induced by the very free life she had led; and she died on the 4th of February, 1808, having just completed her thirtieth year.

It is not to be thought that England enjoyed the monopoly of these viragos—the country of Jeanne d'Arc was quite equal to the occasion, and Renée Bordereau affords an illustration for the last century.

She was born, of peasant parents, in 1770, at the village of Soulaine, near Angers; and at the time of the insurrection in La Vendée, when the royalists were so cruelly punished, she lost forty-two relations in the struggle, her father being murdered before her eyes.

This crushed out of her any soft and feminine feelings she might have possessed, and she vowed vengeance on the hated Republicans. She obtained a musket, taught herself how to use it, learned some elementary drill, and then, donning man's attire, joined the royalists. Among them she was known by the name of Langevin, and where the fight was fiercest, there she would be, and none suspected that the daring trooper was a woman. On horseback, and on foot, she fought in above two hundred battles and skirmishes, frequently wounded, but seldom much hurt. Such was the terror with which she inspired the Bonapartists, that, when the rebellion was put down, Napoleon specially exempted Langevin from pardon, and she languished in prison until the Restoration. She died in 1828.

THE 'TIMES' AND ITS FOUNDER.

 DISCURSIVE book anent the eighteenth century, as this is, would be incomplete without a mention of one of the greatest powers which it produced. This marvellous newspaper, whose utterances, at one time, exercised a sensible influence over the whole of the civilised world, and which, even now, is the most potent of all the English press, was founded by Mr. John Walter, on January 1, 1788.

This gentleman was born either in 1738 or 1739, and his father followed the business of a 'coal buyer,' which meant that he bought coals at the pit's mouth, and then shipped them to any desired port, or market. In those days almost all coals came, by sea, from Newcastle, and its district, because of the facility of carriage; the great inland beds being practically unworked, and in many cases utterly unknown: it being reserved for the giant age of steam to develop their marvellous resources.

His father died in 1755, John Walter then being seventeen and, boy though he was, he at once succeeded to his father's business. In it he was diligent and throve well, and he so won the confidence and respect of his brother 'coal buyers' that when a larger Coal Exchange was found necessary, in order to accommodate, and keep pace with its increasing business, the whole of the arrangements, plans, and directions were left in his hands. When the building was completed, he was rewarded by his brethren in trade with the position of manager, and afterwards he became Chairman to the Body of Coal Buyers.

He married, and, in 1771, things had gone so prosperously with him that he bought a house with some ground at Battersea Rise, and here he lived, and reared his family of six children, until his bankruptcy, when it was sold. He also took unto himself partners, and was the head of the firm of Walter, Bradley, and Sage. For some time all went well, but competition arose, and the old-fashioned way of doing business could not hold its own against the keenness, and cutting, of the new style. Let us hear him tell his own story.[1]

'I shall forbear relating the various scenes of business I was engaged in prior to my embarking in Lloyd's Rooms; sufficient it is to remark that a very extensive trade I entered into at the early age of seventeen, when my father died, rewarded a strong spirit of industry, and, for the first ten or twelve years, with a satisfactory increase of fortune; but a number of inconsiderable dealers, by undermining the fair trader, and other dishonourable practices, reduced the profits, and made them inadequate to the risque and capital employed. It happened unfortunately for me, about that time, some policy brokers, who had large orders for insurances on foreign Indiamen and other adventures, found their way to the Coal Market, a

[1] 'The case of Mr. John Walter, of London, Merchant.' London, 1781.

building of which I was the principal planner and manager.

'I was accustomed, with a few others, to underwrite the vessels particularly employed in that trade, and success attended the step, because the risque was fair, and the premiums adequate. This was my temptation for inclining to their solicitations of frequenting Lloyd's Rooms.[1] With great reluctance I complain that I quitted a trade where low art and cunning combated the fair principles of commerce, which my mind resisted as my fortune increased; but from the change I had to encounter deception and fraud, in a more dangerous but subtle degree.

'The misfortunes of the war were of great magnitude to the Underwriters, but they were considerably multiplied by the villainy and depravity of Mankind. In the year 1776, at a time when they received only peace premiums, American privateers swarmed on the seas, drove to desperation by the Boston port act passing at the close of the preceding year, to prohibit their fisheries, and our trade fell a rapid prey before government had notice to apply the least protection. Flushed with success, it increased the number of their armed vessels, and proved such a source of riches as enabled them to open a trade with France, who had, hitherto, been only a silent spectator, and produced the sinews of a war which then unhappily commenced.'

He then details the causes which led to his bankruptcy—how the wars with the French, Spaniards, and Dutch, all of whom had their men-of-war and privateers, which preyed upon our commerce, ruined the underwriters, and continues,

[1] Then in Lombard Street.

'In two years only of the war I lost, on a balance, thirty-one thousand pounds, which obliged me, in 1781, to quit the Coal Trade, after carrying it on so many years, when I had returned' (? turned over) ' above a Million of money, the profits of which have been sunk as an Underwriter, that I might have the use of my capital employed in it, to pay my unfortunate losses . . . . Last year, I was obliged to make a sacrifice of my desirable habitation at Battersea Rise, where I had resided ten years, and expended a considerable sum of money, the fruits of many years of industry, before I became acquainted with Lloyd's Rooms.

'These reserves, however, proved ineffectual, and I found it necessary, on examining the state of my accounts early in January last, to call my Creditors together; for, though some months preceding I found my fortune rapidly on the decline, I never suspected my being insolvent till that view of my affairs, when I found a balance in my favour of only nine thousand pounds, from which was to be deducted a fourth part owing me by brokers, who, unfortunately for me as well as themselves, were become bankrupts. This surplus, it was clear, would not bear me through known, though unsettled, losses, besides what might arise on unexpired risques. I therefore, without attempting to borrow a shilling from a friend, resorting to false Credit, or using any subterfuge whatever, after depositing what money remained in my hands, the property of others, laid the state of my affairs before my Creditors.

'This upright conduct made them my friends; they immediately invested me with full power to settle my own affairs, and have acted with liberality and kindness. They were indebted for the early knowledge I gave them of my affairs to the regularity of my accounts; for, had I rested my inquiry till after the broker's yearly accounts were chequed, in all probability a very trifling dividend would have ensued. Had the merchant been obliged to stand his own risque during the late war, few concerned on the seas would have been able to withstand the magnitude of their losses.

'The only alleviation to comfort me in this affliction has arose from the consideration that I have acted honourably by all men; that, neither in prosperity nor adversity, have I ever been influenced by mean or mercenary motives in my connections with the world, of which I can give the most satisfactory proofs; that, when in my power, benevolence ever attended my steps; the deserving and needy never resorted to me in vain, nor has gratitude ever been wanting to express any obligations or kindnesses received from those I have had transactions with by every return in my power. I have the further consolation of declaring that, in winding up my affairs, I have acted with the strictest impartiality in every demand both for and against my estate; that I have (unsolicited) attended every meeting at Guildhall to protect it against plunder. A dividend was made as soon as the bankrupt laws would permit, and the surplus laid out in interest for the benefit of the estate, till a fair time is allowed to know what demands may come against it. I am fully convinced that it will not be £15,000 deficient; above double that sum I have left in Lloyd's Rooms as a profit among the brokers.

'No prospect opening of embarking again in business for want of Capital to carry it on, I was advised to make my case known to the administration, which has been done both by public and private application of my friends, who kindly interceded in my behalf for some respectable post under Government, and met with that kind reception from the Minister which gave me every prospect of success, which I flatter myself I have some natural claim to, from the consideration that, as trade is the support of the nation, it could not be carried on without Underwriters.

'And as the want of protection to the trade of the Country, from the host of enemies we had to combat, occasioned by misfortunes, whom could I fly to with more propriety than to Government? as, by endeavouring to protect commerce, I fell a martyr on the conclusion of an unfortunate war. I was flattered with hopes that my pretensions to an appointment were not visionary, and that I was not wanting in ability to discharge the duties of any place I might have the honour to fill. The change of administration[1] which happened soon after was death to my hopes, and, as I had little expectation of making equal interest with the Minister who succeeded, I have turned my thoughts to a matter which appeared capable of being a most essential improvement in the conduct of the Press;[2] and, by great attention and assiduity for a year past, it is now reduced from a very voluminous state and great incorrectness to a system which, I hope, will meet the public approbation and countenance.

[1] Lord North resigned, and Lord Rockingham succeeded as Premier, 1782.

[2] Logotypes—or printing types in which words, etc., were cast, instead of single letters.

'Such is the brief state of a Case which I trust humanity will consider deserving a better fate. Judge what must be my sensations on this trying occasion : twenty-six years in the prime of life passed away, all the fortune I had acquired by a studious attention to business sunk by hasty strides, and the world to begin afresh, with the daily introduction to my view of a wife and six children unprovided for, and dependent on me for support. Feeling hearts may sympathise at the relation, none but parents can conceive the anxiety of my mind in such a state of uncertainty and suspense.'

From an unprejudiced perusal of this 'case,' the reader can but come to the conclusion that Mr. John Walter was not overburdened with that inconvenient commodity—modesty; and that his logic—judged by ordinary rules—is decidedly faulty. But that he did try to help himself, is evidenced by the following advertisement in the *Morning Post* of July 21, 1784 :

'*To the Right Hon. the Lord Mayor, Aldermen, and Common-councilmen of the City of London.*

'MY LORD AND GENTLEMEN,

'The Office of Principal Land Coal Meter of this City being at present vacant by the death of Mr. John Evans, permit me to solicit the honour of succeeding him. My pretensions to your countenance on this occasion are the misfortunes in which (in common with many other respectable Citizens) I have been involved by the calamities of the late war, and an unblemished reputation, which has survived the wreck of my fortune. Having been a Liveryman twenty-four years, during which time I carried on an extensive branch of the coal trade, my fellow-citizens cannot well be unacquainted with my character; and my having been greatly instrumental in establishing the very office which I solicit your interest to fill, will, I hope, be deemed an additional recommendation to your patronage.

'If my pretensions should meet your approbation, and be crowned with success, I shall ever retain a lively sense of so signal an obligation on,

'My Lord and Gentlemen,
'Your most obedient, devoted, humble servant,
'JOHN WALTER.
'Printing House Square, Blackfriars.'

We hear of him again in connection with this situation, which he did not suceeed in obtaining, in an advertisement in the *Morning Post*, 30th of July, 1784.

'*To the Right Hon. the Lord Mayor, &c.*

'The Report, which a few days ago was credited by few, is now confirmed by many, and believed by all men, that a Coalition has been formed for the purpose of forcing you to bestow the emoluments of the Principal Land Coal Meter Office on two Aldermen, and it has been agreed that, on the day of the Election, one of them shall decline the Contest, and make a transfer to the other of the votes which some of you were pleased to engage to him . . .

'My pretensions I submit to the Corporation at large, and I strongly solicit the assistance of the merchants and traders of the Metropolis to join their efforts, and endeavour to wrest the power of appointment from the hands of a Junto, and restore the freedom of Election. Assert your independence,

and consequence, in time; with your breath you can blast the Coalition in its infancy; but, if you suffer it to conquer you in its present state, it will become a Hydra that will swallow up your Franchises, and leave you, like a Cathedral Chapter, the liberty of obeying a *congé d'èlire* sent to you by a self-constituted faction.
'I am, &c., &c.,
'JOHN WALTER.
'Printing House Square, Blackfriars.'

How did he come to this (to us) familiar address? It was by a chance which came in his way, and he seized it. In 1782 he, somehow, became acquainted with a compositor named Henry Johnson, who pointed out the trouble and loss of time occasioned by setting up words with types of a single letter, and proposed that at all events those words mostly in use should be cast in one. These were called 'Logotypes' (or word types), and printing, therefore, was called 'Logography.' Caslon at first made the types—but there is evidence that they quarrelled, for in a letter of August 12, 1785, in the *Daily Universal Register* of that date, which he reprinted in broadside form, he says, 'Mr. Caslon, the founder (whom I at first employed to cast my types), calumniated my plan, he censured what he did not understand, wantonly disappointed me in the work he engaged to execute, and would meanly have sacrificed me, to establish the fallacious opinion he had promulgated.'

People had their little jokes about the 'Logotypes,' and Mr. Knight Hunt, in his 'Fourth Estate,' writes, 'It was said that the orders to the type-founder ran after this fashion, "Send me a hundred-weight of heat, cold, wet, dry, murder, fire, dreadful robbery, atrocious outrage, fearful calamity, and alarming explosion."' That he obtained not only literary, but royal recognition of his pet type, is shown by a footnote to the letter above quoted (respecting Mr. Caslon),

'Any gentleman who chuses may inspect the Logographic Founts and Types, at the Printing-office, or at the British Museum, to which place they have been removed from the Queen's Palace.'

Where he got his money from he does not say, but on the 17th of May, 1784, he advertised that 'Mr. Walter begs to inform the public that he has purchased the printing-house formerly occupied by Mr. Basket near Apothecaries Hall, which will be opened on the first day of next month for printing words entire, under his Majesty's Patent;' and he commenced business June 1, 1784.

Printing House Square stands on the site of the old Monastery of Blackfriars. After the dissolution of the monasteries, in Henry the Eighth's time, it passed through several hands, until it became the workshop of the royal printer. Here was printed, in 1666, the *London Gazette*, the oldest surviving paper in England; and, the same year, the all-devouring Great Fire completely destroyed it. Phœnix-like, it arose from its ashes, more beautiful than before—for the writer of 'A New View of London,' published in 1708, thus describes it: *Printing House Lane*, on the E side of Blackfryars: a passage to the *Queen's Printing House* (which is a stately building).'

'Formerly occupied by Mr. Basket,' a printer, under the royal patent, of Bibles and Prayer-books. To him succeeded other royal and privileged printers. Eyre and Strahan, afterwards Eyre, Strahan, and

Spottiswoode, now Spottiswoode and Co., who, in 1770, left Printing House Square, and moved to New Street, Fleet Street, a neighbourhood of which, now, that firm have a virtual monopoly.

John Walter could not have dreamed of the palace now built at Bearwood; for, like most mercantile men of his day, he was quite content to 'live over the shop'; and there, in Printing House Square, his son, and successor, John (who lived to build Bearwood), was born, and there James Carden, Esq., received his bride, John Walter's eldest daughter, who was the mother of the present venerable alderman, Sir Robert Carden. There, too, died his wife, the partner of his successes and his failures, in the year 1798.

The first work printed at this logographic printing establishment was a little story called, 'Gabriel, the Outcast.' Many other slight works followed; but these were not enough to satisfy the ambitions of John Walter, who, six months after he commenced business, started a newspaper, the *Daily Universal Register*, on the 1st of January, 1785.[1] Even at that date there was no lack of newspapers, although our grandfathers were lucky to have escaped the infliction of the plague of periodicals under which we groan; for there were the *Morning Post*, the *Morning Chronicle*, the *General Advertiser*, *London Gazette*, *London Chronicle*, *Gazetteer*, *Morning Herald*, *St. James's Chronicle*, *London Recorder*, *General Evening Post*, *Public Advertiser*, *Lounger*, *Parker's General Advertiser*, &c. So we must conclude that John Walter's far-seeing intelligence foretold that a good

[1] The centenary of the *Times* was improperly celebrated in that paper on the 1st of January, 1885.

daily paper, ably edited, would pay. It was logographically printed, and was made the vehicle of puffs of the proprietor's hobby. The *Times* was also so printed for a short period, but, eventually, it proved so cumbersome in practice, as absolutely to hinder the compositors, instead of aiding them.

On the 1st of January, 1788, was born a baby that has since grown into a mighty giant. On that day was published the first number of THE TIMES, *or Daily Universal Register*, for it had a dual surname, and the reasons for the alteration are given in the following ' editorial.'

'THE TIMES.

' Why change the head?

' This question will naturally come from the Public —and *we*, the *Times*, being the PUBLIC'S most humble and obedient Servants, think ourselves bound to answer:—

' All things have *heads*—and all *heads* are liable to *change*.

' Every sentence and opinion advanced by Mr. *Shandy* on the influence and utility of a well-chosen surname may be properly applied in showing the recommendations and advantages which result from placing a striking title-page before a book, or an inviting HEAD on the front page of a *Newspaper*.

' A HEAD so placed, like those *heads* which once ornamented *Temple Bar,* or those of the *great Attorney*, or *great Contractor*, which, not long since, were conspicuously elevated for their *great actions*, and were exhibited, in wooden frames, at the *East* and *West* Ends of this Metropolis, never fails of attracting the eyes of passengers—though, indeed, we do not expect to experience the lenity shown to these *great exhibitors*, for probably the TIMES will be pelted without mercy.

'But then, a *head* with a *good face* is a harbinger, a gentleman-usher, that often strongly recommends even DULNESS, FOLLY, IMMORALITY, or VICE. The immortal Locke gives evidence to the truth of this observation. That great philosopher has declared that, though repeatedly taken in, he never could withstand the solicitations of a well-drawn title-page —authority sufficient to justify *us* in assuming a *new head* and a *new set of features*, but not with a design to impose; for we flatter ourselves the HEAD of the TIMES will not be found deficient in *intellect*, but, by putting a *new face* on affairs, will be admired for the *light of its countenance*, whenever it appears.

'To advert to our first position.

'The UNIVERSAL REGISTER has been a name as injurious to the *Logographic Newspaper*, as TRISTRAM was to MR. SHANDY'S SON. But OLD SHANDY forgot he might have rectified by *confirmation* the mistakes of the *parson* at *baptism* with the touch of a *Bishop* have changed TRISTRAM to Trismegistus.

'The UNIVERSAL REGISTER, from the day of its first appearance to the day of its *confirmation*, has, like TRISTRAM, suffered from unusual casualties, both laughable and serious, arising from its name, which, on its introduction, was immediately curtailed of its fair proportion by all who called for it—the word *Universal* being *Universally* omitted, and the word *Register* being only retained.

'" Boy, bring me the *Register*."

'The waiter answers: " Sir, we have not a library, but you may see it at the *New Exchange Coffee House*."

'"Then I'll see it there," answers the disappointed politician; and he goes to the *New Exchange*, and calls for the *Register;* upon which the waiter tells him he cannot have it, as he is not a subscriber, and presents him with the *Court and City Register*, the *Old Annual Register*, or, if the Coffee-house be within the Purlieus of Covent Garden, or the hundreds of Drury, slips into the politician's hand *Harris's Register* of Ladies.

'For these and other reasons the parents of the UNIVERSAL REGISTER have added to its original name that of the

TIMES,

Which, being a *monosyllable*, bids defiance to *corrupters* and *mutilaters* of the language.

'THE TIMES! What a monstrous name! Granted, for THE TIMES *is* a many-headed monster, that speaks with an hundred tongues, and displays a thousand characters, and, in the course of *its* transformations in life, assumes innumerable shapes and humours.

'The critical reader will observe we personify our *new name;* but as we give it no distinction of sex, and though *it* will be *active* in *its* vocations, yet we apply to *it* the *neuter gender*.

'THE TIMES, being formed of materials, and possessing qualities of opposite and heterogeneous natures, cannot be classed either in the animal or vegetable *genus;* but, like the *Polypus*, is doubtful, and in the discussion, description, dissection, and illustration will employ the pens of the most celebrated among the *Literati*.

'The HEADS OF THE TIMES, as has been said, are many; they will, however, not always appear at the same time, but casually, as public or private affairs may call them forth.

'The principal, or leading heads are—

>The Literary;
>Political;
>Commercial;
>Philosophical;
>Critical;
>Theatrical;
>Fashionable;
>Humorous;
>Witty, &c.

'Each of which are supplied with a competent share of intellects for the pursuit of their several functions; an endowment which is not in *all times* to be found even in the HEADS of the *State*, the *heads* of the *Church*, the *heads* of the *Law*, the *heads* of the *Navy*, the *heads* of the *Army*, and though *last*, not least, the great *heads* of the *Universities*.

'The *Political Head* of THE TIMES, like that of *Janus*, the Roman Deity, is doubly faced; with one countenance it will smile continually on the friends of *Old England*, and with the other will frown incessantly on her *enemies*.

'The alteration we have made in our *head* is not without precedents. The WORLD has parted with half its CAPUT MORTUUM, and a moiety of its brains. The HERALD has cut off half its head, and has lost its original humour. The POST, it is true, retains its whole head and its old features; and, as to the other public prints, they appear as having neither *heads* nor *tails*. On the PARLIAMENTARY HEAD every communication that ability and industry can produce

may be expected. To this great *National object*, THE
TIMES will be most sedulously attentive, most accurately correct, and strictly impartial in its *reports*.'

The early career of the *Times* was not all prosperity, and Mr. Walter was soon taught a practical lesson in keeping his pen within due bounds, for, on July 11th, 1788, he was tried for two libellous paragraphs published in the *Times*, reflecting on the characters of the Duke of York, Gloucester, and Cumberland, stating them to be 'insincere' in their profession of joy at his Majesty's recovery. It might have been an absolute fact, but it was impolitic to print it, and so he found it, for a jury found him guilty.

He came up for judgment at the King's Bench on the 23rd of November next, when he was sentenced by the Court to pay a fine of fifty pounds, to be imprisoned twelve months in Newgate, to stand in the pillory at Charing Cross, when his punishment should have come to an end, and to find security for his good behaviour.

He seems to have ridden a-tilt at all the royal princes, for we next hear of him under date of 3rd of February, 1790, being brought from Newgate to the Court of King's Bench to receive sentence for the following libels:

For charging their Royal Highnesses the Prince of Wales and Duke of York with having demeaned themselves so as to incur the displeasure of his Majesty. This, doubtless, was strictly true, but it cost the luckless Walter one hundred pounds as a fine, and another twelve months' imprisonment in Newgate.

This, however, was not all; he was arraigned on another indictment for asserting that His Royal Highness the Duke of Clarence returned from his station without leave of the Admiralty, or of his commanding officer, and for this he was found guilty, and sentenced to pay another hundred pounds.

Whether he made due submission, or had powerful friends to assist him, I know not,—but it is said that it was at the request of the Prince of Wales—at all events, he received the king's pardon, and was released from confinement on 7th of March, 1791, after which time he never wrote about the king's sons in a way likely to bring him within the grip of the Law.

From time to time we get little *avisos* as to the progress of the paper, for John Walter was not one of those who hide their light under a bushel. Contrast the printing power then with the magnificent 'Walter' machines of the present day, which, in their turn, will assuredly be superseded by some greater improvement.

The *Times*, 7th of February, 1794. ' The Proprietors have for some time past been engaged in making alterations which they trust will be adequate to remedy the inconvenience of the late delivery complained of; and after Monday next the TIMES will be worked off with three Presses, and occasionally with four, instead of TWO, as is done in all other Printing-offices, by which mode two hours will be saved in printing the Paper, which, notwithstanding the lateness of the delivery, is now upwards of FOUR THOUSAND THREE HUNDRED in sale, daily.'

The following statement is curious, as showing us some of the interior economy of the newspaper in its early days. From the *Times*, April 19, 1794:

'TO THE PUBLIC.

'It is with very great regret that the Proprietors

of this Paper, in Common with those of other Newspapers, find themselves obliged to increase the daily price of it ONE HALFPENNY, a measure which they have been forced to adopt in consequence of the Tax laid by the *Minister* on *Paper*, during the present Session of Parliament, and which took place on the 5th instant.

'While the Bill was still pending, we not only stated in our Newspaper, but the Minister was himself informed by a Committee of Proprietors, that the new Duty would be so extremely oppressive as to amount to a necessity of raising the price, which it was not only their earnest Wish, but also their Interest, to avoid. The Bill, however, passed, after a long consideration and delay occasioned by the great doubts that were entertained of its efficacy. We wish a still longer time had been taken to consider it; for we entertain the same opinion as formerly, that the late Duty on Paper will not be productive to the Revenue, while it is extremely injurious to a particular class of Individuals, whose property was very heavily taxed before.

'In fact, it amounts either to a Prohibition of printing a Newspaper at the present price, or obliges the Proprietors to advance it. There is no option left; the price of Paper is now so high that the Proprietors have no longer an interest to render their sale extensive, as far as regards the profits of a large circulation. The more they sell at the present price, the more they will lose; to us alone the *Advance* on Paper will make a difference of £1,200 sterling per Annum more than it formerly cost us—a sum which the Public must be convinced neither can, nor ought to be afforded by any Property of the limited nature of a Newspaper, the profits on the sale of which are precisely as follows:

'SALE.

2,000 Newspapers sold to the Newshawkers at 3½d., with a further deduction of allowing them a Paper in every Quire of 24 ... ... £26 18 6.

'COST OF 2,000 PAPERS.

A Bundle of Paper containing 2,000 Half-sheets, or 2,000 Newspapers at Four Guineas per Bundle, which is the price it will be sold at under the new Duty is £4 4 0.

	£4	4	0	£26	18	6
2,000 Stamps at 2d., deducting discount	16	0	0	20	4	0
Profits				£6	14	6

'This is the whole Profit on the sale of two thousand Newspapers, out of which is to be deducted the charges of printing a Newspaper (which, on account of the Rise in Printers' Wages last year, is £100 a year more than it ever was before), the charges of Rent, Taxes, Coals, Candles (which are very high in every Printing-office), Clerks, general Superintendance, Editing, Parliamentary and Law Reports, and, above all, the Expenses of FOREIGN CORRESPONDENCE, which, under the present difficulties of obtaining it, and the different Channels which must be employed to secure a regular and uninterrupted Communication, is immense. If this Paper is in high estimation, surely the Proprietors ought to receive the advantage of their success, and not the Revenue, which already monopolises such an immense income from this property, no less than to the amount of £14,000 sterling during last year only. We trust that these reasons will have sufficient weight with the Public to excuse us when we announce, though with very great regret, that on

Monday next the price of this Paper will be *Fourpence Halfpenny.*'

Occasionally, the proprietor fell foul of his neighbours; vide the *Times,* November 16, 1795:

' All the abuse so lavishly bestowed on this Paper by other Public Prints, seems as if designed to betray, that in proportion as our sale is *good,* it is *bad* TIMES with them.'

In the early part of 1797, Pitt proposed, among other methods of augmenting the revenue, an additional stamp of three halfpence on every newspaper. The *Times,* April 28, 1797, groaned over it thus:

'The present daily sale of the TIMES is known to be between four and five thousand Newspapers. For the sake of perspicuity, we will make our calculation on four thousand only, and it will hold good in proportion to every other Paper.

'The Newsvendors are now allowed by the Proprietors of every Newspaper two sheets in every quire, viz., twenty-six for every twenty-four Papers sold. The stamp duty on two Papers in every quire in four thousand Papers daily at the old Duty of 2d., amounts to £780 a year, besides the value of the Paper. An additional Duty of 1½d. will occasion a further loss of £585 in this one instance only, for which there is not, according to Mr. PITT's view of the subject, to be the smallest remuneration to the Proprietors. Is it possible that anything can be so unjust? If the Minister persists in his proposed plan, it will be impossible for Newspapers to be sold at a lower rate than sixpence halfpenny per Paper.'

Pitt, of course, carried out his financial plan, and the newspapers had to grin, and bear it as best they could—the weaker going to the wall, as may be seen by the following notices which appeared in the *Times*, July 5 :

'To the Public.

' We think it proper to remind our Readers and the Public at large that, in consequence of the heavy additional Duty of Three Half-pence imposed on every Newspaper, by a late Act of Parliament, which begins to have effect from and after this day, the Proprietors are placed in the very unpleasant position of being compelled to raise the price of their Newspapers to the amount of the said Duty. To the Proprietors of this Paper it will prove a very considerable diminution of the fair profits of the Trade ; they will not, however, withdraw in the smallest degree any part of the Expenses wl .ch they employ in rendering the Times an Intelligent and Entertaining source of Information : and they trust with confidence that the Public will bestow on it the same liberal and kind Patronage which they have shown for many years past ; and for which the Proprietors have to offer sentiments of sincere gratitude. From this day, the price of every Newspaper will be Sixpence.'

July 19, 1797. ' Some of the Country Newspapers have actually given up the Trade, rather than stand the risk of the late enormous heavy Duty : many others have advertised them for Sale : some of those printed in Town must soon do the like, for the fair profits of Trade have been so curtailed, that no Paper can stand the loss without having a very large proportion of Advertisements. We have very little doubt but that, so far from Mr. Pitt's calculation of a profit of £114,000 sterling by the New Tax on

Newspapers, the Duty, the same as on WINE, will fall very short of the original Revenue.'

July 13, 1797. 'As a proof of the diminution in the general sale of Newspapers since the last impolitic Tax laid on them, we have to observe, as one instance, that the number of Newspapers sent through the General Post Office on Monday the 3rd instant, was 24,700, and on Monday last, only 16,800, a falling off of nearly *one-third.*'

Once again we find John Walter falling foul of a contemporary—and indulging in editorial amenities.

July 2, 1798. 'The *Morning Herald* has, no doubt, acted from *very prudent motives* in declining to state any circumstances respecting its sale. All that we hope and expect, in future, is—that it will not attempt to injure this Paper by insinuating that it was in a declining state; an assertion which it knows to be false, and which will be taken notice of in a different way if repeated. The *Morning Herald* is at liberty to make any other comments it pleases.'

Have the *Daily Telegraph* and the *Standard* copied from John Walter, when they give public notice that their circulation is so-and-so, as is vouched for by a respectable accountant? It would seem so, for this notice appeared in the *Times*:

'We have subjoined an Affidavit sworn yesterday before a Magistrate of the City, as to the present sale of the TIMES.

'" We, C. Bentley and G. Burroughs, Pressmen of the *Times*, do make Oath, and declare, That the number printed of the *Times* Paper for the last two months, has never been, on any one day, below 3 thousand, and has fluctuated from that number to three thousand three hundred and fifty."

'And, in order to avoid every subterfuge, I moreover attest, That the above Papers of the TIMES were paid for to me, previous to their being taken by the Newsmen from the Office, with the exception of about a dozen Papers each morning which are spoiled in Printing.

'J. BONSOR, Publisher.

'Sworn before me December 31, 1798.

'W. CURTIS.'

From this time the career of the *Times* seems to have been prosperous, for we read, January 1, 1799,

'THE NEW YEAR.

'The New Year finds the TIMES in the same situation which it has invariably enjoyed during a long period of public approbation. It still continues to maintain its character among the Morning Papers, as the most considerable in point of sale, as of general dependence with respect to information, and as proceeding on the general principles of the British Constitution. While we thus proudly declare our possession of the public favour, we beg leave to express our grateful sense of the unexampled patronage we have derived from it.'

Mr. John Walter was never conspicuous for his modesty, and its absence is fully shown in the preceding and succeeding examples (January 1, 1800):

'It is always with satisfaction that we avail ourselves of the return of the present Season to acknowledge our sense of the obligation we lay under to the Public, for the very liberal Patronage with which they have honoured the TIMES, during many years; a constancy of favour, which, we believe, has never before distinguished any Newspaper, and for which the Proprietors cannot sufficiently express their most grateful thanks.

'This Favour is too valuable and too honourable to excite no envy in contemporary Prints, whose frequent habit it is to express it by the grossest calumnies and abuse. The Public, we believe, has done them ample justice, and applauded the contempt with which it is our practice to receive them.'

As this self-gratulatory notice brings us down to the last year of the eighteenth century, I close this notice of 'The *Times* and its Founder.' John Walter died at Teddington, Middlesex, on the 26th of January, 1812.

IMPRISONMENT FOR DEBT.

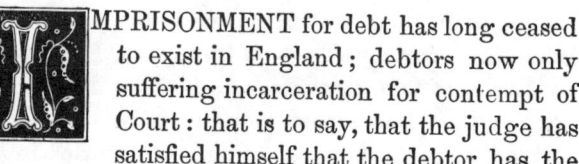MPRISONMENT for debt has long ceased to exist in England; debtors now only suffering incarceration for contempt of Court: that is to say, that the judge has satisfied himself that the debtor has the means to pay, and will not. But, in the eighteenth century, it was a fearful fact, and many languished in prison for life, for most trifling sums. Of course, there were debtors *and* debtors. If a man had money or friends, much might be done to mitigate his position; he might even live outside the prison, in the Rules, as they were called, a limited district surrounding the prison; but for this advantage he must find substantial bail—enough to cover his debt and fees. But the friendless poor debtor had a very hard lot, subsisting on charity, going, in turn, to beg of passers-by for a coin, however small, rattling a box to call attention, and dolorously repeating, 'Remember the poor prisoners.'

There were many debtors' prisons, and one of the principal, the Fleet, was over-crowded; in fact, they all were full. Newgate, the Marshalsea, the Gate House, Westminster, the Queen's Bench, the Fleet, Ludgate, Whitecross Street, Whitechapel, and a peculiar one belonging to St. Katharine's (where are now the docks).

Arrest for debt was very prompt; a writ was taken out, and no poor debtor dare stir out without walking 'beard on shoulder,' dreading a bailiff in every passer-by. The profession of bailiff was not an honoured one, and, probably, the best men did not enter it; but they had to be men of keen wit and ready resource, for they had equally keen wits, sharpened by the dread of capture, pitted against them. Some rose to eminence in their profession, and as, occasionally, there is a humorous side even to misery, I will tell a few stories of their exploits. As I am not inventing them, and am too honest to pass off another man's work as my own, I prefer telling the stories in the quaint language in which I find them.

'*Abram Wood* had a Writ against an *Engraver*, who kept a House opposite to *Long Acre* in *Drury Lane*, and having been several times to serve it, but could never light on the Man, because he work'd at his business above Stairs, as not daring to shew his Head for fear of being arrested, for he owed a great deal of Money, Mr. *Bum* was in a Resolution of spending no more Time over him; till, shortly after, hearing that one *Tom Sharp*, a House-breaker, was to be hang'd at the end of *Long Acre*, for murdering a Watchman, he and his Follower dress'd themselves like Carpenters, having Leather Aprons on, and Rules tuck'd in at the Apron Strings: then going early the morning or two before the Malefactor was to be executed, to the place appointed for Execution, they there began to pull out their Rules, and were very busie in marking out the Ground where they thought best for erecting the Gibbet. This drew several of the Housekeepers about 'em presently, and among the rest the *Engraver*, who, out of a selfish humour of thinking he might make somewhat the more by People standing in his House to see the Execution, in Case this Gibbet was near it, gave *Abram* a Crown, saying,

"'*I'll give you a Crown more if you'll put the Gibbet hereabouts;*" at the same time pointing where he would have it.

'Quoth *Abram*: "*We must put it fronting exactly up* Long Acre; *besides, could I put it nearer your door, I should require more Money than you propose, even as much as this*" (at the same time pulling it out of his pocket) "*Writ requires, which is twenty-five Pounds.*" So, taking his prisoner away, who could not give in Bail to the Action, he was carried to Jayl, without seeing *Tom Sharp* executed.'

'*William Browne* had an Action given him against one *Mark Blowen*, a Butcher, who, being much in debt, was never at his Stall, except on *Saturdays*, and then not properly neither, for the opposite side of the way to his Shop being in the Duchy Liberty[1] (with the Bailiff whereof he kept in Fee) a Bailiff of the Marshal's Court could not arrest him. From hence he could call to his Wife and Customers as there was occasion; and there could *Browne* once a week see his Prey, but durst not meddle with him. Many a Saturday his Mouth watered at him; but one Saturday above the rest, *Browne*, stooping for a Purse, as if he found it, just by his Stall, and pulling five or six guineas out of it, the Butcher's Wife cry'd "Halves;"

---

[1] *i.e.*, in the liberty or Rules of the Fleet.

his Follower, who was at some little distance behind him, cry'd out, "Halves" too.

'*Browne* refused Halves to either, whereupon they both took hold of him, the Woman swearing it was found by her Stall, therefore she would have half; and the Follower saying, As he saw it as soon t'other, he would have a Share of it too, or he would acquaint the Lord of the Mannor with it. *Mark Blowen*, in the meantime, seeing his Wife and another pulling and haling the Man about, whom he did not suspect to be a Bailiff, asked, "What's the Matter?" His wife telling him the Man had found a Purse with Gold in it by her Stall, and therefore she thought it nothing but Justice but she ought to have some of it.

"'*Ay ay*,' (quoth the Butcher), "*and nothing but Reason, Wife.*"

' So, coming from his privileged side of the Way, he takes hold of *Browne* too, bidding his Wife look after the Shop, for he would take care of him before they parted.

'*Brnwne*, being thus hemm'd in by his Follower and the Butcher, quoth he:

'" *Look'ee here, Gentlemen, I have Six Guineas here, 'tis true, but, if I should give you one half of it, why, then there is but a quarter Share of the other two.*"

'" *No, no*," (replyed they), '*we'll have Man and Man alike, which is Two Guineas apiece.*"

'" *Well*," (quoth Browne), "*if it must be so, I'm contented; but, then, I'll tell you what, I'll have the odd Eighteen Pence spent.*"

'" *With all my heart*," said Blowen. " *We'll never make a dry Bargain on't.*"

'They are all agreed, and *Browne* leads them up to the *Blackmore's Head* Alehouse, in *Exeter Street*, where a couple of Fowls are ordered to be laid down, and Stout and Ale is called for by wholesale. At last they went to Dinner, and, afterwards, *Browne*, changing his Six Guineas for Silver, gave his Follower (to carry on the jest) Forty Shillings, and put the rest in his pocket. *Mark Blowen*, seeing that, began to look surly, and asked for his Share.

'Said *Browne*: " *What Share, friend?*"

'Quoth *Mark Blowen*: " *Forty Shillings, as you gave this Man here.*"

'*Browne* reply'd: " *Why, truly, Sir, I shall have an urgent Occasion to Night for what Sum I have about me, and if you'll be pleas'd to lend me your Share but till* Monday *Morning, I'll come and pay you then at this House without fail, and return you, with infinite thanks, for the Favour.*"

'Quoth *Mark* (who was a blundering, rustical sort of a Fellow): " *D—— me, Sir, don't think to Tongue-Pad me out of my Due. I'll have my Share now, or else he that's the best Man here of us three shall have it all, win it, and wear it.*"

' " *Pray, Sir,*" (said *Browne*), " *don't be in this Passion. I'll leave you a sufficient Pledge for it till* Monday.*"

'Quoth *Mark*: " *Let's see it.*"

'Hereupon *Browne* pulls out his Tip-Staff, and lays it on the Table; but the Butcher, not liking the Complexion of it, began to be moving, when the Follower, laying Hands on him, they arrested him in an Action of Eighteen Pounds, and carried him to the *Marshalsea*, where, after a Confinement of Nine Months, he ended his Days.'

There is another famous bailiff on record, named Jacob Broad; and of him it is narrated that, 'being employed to arrest a Justice of the Peace living near

Uxbridge, he went down there very often, and had us'd several Stratagems to take him, but, his Worship being very cautious in conversing with any of *Jacob's* Fraternity, his Contrivances to nap him prov'd always abortive. However, a great deal of Money was proffer'd by the Creditor to take the worshipful Debtor; so one Day *Jacob*, with a couple of his Followers, took a Journey in the Country, and, being near the end of their Journey, *Jacob* alights, and flings his Bridle, Saddle, and Boots into a Thick Hedge, and then puts a Fetlock[1] on his Horse. The Followers tramp'd it a-foot, to one of whom giving the Horse, he leads it to a Smith at *Uxbridge*, and, telling him he had lost the Key of the Fetlock, he desir'd him to unlock it, whilst he went to a neighbouring Alehouse, where he would give him a Pot or two of Drink for his Pains. Accordingly the Smith unlockt it, and carried the Horse to the Alehouse; and, after he had drank Part of half-a-dozen of Drink, return'd to his Work again. Shortly after, came the other Follower to the Smith, inquiring if he did not see such a Horse come by that way, describing at the same time the Colour and Marks of it, and how his Master had lost him out of his Grounds that Morning. The Smith reply'd, that such a Horse was brought to him but a little before, to have a Fetlock taken off, and that he did imagine the Fellow to be a Rogue that had him; but, however, he believ'd he was still at such an Alehouse hard by, and might be there apprehended. Hereupon the Smith and Follower went to the Alehouse, where they found the Horse standing at the Door, and the other Follower in the House, whom they call'd a thousand

---

[1] A foot-lock or hobble.

Rogues, and charg'd with a Constable for a Thief. In the meantime, came *Jacob Broad*, who own'd the Horse to be his, and the Town-People, being all in a hurly-burly, they carried him before the Justice whom *Jacob* wanted; but no sooner were *Jacob*, the supposed Thief, and the other Follower entered the House, but charging the Constable to keep the Peace, they arrested his Worship, and brought him forthwith to *London*, where he was forc'd to pay the Debt of two hundred and thirty-four Pounds before he could reach home again.'

Another story is related of Jacob Broad.

'A certain Gentleman who liv'd at *Hackney*, and had been a Collector of the late Queen's Duties, but cheated her of several thousands of Pounds, goes home, and pretends himself sick. Upon this he keeps his Bed, and, after a Fortnight's pretended Illness, it was given out that he was Dead. Great preparations were then made for his Funeral. His Coffin, which was filled with Bricks and Saw-Dust, was covered with black Velvet, and his Wife, and Six Sons and Daughters, all in deep Mourning, follow'd it to the Grave, which was made in St. *John's* Church, at *Hackney*. This sham Funeral was so well carried on, that all the People of the Town would have sworn the Collector was really Dead. About a Week after his supposed Interment, *Jacob Broad* had an Action of one hundred and fifty Pounds against him. He went to *Hackney* to serve the Writ, but, enquiring after the Person he was to arrest, and being told that he was dead and buried, he return'd home again.

'About Seven Years afterwards, the Creditor being certainly inform'd that the Collector was alive and well in his own House, he employed *Jacob* again to arrest him, and accordingly he and another went to execute the Writ. *Jacob* planted himself in an Alehouse adjacent to the long-supposed Deceased's Habitation, and, while his Aid-de-Camp, or Follower, was doing something else, he told a Woman, coming by with a great Load of Turnips on her Head, that the People of such a House wanted some, which was the House where the Seven Years dead Man dwelt. She went forthwith and knockt at the Door, which was open'd to let her in, and the Follower, who was close at her Heels, rush'd in after her, and ran into a Back Parlour, where he saw the Person (according to the Description of him) whom he wanted sitting by the Fire Side. It happening then to be a festival Day, for the Entertainment of the Collector's Children, and Grand Children, the Table was spread with Variety of Dainties; the Follower leapt over the Table, overthrowing the Viands on it, and laying hold of the Prisoner, all their Mirth was spoilt at once. In the mean Time came *Jacob Broad*, and, taking out the supposed dead Man, he seem'd to be overjoy'd at his Resurrection from a Seven Years' Confinement and for tasting the fresh Air. *Jacob* brings him to *London*, whence he remov'd himself by a Writ of *Habeas Corpus* to the King's Bench Prison in *Southwark*, where he died again in a Week's time, for he was never heard of till he was seen about Three Years after in *Denmark*.

'*Jacob Broad* was always very happy in having Followers as acute as himself in any sort of Roguery, especially one *Andrew Vaughan*, afterwards a Bailiff himself on Saffron Hill, and one *Volly Vance*, otherwise call'd *Glym Jack* from his having been a Moon

Curser,[1] or Link Boy . . . From a Link Boy *Glym Jack* came to be *Jacob Broad's* Follower, who, together with *Andrew Vaughan*, he once took into the Country along with him to arrest a Justice of Peace, who was one of the shyest cocks that ever *Jacob* had to take by Stratagem. In order to accomplish this Undertaking, *Jacob*, *Andrew*, and *Glym Jack* were very well drest in Apparel, and mounted on good Geldings, having fine Hangers on their Sides, and Pistols in their Holsters, beside Pocket Pops sticking in their Bosoms. Being thus accoutred they rid into an Inn in the Town where the Justice of Peace they wanted dwelt, and, putting up their Horses, they ask'd the Landlord for a private Room, which, being accommodated with, they refresh'd themselves with a good Dinner, and afterwards set to play.

'Whilst they were shaking their Elbows at 7 or 11 nick it, a great deal of Money and three or four Watches lying on the Table, when at last one of 'em cry'd, this Watch is my Snack, for I'm sure I first attackt the Gentleman from whom we took it; another swore such a Purse of Gold was his, which they had taken that Morning from a Gentlewoman, and, in short, everyone of 'em was swearing such a Prize was his, all which the Landlord (who listened at the Door) overhearing, thought to himself they were all Highwaymen. Hereupon he goes and acquaints the shy Justice of Peace with the matter, who ask'd *If he were sure they were Rogues.*

' " *Nothing*," (quoth the Innkeeper), " *is more certain, for they are all arm'd with more Pistols than ordinary,*

---

[1] From the link-boy's natural hatred of 'the Parish Lantern,' which would deprive him of his livelihood.

swearing, damning, cursing, and sinking every Word they speak, and falling out about dividing their Booty."

'"Ay, ay," (reply'd the Justice), "they are then certainly Highwaymen," and so order'd him to secure them.

'The Innholder went for a Constable, who, with a great many Rusticks, arm'd with Pitch Forks, long Poles, and other Country Weapons, went with the Landlord to the Inn, suddenly rush'd into the Room, and surpriz'd *Jacob* and his Followers, with Money and Watches lying before them.

'" So," (says the Constable), "*pretty Gentlemen, are not ye, that honest people can't travel the Country without being robb'd by such villains as you are?—Well,*" (quoth the Constable to *Jacob*), "*what's your Name?*"

'His answer was *Sice-Ace*.[1]

'" *A fine Rogue, indeed!*" said the Constable, at the same time asking *Andrew* his Name, whose answer was,

'" *Cinque-Duce.*"

'" *Another Rogue in Grain!*" quoth the Constable; and then ask'd *Glym Jack* what his Name was, who reply'd,

'" *Quater-Tray.*"

'" *Rogues! Rogues all!*" said the Constable; " ay, worse than all, they are mear Infidels, Heathens, for I never heard such names before in a Christian Country. Come, Neighbours, bring 'em away before Mr. Justice, his Worship will soon make them change their Notes."

'Accordingly the Rusticks haled them along the Town to his Worship's House, into which they were no sooner enter'd but he began to revile *Jacob* and

---

[1] In throwing dice a corruption of the French numerals is used, as ace (one), deuce (two), tray (three), &c.

his Brethren for Highwaymen, and asking them their Names, they still were in the same Tone of *Sice-Ace, Cinque-Duce,* and *Quater-Tray,* at which the Justice, lifting up his Hands and Eyes to the Ceiling, cry'd out, *Such audacious Rogues as these were never seen before.*

'" *Here, Tom,*" (quoth his Worship to his Clerk), "*write their* Mittimus, *for 1 will send them everyone to* Newgate."

'Whilst their Commitment was writing, *Jacob* pulls a Bit of Parchment out of his Pocket, and, asking the Constable if he could read it, he put on his Spectacles, and posing and mumbling over it a Minute or two, said,

'" *I cannot tell what to make of it. It is Latin, I think.*"

'" *Well, then,*" (quoth Jacob), " *I'll tell you what it is, it is the King's Process against this Gentleman that is going to commit us to* Newgate; *therefore, in my Execution of it, I require you, as you are a Constable, to keep the Peace.*"

'This turn of the Dice made the Magistrate, the Peace Officer, and all the Rusticks stare at one another as if they were out of their Senses. However, *Jacob* brought his Prisoner to *London,* and oblig'd him to make Satisfaction before he got out of his Clutches.'

The above anecdotes illustrate the humorous side of a bailiff's life, but sometimes they met with very rough treatment, nay, were even killed. On the 4th of August, 1722, a bailiff named Boyce was killed by a blacksmith, who ran a red-hot iron into him; and the book I have quoted from thus speaks of bailiffs as 'such Villains, whose Clan is suppos'd to descend from the cursed Seed of *Ham*, and therefore stinks in the Nostrils of all honest Men. Some of them have been paid in their own Coyn, for Captain *Bew* kill'd a Sergeant of one of the Compters. Shortly after, a Bailiff was kill'd in *Grays-Inn* Walks; another Bailiff had his Hand chopt off by a Butcher in *Hungerford* Market, in the *Strand*, of which Wound he dyed the next Day, and another Man kill'd two Bailiffs at once with a couple of Pistols in *Houghton Street*, by *Clare Market*, for which he was touch'd with a cold iron[1] at the Sessions House at the *Old Baily*, besides several others of that detestable Tribe have deservedly suffer'd the same fate . . . . . .

'But, by the way, we must take Notice that a Bailiff is Universally hated by Man, Woman, or Child, who dearly love to see them duckt (Pick-pocket like) in the *Muse* Pond,[2] or the cleanly Pond of the Horse Guards, at *Whitehall*, and sometimes well rinsed at the *Temple*, or *Grays-Inn* Pump; and if any of these napping Scoundrels is taken within the Liberty of the *Mint*, the enraged Inhabitants of this Place tye him fast with Ropes in a Wheelbarrow; then they trundle him about the Streets, with great Shouts and Huzzas . . . . . . After he is convey'd in the like Order to a stinking Ditch, near *St. George's* Fields, where he is plunged over Head and Ears, *à la mode de Pickpocket;* and then, to finish the Procession, he is solemnly convey'd to a Pump, according to the

---

[1] *I.e.*, That sentence of death, owing to his pleading benefit of clergy, or ability to read, was commuted to imprisonment, and branding on the face with a red-hot iron. By degrees, however, the iron got colder, until, at last, it was barely warm.

[2] Mews, or horse-pond.

antient Custom of the Place, where he is sufficiently drench'd for all his dirty Doings.'

This, as I have said, shows the humorous side of imprisonment for debt. An unimpeachable and veracious authority, one who only gave dry statistics, and did not draw upon his imagination for his facts, was John Howard, the philanthropist, who published, in 1777, 'The State of the Prisons in England and Wales.' From his report we learn that the allowance to debtors was a penny loaf a day—and when we consider that, during the French war, bread at one time rose to a price equivalent to our half-crown per quartern loaf, it could hardly be called a sufficient diet. But the City of London, generous then, as ever, supplemented this with a daily (? weekly) supply of sixteen stone, or one hundred and twenty-eight pounds, of beef, which, as Howard gives the average of debtors in two years (1775-6) at thirty-eight, would be more than ample for their needs—and there were other charities amounting to fifty or sixty pounds a year but, before they were discharged, they were compelled to pay the keeper a fee of eight shillings and tenpence.

In the Fleet Prison they had no allowance, but, if they made an affidavit that they were not worth five pounds, and could not subsist without charity, they had divided amongst them the proceeds of the begging-box and grate, and the donations which were sent to the prison. Of these, Howard says, at the time of his visit, there were seventeen. But the other prisoners who had any money had every facility afforded them to spend it. There was a tap, at which they could purchase whatever liquor they required; there was a billiard-table, and, in the yard, they could play at skittles, Mississipi, fives, tennis, &c. On Monday nights there was a wine club, and on Thursday nights a beer club, both of which usually lasted until one or two in the morning; and pretty scenes of riot and drunkenness took place. The prisoners were allowed to have their wives and children to live with them.

Ludgate had ceased to exist, and the debtors were transferred to New Ludgate, in Bishopsgate Street. It was a comparatively aristocratic debtors' prison, for it was only for debtors who were free of the City, for clergymen, proctors, and attorneys. Here, again, the generosity of the City stepped in; and, for an average number of prisoners of twenty-five, ten stone, or eighty pounds of beef, were given weekly, together with a daily penny loaf for each prisoner. The lord mayor and sheriffs sent them coals, and Messrs. Calvert, the brewers, sent weekly two barrels of small beer, besides which, there were some bequests.

The Poultry Compter was in the hands of a keeper who had bought the place for life, and was so crowded that some of the prisoners had to sleep on shelves over the others, and neither straw nor bedding was allowed them. The City gave a penny loaf daily to the prisoners, and remitted for their benefit the rent of thirty pounds annually; the Calverts also sent them beer. At Howard's visits, eight men had their wives and children with them.

Wood Street Compter was not a pleasant abode, for Howard says the place swarmed with bugs. There were thirty-nine debtors, and their allowance was a daily penny loaf from the City, two barrels of beer weekly from the Calverts; the sheriffs gave them thirty-two pounds of beef on Saturdays, and for some

IMPRISONMENT FOR DEBT. 241

years a benevolent baker sent them, weekly, a large leg and shin of beef.

At Whitechapel was a prison for debtors, in the liberty and manor of Stepney and Hackney, but it was only for very small debtors, those owing above two pounds, and under five. Howard's story of this prison is a very sad one, the occupants being so very poor:

'The Master's-side Prisoners have four sizeable chambers fronting the road—*i.e.*, two on each storey. They pay two shillings and sixpence a week, and lie two in a bed; two beds in a room. The Common-side Debtors are in two long rooms in the Court Yard, near the Tap-room. Men in one room, women in the other: the Court Yard in common. They hang out a begging-box from a little closet in the front of the House, and attend it in turn. It brings them only a few pence a day, and of this pittance none partake but those who, at entrance, have paid the keeper two shillings and sixpence, and treated the Prisoners with half a gallon of beer. The last time I was there, no more than three had purchased this privilege . . .

'At my first visit there were, on the Common-side, two Prisoners in Hammocks, sick and very poor. No chaplain. A compassionate Man, who is not a regular Clergyman, sometimes preaches to them on Sunday, and gives them some small relief. Lady Townsend sends a Guinea twice a year, which her Servant distributes equally among the Prisoners.

'As Debtors here are generally very poor, I was surprised to see, once, ten or twelve noisy men at skittles; but the Turnkey said they were only visitants. I found they were admitted here as at another public-house. No Prisoners were at play with them.'

At St. Catharine's, without the Tower, was another small debtors' prison. This parish was a '*peculiar*,' the Bishop of London having no jurisdiction over it, and the place was under the especial patronage of the Queens of England ever since the time of Matilda, the wife of Stephen, who founded a hospital there, now removed to Regent's Park. It was a wonderful little parish, for there people could take sanctuary— and there also were tried civil and ecclesiastical cases. Howard says that the prison for debtors had been rebuilt seven years before he wrote. It was a small house of two storeys; two rooms on a floor. In April, 1774, there was a keeper, but no prisoners. ' I have since called two or three times, and always found the House uninhabited.'

No notice of debtors' prisons would be complete without mention of the King's Bench, which was in Southwark. Howard reports:

'The Prisoners are numerous. At more than one of my visits, some had the Small Pox. It was so crowded this last summer, that a Prisoner paid five shillings a week for half a bed, and many lay in the chapel. In May, 1766, the number of Prisoners within the Walls was three hundred and ninety-five, and, by an accurate list which I procured, their wives (including a few only called so) were two hundred and seventy-nine, children seven hundred and twenty-five—total, one thousand and four; about two-thirds of these were in the Prison.'

The prisoners had, as in the Fleet, their weekly wine and beer clubs, and they also indulged in similar outdoor sports. The Marshalsea and Horsemonger Lane gaol complete the list of London debtors' prisons.

Howard's description of the county prisons is something appalling. Gaol-fever, distemper, or small-pox being recorded against most of them. At Chelmsford there had been no divine service for above a year past, except to condemned criminals. At Warwick the debtors' common day-room was the hall, which was also used as a chapel. At Derby a person went about the country, at Christmas-time, to gentlemen's houses, and begged for the benefit of the debtors. The donations were entered in a book, and signed by each donor. About fourteen pounds were generally collected in this manner.

Chesterfield gaol was the property of the Duke of Portland, and Howard describes it thus:

'Only one room, with a cellar under it, to which the Prisoners occasionally descend through a hole in the floor. The cellar had not been cleaned for many months. The Prison door had not been opened for several weeks, when I was there first. There were four Prisoners, who told me they were almost starved; one of them said, with tears in his eyes, " he had not eaten a morsel that day,"—it was afternoon. They had borrowed a book of Dr. Manton's; one of them was reading it to the rest. Each of them had a wife, and they had, in the whole, thirteen children, cast on their respective parishes. Two had their groats from the Creditors, and out of that pittance they relieved the other two. No allowance: no straw: no firing: water a halfpenny for about three gallons, put in (as other things are) at the window. Gaoler lives distant.'

At Salisbury gaol, just outside the prison gate, a

round staple was fixed in the wall, through which was passed a chain, at each end of which was a debtor padlocked by the leg, who offered for sale to the passers-by, nets, laces, purses, etc., made in the prison. At Knaresborough the debtors' prison is thus described:

'Of difficult access; the door about four feet from the ground. Only one room, about fourteen feet by twelve. Earth floor: no fireplace: very offensive: a common sewer from the town running through it uncovered. I was informed that an Officer confined here some years since, for only a few days, took in with him a dog to defend him from vermin; but the dog was soon destroyed, and the Prisoner's face much disfigured by them.'

The gaolers were not always the most gentle of men, as may be seen by the trial of one Acton, deputy-keeper and turnkey of the Marshalsea, for the murder of a prisoner named Thomas Bliss. The indictment will briefly tell the story:

'That the said *William Acton*, being Deputy Keeper, under *John Darby*, of the said prison, being a person of inhuman and cruel disposition, did, on the 21st of October, in the Year of our Lord, 1726, cruelly, barbarously, and feloniously Beat, Assault, and Wound the said *Thomas Bliss* in the said Prison, *viz.*, in the Parish of Saint George's-in-the-Fields, in the Borough of *Southwark*, in the County of *Surrey*, and did put Irons and Fetters of great and immense weight upon his legs, and an Iron Instrument, and Engine of Torture, upon the Head of the said *Thomas Bliss*, called the Scull-cap, and also Thumb-screws upon his Thumbs; and the said *Thomas Bliss* was so wounded, fettered, tortured and tormented in the Strong Room of the said Prison (which is a dangerous, damp, noisome, filthy, and unwholesome place) did put, and him did there detain several days; by means of which excruciating Tortures, close Confinement, Duress, and cruel Abuses, the said *Thomas Bliss* got so ill an Habit of Body, that he continued in a languishing Condition till the 25th Day of *March* following, and then died.'

Although the facts of the indictment were fully borne out by the evidence, the jury acquitted Acton. I should mention that Bliss had twice attempted to escape from the prison.

Let us pass to a pleasanter theme, and see what was the inner life of a debtor's prison about 1750, the story of which is told in a little book undated.[1] The foot-notes are taken from the book.

. . . .

Close by the Borders of a slimy Flood,
Which now in secret rumbles through the Mud;
(Tho' heretofore it roll'd expos'd to light,
Obnoxious to th' offended City's Sight).[2]

Twin Arches now the sable Stream enclose,
Upon whose Basis late a Fabrick rose;
In whose extended oblong Boundaries,
Are Shops and Sheds, and Stalls of all Degrees,
For Fruit, Meat, Herbage, Trinkets, Pork and Peas.
A prudent City Scheme, and kindly meant;
The Town's oblig'd, their Worships touch the Rent.

[1] 'The Humours of the Fleet.' A Poem, by W. Paget, Comedian, &c. Birmingham.

[2] Where the Fleet Market is now, there was, a few Years since, a Ditch, with a muddy Channel of Water. The Market was built at the Expense of the Lord Mayor and Court of Aldermen, who receive the Rent for it.

Near this commodious Market's miry Verge,
The Prince of Prisons stands, compact and large;
Where by the Jigger's[1] more than magick Charm,
Kept from the Power of doing Good—or Harm,
Relenting Captives inly ruminate
Misconduct past, and curse their present State;
Tho' sorely griev'd, few are so void of Grace,
As not to wear a seeming cheerful face:
In Drink or Sports ungrateful Thoughts must die,
For who can bear Heart-wounding Calumny?
Therefore Cabals engage of various Sorts,
To walk, to drink, or play at different Sports,
Here oblong Table's verdant Plain,
The ivory Ball bounds and rebounds again[2];
There at Backgammon two sit *tête-à-tête*,
And curse alternately their adverse fate;
These are at Cribbage, those at Whist engag'd,
And, as they lose, by turns become enrag'd;
Some of more sedentary Temper, read
Chance-medley Books, which duller Dulness breeds;
Or Politick in Coffee-room, some pore
The Papers and Advertisements thrice o'er;
Warm'd with the Alderman,[3] some sit up late,
To fix th' Insolvent Bill, and Nation's fate:
Hence, Knotty Points at different Tables rise,
And either Party's wond'rous, wond'rous wise;
Some of low Taste, ring Hand-Bells, direful Noise!
And interrupt their Fellows' harmless Joys;
Disputes more noisy now a Quarrel breeds,
And Fools on both Sides fall to Loggerheads;
Till, wearied with persuasive Thumps and Blows,
They drink, are Friends, as tho' they ne'er were Foes.

[1] The Door-keeper, or he who opens and shuts the Jigg, is call'd the Jigger.
[2] Billiards is a very common game here.
[3] Fine Ale drank in the Coffee-room, call'd the 'Alderman,' because brew'd by Alderman Parsons.

Without distinction, intermixed is seen,
A 'Squire dirty, and Mechanick clean:
The Spendthrift Heir, who in his Chariot roll'd,
All his Possessions gone, Reversions sold,
Now mean, as one profuse, the stupid Sot
Sits by a Runner's Side,[1] and shules[2] a Pot.

Some Sots, ill-mannered, drunk, a harmless Flight!
Rant noisy thro' the Galleries all Night;
For which, if Justice had been done of late,
The Pump[3] had been three pretty Masters' Fate.
With Stomach's empty, and Heads full of Care,
Some Wretches swill the Pump, and walk the Bare.[4]
Within whose ample Oval is a Court,
Where the more Active and Robust resort,
And glowing, exercise a manly Sport.
(Strong Exercise with mod'rate Food is good,
It drives in sprightful Streams the circling Blood;)
While these, with Rackets strike the flying Ball,
Some play at Nine-pins, Wrestlers take a Fall;
Beneath a Tent some drink, and some above
Are slily in their Chambers making Love;
Venus and Bacchus each keeps here a Shrine,
And many Vot'ries have to Love and Wine.

Such the Amusements of this merry Jail,
Which you'll not reach, if Friends or Money fail;
For e'er it's threefold Gates it will unfold,
The destin'd Captive must produce some Gold;

---

[1] A Runner is a Fellow that goes abroad of Errands for the Prisoners.

[2] Begs.

[3] Persons who give any Considerable offence are often try'd, and undergo the Discipline of the Pump. The Author was one of these in a drunken Frolick, for which he condemns himself.

[4] A Spacious place, where there are all sorts of Exercises, but especially Fives.

Four Guineas at the least for diff'rent Fees,
Compleats your *Habeas*, and commands the Keys;
Which done, and safely in, no more you're led,
If you have Cash, you'll find a Friend and Bed;
But, that deficient, you'll but ill betide,
Lie in the Hall,¹ perhaps on Common Side.²

But now around you gazing Jiggers swarm,³
To draw your Picture, that's their usual Term;
Your Form and Features strictly they survey,
Then leave you (if you can) to run away.

To them succeeds the Chamberlain, to see
If you and he are likely to agree;
Whether you'll tip,⁴ and pay you're Master's Fee.⁵
Ask him how much? 'Tis one Pound, six, and eight;
And, if you want, he'll not the Twopence bate;
When paid, he puts on an important Face,
And shows Mount-scoundrel⁶ for a charming Place;
You stand astonish'd at the darken'd Hole,
Sighing, the Lord have Mercy on my Soul!
And ask, Have you no other Rooms, Sir, pray?
Perhaps inquire what Rent, too, you're to pay:

¹ A Publick Place, free for all Prisoners.
² Where those lie who can't pay their Master's Fee.
³ There are several of these Jiggers, or Door-keepers, who relieve one another, and, when a Prisoner comes first in, they take a nice Observation of him, for fear of his escaping.
⁴ A cant Word for giving some Money in order to show a Lodging.
⁵ Which is One Pound, Six, and Eightpence, and then you are entitled to a bed on the Master's-side, for which you pay so much per Week.
⁶ Mount-scoundrel, so-call'd from its being highly situated, and belonging, once, to the Common-side, tho' lately added to the Master's; if there be room in the House, this Place is first empty, and the Chamberlain commonly shows this to raise his Price upon you for a better.

IMPRISONMENT FOR DEBT.

Entreating that he would a better seek;
The Rent (cries gruffly) 's Half-a-Crown a Week.
The Rooms have all a Price, some good, some bad,
But pleasant ones, at present, can't be had;
This Room, in my Opinion's not amiss;
Then cross his venal Palm with Half a Piece,[1]
He strait accosts you with another face.

How your Affairs may stand, I do not know;
But here, Sir, Cash does frequently run low.
I'll serve you—don't be lavish—only mum!
Take my Advice, I'll help you to a Chum.[2]
A Gentleman, Sir, see—and hear him speak,
With him you'll pay but fifteen Pence a Week,[3]
Yet his Apartments on the Upper Floor,[4]
Well-furnished, clean and nice; who'd wish for more?
A Gentleman of Wit and Judgement too!
Who knows the Place,[5] what's what, and who is who;
My Praise, alas! can't equal his Deserts;
In brief—you'll find him, Sir, a Man of Parts.

Thus, while his fav'rite Friend he recommends,
He compasses at once their several Ends;
The new-come Guest is pleas'd that he shou'd meet
So kind a Chamberlain, a Chum so neat;
But, as conversing thus, they nearer come,
Behold before his Door the destin'd Chum.

[1] Half-a-guinea.
[2] A Bed-fellow so call'd.
[3] When you have a Chum, you pay but fifteen Pence per Week each, and, indeed, that is the Rent of a whole Room, if you find Furniture.
[4] The Upper Floors are accounted best here, for the same Reason as they are at Edinburgh, which, I suppose, every Body knows.
[5] It is common to mention the Fleet by the name of the Place, and I suppose it is call'd the Place by way of Eminence, because there is not such another.

Why he stood there, himself cou'd scarcely tell,
But there he had not stood had Things gone well;
Had one poor Half-penny but blest his Fob,
Or if in prospect he had seen a Job,
H' had strain'd his Credit for a Dram of Bob.[1]
But now, in pensive Mood, with Head downcast,
His Eyes transfix'd as tho' they look'd their last;
One Hand his open Bosom lightly held,
And one an empty Breeches Pocket fill'd;
His Dowlas Shirt no Stock, nor Cravat, bore,
And on his Head, no Hat, nor Wig he wore,
But a once black shag Cap, surcharg'd with Sweat;
His Collar, here a Hole, and there a Pleat,
Both grown alike in Colour, that—alack!
This neither now was White, nor was that Black,
But matched his dirty yellow Beard so true,
They form'd a threefold Cast of Brickdust Hue.
Meagre his Look, and in his nether Jaw
Was stuff'd an eleemosynary Chaw.[2]
(Whose Juice serves present Hunger to asswage,
Which yet returns again with tenfold Rage.)
His Coat, which catch'd the Droppings from his Chin,
Was clos'd, at Bottom, with a Corking Pin;

. . . .

Loose were his Knee-bands, and unty'd his Hose,
Coax'd[3] in the Heel, in pulling o'er his Toes;
Which, spite of all his circumspective Care,
Did thro' his broken, dirty Shoes appear.

Just in this hapless Trim, and pensive Plight,

---

[1] A Cant Word for a Dram of Geneva.
[2] A Chew of Tobacco—supposed to be given him.
[3] When there are Holes above Heel, or the Feet are so bad in a Stocking that you are forced to pull them to hide the Holes, or cover the Toes, it is call'd Coaxing.

The old Collegian[1] stood confess'd to Sight;
Whom, when our new-come Guest at first beheld,
He started back, with great Amazement fill'd;
Turns to the Chamberlain, says, Bless my Eyes!
Is this the Man you told me was so nice?
I meant, his Room was so, Sir, he replies;
The Man is now in Dishabille and Dirt,
He shaves To-morrow, tho', and turns his Shirt;
Stand not at Distance, I'll present you—Come,
My Friend, how is't? I've brought you here a Chum;
One that's a Gentleman; a worthy Man,
And you'll oblige me, serve him all you can.

The Chums salute, the old Collegian first,
Bending his Body almost to the Dust;
Upon his Face unusual Smiles appear,
And long-abandon'd Hope his Spirits cheer;
Thought he, Relief's at hand, and I shall eat;
Will you walk in, good Sir, and take a seat?
We have what's decent here, though not compleat.
As for myself, I scandalize the Room,
But you'll consider, Sir, that I'm at Home;
Tho' had I thought a Stranger to have seen,
I should have ordered Matters to 've been clean;
But here, amongst ourselves, we never mind,
Borrow or lend—reciprocally kind;
Regard not Dress, tho', Sir, I have a Friend
Has Shirts enough, and, if you please, I'll send.
No Ceremony, Sir,—You give me Pain,
I have a clean Shirt, Sir, but have you twain?
Oh yes, and twain to boot, and those twice told,
Besides, I thank my Stars, a Piece of Gold.

---

[1] As the Prison is often called the College, so it is common to call a Prisoner a Collegian; and this Character is taken from a Man who had been many Years in the Place, and like to continue his Life.

Why then, I'll be so free, Sir, as to borrow,
I mean a Shirt, Sir—only till To-morrow.
You're welcome, Sir;—I'm glad you are so free;
Then turns the old Collegian round with Glee,
Whispers the Chamberlain with secret Joy,
We live To-night!—I'm sure he'll pay his Foy;
Turns to his Chum again with Eagerness,
And thus bespeaks him with his best Address:

See, Sir, how pleasant, what a Prospect's there;
Below you see them sporting on the Bare;
Above, the Sun, Moon, Stars, engage the Eye,
And those Abroad can't see beyond the Sky;
These Rooms are better far than those beneath,
A clearer Light, a sweeter Air we breathe;
A decent Garden does our Window grace
With Plants untainted, undisturb'd the Glass;
In short, Sir, nothing can be well more sweet;
But I forgot—perhaps you chuse to eat,
Tho', for my Part, I've nothing of my own,
To-day I scraped my Yesterday's Blade-bone;
But we can send—Ay, Sir, with all my Heart,
(Then, very opportunely, enters Smart[1])
Oh, here's our Cook, he dresses all Things well;
Will you sup here, or do you chuse the Cell?
There's mighty good Accommodations there,
Rooms plenty, or a Box in Bartholm'[2] Fair;
There, too, we can divert you, and may show
Some Characters are worth your while to know.
Replies the new Collegian, Nothing more
I wish to see, be pleas'd to go before;
And, Smart, provide a handsome Dish for Four.

. . . .

[1] The Name of the Cook of the Kitchen.
[2] A place in the Cellar call'd Bartholomew Fair.

But I forget; the Stranger and his Chum,
With t'other two, to Barth'lomew Fair are come;
Where, being seated, and the supper past,
They drink so deep, and put about so fast,
That, e're the warning Watchman walks about,
With dismal tone Repeating, Who goes out?[1]
Ere St. Paul's Clock no longer will withold
From striking Ten, and the voice cries—All told;[2]
Ere this, our new Companions, everyone
In roaring Mirth and Wine so far were gone,
That ev'ry Sense from ev'ry Part was fled,
And were with Difficulty got to Bed;
Where, in the Morn, recover'd from his Drink,
The new Collegian may have Time to think;
And recollecting how he spent the Night,
Explore his Pockets, and not find a Doit.

Too thoughtless Man! to lavish thus away
A Week's support in less than half a Day,
But 'tis a Curse attends this wretched Place,
To pay for dear-bought Wit in little Space,
Till Time shall come when this new Tenant here,
Will in his turn shule for a Pot of Beer,
Repent the melting of his Cash too fast,
And Snap at Strangers for a Night's Repast.

[1] Who goes out? is repeated by Watchmen Prisoners from half-an-hour after nine till St. Paul's Clock strikes Ten, to give Visitors Notice to depart.

[2] While St. Paul's is striking Ten, the Watchman don't call Who goes out? but when the last stroke is given they cry All told! at which time the Gates are lock'd and nobody suffer'd to go out upon any Account.

JONAS HANWAY.

IF Jonas Hanway had lived before Fuller, he certainly would have been enshrined among his ' Worthies;' and it is astonishing to find how comparatively ignorant of him and his works are even well-read men. Ask one about him, and he will reply that he was a philanthropist, but he will hardly be able to say in what way he was philanthropic: ask another, and the reply will be that he was the man who introduced umbrellas into England—but it is very questionable if he could tell whence he got the umbrella to introduce. But in his time he was a man of mark, and his memory deserves more than a short notice in ' Chalmers,' the ' Biographie Universelle,' or any other biographical dictionary.

He was born at Portsmouth on the 12th of August, 1712, in the reign of ' good Queen Anne.' History is silent as to his pedigree, save and except that his father was connected with the navy, and was for some years store-keeper to the dockyard at Portsmouth, and his uncle by the father's side was a Major John Hanway, who translated some odes of Horace, &c. His father died whilst Jonas was still a boy, and Mrs. Hanway had much trouble to bring up her young family, who all turned out well, and were prosperous in after life: one son, Thomas, filling the post of commander-in-chief of his Majesty's ships at Plymouth, and afterwards commissioner of the dockyard at Chatham.

On his father's death, his mother removed to London, where, somehow or other, she brought up her children by her own exertions, and with such care and affection that Jonas never spoke, or wrote, of his mother but in terms of the highest reverence and gratitude. He was sent to school, where he was not only educated commercially, but classically. Still, he had his bread to win, and, when he was seventeen years of age, he was sent to Lisbon, which he reached June, 1729, and was bound apprentice to a merchant, under whose auspices he developed the business qualities which afterwards stood him in good stead. At the end of his apprenticeship he set up in business for himself in Lisbon, but soon removed to the wider field of London. What pursuit he followed there, neither he, nor any biographer of his, has told us, but in 1743 he accepted the offer of a partnership in Mr. Dingley's house at St. Petersburg.

What a difference in the voyage from London to St. Petersburg, then and now! Now, overland: it only takes two days and a half.

Then, in April, 1743, he embarked on the Thames in a crazy old tub, bound for Riga, and got to Elsinore in May. As everything then was done in a leisurely manner, they stopped there for some days, arriving at Riga by the end of May, having taken twenty-six days to go from Elsinore to Riga, now done by steam, under fair conditions, in two days.

Here he found, as most people do, the Russian spring as hot as he ever remembered summer in

Portugal, and was most hospitably entertained by the British factors. But Russia was at war with Sweden, and, although he had plenty of letters of recommendation, the Governor of Riga would not allow him to proceed on his journey, until he had communicated with the authorities at St. Petersburg, thus causing a delay of a fortnight, and he did not leave until the 7th of June. His sojourn at Riga, however, was not lost, for he kept his eyes open, and looked about him.

Travelling by post in Russia, even now, is not a luxury; it must have been ten times worse then, when he started on his journey in his sleeping-wagon, which was 'made of leather, resembling a cradle, and hung upon braces,' and his report of his journey was that 'the post-horses are exceedingly bad, but as the stages are short, and the houses clean, the inconvenience is supportable.' He made the journey in four days.

On his arrival, he soon set to work on the business that he came out to execute namely, the opening of trade through the Caspian Sea to Persia, a journey which involved crossing Russia in Europe from the north-west to the south-east. This route had already been trodden by a sailor named Elton, who had spent some years among the nomadic Tartar tribes, and had, in 1739, descended the Volga with a cargo of goods, intending to go to Mesched; but he sold them before he reached there, at Resched, for a good price, and obtained leave to trade for the future. He returned to St. Petersburg, went again to Persia, and remained there in the service of Nadir Shah. It was to supply his defection that Jonas Hanway went out to Russia.

On the 10th of September, 1743, he set out on his veritably perilous journey, and it is really worth while to describe the despatch of goods in Russia at that day. 'In Russia carriages for merchandize are drawn only by one horse. These vehicles are nine or ten feet long, and two or three broad, and are principally composed of two strong poles, supported by four wheels, of near an equal size, and about as high as the fore wheels of our ordinary coaches, but made very slight, many of the rounds of the wheels are of a single piece of wood, and open, in one part, for near an inch, and some of them are not shod with iron.

'The first care is to lay the bales as high as the cart will admit on a bed of mats of the thickest sort. Besides the original package, which is calculated to stand the weather, the bales are usually covered with very thick mats, and over these other mats are laid to prevent the friction of the ropes; lastly, there is another covering of mats, in the want of raw cowhides, which are always best to defend goods from rain, or from the snow, which, when it melts, is yet more penetrating. Each bale is sealed up with a leaden seal, to prevent its being opened on the road, or any of the goods vended in the Country, that is, when they are intended for Persia . . . . . .

'The Caravans generally set out about twelve, both in the night and day, except in the heat of summer. In the winter, between St. Petersburg and Mosco, they usually travel seventy wersts[1] (about forty-seven English miles) in twenty-four hours, but from Moscow to Zaritzen only forty or fifty wersts: in summer their stages are shorter. Great part of the last-mentioned

[1] A werst is one thousand and sixty-seven metres.

road being through an uninhabited country, makes the Carriers cautious not to jade their horses. Every time they set out, the conductors ought to count the loads. When necessity requires that the Caravan should be drawn within fences, or into yards, the heads of the waggons ought to stand towards the door in regular order, and a guard, who will keep a better watch than an ordinary carrier, should be set over it: for want of this precaution, whole Caravans in Russia have been sometimes consumed by fire. It is most eligible to stop in the field, where the usual method is to form the Carriages into a ring, and bring the horses, as well as the men, within it, always observing to keep in such a position as best to prevent an attack, or repulse an enemy.

'The Khalmucks on the banks of the Volga are ever ready to embrace an opportunity of plundering and destroying passengers; therefore, when there is any occasion to travel on those banks, which should be avoided as much as possible, an advance guard of at least four Cossacks is of great use, especially to patrole in the night; it is not often practised, but I found it indispensably necessary when I travelled on those banks . . . . .

'A hundred carriages take up two-thirds of a mile in length, so that, when no horseman is at hand to spread the alarm, the rear might be easily carried off. They have not even a trumpet, horn, or other instrument for this purpose; they trust in providence, and think any care of this kind unnecessary, though the neglect has sometimes proved of fatal consequence.'

In this primitive style he set forth on his trading venture to Persia, taking with him a clerk, a Russian, as menial servant, a Tartar boy, and a soldier, by way of guard, He had 'a convenient sleeping-waggon' for himself, and another for his clerk—the Russ, the Tartar, and the soldier evidently having to shift as the drivers of the twenty loads of goods (consisting of thirty-seven bales of English cloth) did. It is interesting to follow out this little venture. The caravan started on the 1st of September, 1743, and ten days afterwards he set out to join it, which he did at Tver, arriving at Moscow on the 20th of September.

Here he looked about him, saw the Great Bell, &c. received no little hospitality, and repaired the defects of his caravan, starting again on the 24th of September, and his instructions to his limited suite were to avoid all occasion of dispute, and, should such unfortunately arise, he should be informed of it, in order that he might deal with it according to the best of his judgment. But he went among the Tartars without any misadventure, noting some very curious facts, until he came to Tzaritzin, on the Volga, whence he proposed to commence his somewhat perilous journey by water, to the Caspian Sea. He arrived at Tzaritzin on the 9th of October, but, as there was not the same pushing and driving in business then as now, he stopped there for a month to recruit, and hire a vessel. He succeeded in getting one, such a thing as it was, but then he only paid a nominal sum for it. As he justly observes: 'The reader will imagine that forty roubles[1] cannot purchase a good vessel; however, this price produced the best I could find. Their decks were only loose pieces of the barks of trees; they have no knees, and but few beams: hardly any pitch or tar

[1] Then valued at four shillings each, or eight pounds in all.

is used, in place of it are long slips of bark, which they nail over the gaping seams, to prevent the loose and bad corking (caulking) from falling out. Instead of iron bolts, they have spikes of deal with round heads. The method of keeping them clear of water is by a large scoop, which is suspended by the beam over the well-way, and through a scuttle at a proper height they scoop out the water with great facility.'

He bought two of these A.1. vessels, and put a crew of five fishermen on board each, besides his own suite, and, because of the pirates who infested those waters, he hired a guard of six soldiers. By-the-way, they had a rough and ready way of dealing with these pirates when they did catch them. 'As their cruelties are very great, so is the punishment inflicted on them when they are taken. A float is built, in size according to the number of delinquents, and a gallows erected on it, to contain a sufficient number of iron hooks, on which they are hung alive, by the ribs. The float is launched into the stream, with labels over their heads, signifying their crimes; and orders are given to all towns and villages on the borders of the river, upon pain of death, not only to afford no relief to any of these wretches, but to push off the float, should it land near them. Sometimes their partners in wickedness meet them, and, if there are any signs of life, take him down, otherwise they shoot them dead; but, if they are catched in these acts of illegal mercy, they are hung up without the ceremony of a trial, as happened about eight years ago. They tell me of one of these miscreants who had the fortune to disengage himself from the hook, and though naked, and trembling with pain and loss of blood, he got ashore. The first object he saw who could afford him any relief was a poor shepherd, whose brains he beat out with a stone, and took his clothes. These malefactors sometimes hang thus three, four, and five days alive. The pain generally produces a raging fever, in which they utter the most horrid imprecations, and implore the relief of water, or other small liquors.'

He was observant, and, on his journey down the Volga, he noted many things which throw much light on the social life in Russia of these days. Take for instance the following: 'The 14th of October I sent letters to my friends, by messengers who are appointed to attend a box of grapes, which is sent from Astrachan to the Empress's Court every three days during the season. It is carried by two horses, supported in the manner of a litter. The grapes are preserved in sand, but, at best, are ill worth the expense of the conveyance for one thousand two hundred English miles.'

He sailed from Tzaritzin on the 14th of October, and on the 19th of the same month he reached Astrachan, where he was kindly received by Mr. George Thompson, agent to the British merchants trading to Persia; and also by the Russian governor (a quondam page to Peter the Great) who gave him many assurances that every help should be afforded him in his trade with Persia—but candidly informed him what rogues the Armenian traders were: 'They are the most crafty people in all Asia, and delight in fraud. Let them get fifty per Cent. in a fair way, they are not contented without cheating five, and the five is sweeter than the fifty.'

Lapow, even then, was a recognized institution

in Russia, for Hanway observes, 'The Officers of the the Admiralty and Custom-House of Astrachan have very small salaries, which is the case in all other places in Russia: so that, instead of doing their duty to despatch business, they often seek pretences to protract it, in order to obtain the more considerable presents. Upon these occasions French Brandy, white wine, hats, stockings, ribbons, and such like are acceptable.' Now-a-days, things are managed in a less cumbrous form. Rouble Notes take the place of gross material—but the Russian Official is unchanged.

Again, 'Whilst I was busied in getting what informations were necessary, the governor invited me to a feast, at which there were nearly a hundred dishes; here I saw a singular specimen of Russian intemperance, for there were above thirty people who drank to excess, in goblets, a kind of cherry brandy. This feast was made for the birth of his granddaughter, on which occasion the guests presented an offering each according to his rank. This is a civil way of levying a heavy tax on the merchants, and a custom, tho' not elegant, less absurd than that of some politer countries; for here, without disguise or ceremony, you leave one or two ducats, or some richer present on the lady's bed, who sits up with great formality to be saluted.'

From Astrachan he went to Yerkie, at the mouth of the Volga, and virtually on the Caspian Sea, whence he set sail on the 22nd of November, arriving at Astrabad Bay on the 18th of December, where his vessel was taken for a pirate, and signal fires were, in consequence, lit on the hill-tops, etc. So he lay at anchor for a few days, employing his men in packing his goods so that they might be easily carried on land ; and he gives us a curious insight into the life of sailors of that period.

'The 25th being Christmas Day, I excused the seamen from the package of cloth, and prevailed on them to hear prayers, and a sermon. English seamen, of all mankind, seem the most indifferent with regard to religious duties; but their indifference is more the effect of want of reflection than the irreligious carelessness of their leaders. It is not to be imagined they would fight less if they prayed more; at least we find the praying warriors in Cromwell's days fought as if they were sure of becoming saints in heaven. Certain it is our seamen do not entertain the same impressions of religion as the common run of labouring people.'

Hanway had been warned that he must take care of himself at Astrabad ; that, probably, he would be robbed, and most certainly cheated; but never having received such treatment, and with his conscious faith of being an honest Englishman, he gave but little heed to the caution, but spent many days on ship-board, making up his merchandize into suitable packages for land carriage, and when he did land, he went in state, on horseback, to visit the governor, taking with him the invariable Oriental present, which, in his case, consisted of fine cloth, and loaves of sugar. He was kindly received by the governor, but soon having experienced the deceit and duplicity of the people, he hurried forward his departure for Mesched, sending ten camel loads of goods in advance. Luckily he did so, for the next day the town was besieged by Turcomans, who wanted to get possession of the Shah's treasure, then in Astrabad, as well as the English goods, which presented an almost irresistible temptation to them.

Hanway was advised to disguise himself and fly, but he was an Englishman, and had the pluck of his race; so he concluded to stay, in spite of the objurgations and maledictions of some of the inhabitants, who cursed him as being the cause of their misfortunes. The town made but a feeble resistance, and, soon after its fall, Hanway received a visit from the captors, the story of which he thus tells:

'I had collected my servants in one room, from whence I sent a little boy, a servant, who understood the Turkish language, which is most known to the Khajars, to conduct these hostile visitors to us, and to tell them that, as we were at their mercy, we hoped they would treat us with humanity. They immediately entered, and assured us they did not mean to hurt us; on the contrary, that as soon as their government was established, they would pay me for my goods. They demanded, at the same time, where they were lodged; and informed me that the forty bales which I had sent out of the town some days before, were already in their possession. Mahommed Khan Beg then demanded my purse, which I had prepared with about thirty crowns in gold and silver; he contented himself for the present with counting it, and then returned it to me, demanding if I had any more, for that it would be the worse for me if I concealed any. I thought it warrantable, however, to make an evasive answer, though it was a true one as to the fact; *viz.*, that all the town knew very well that I had been searching for money in exchange for my bill on Mr. Elton, not having sufficient to convey my Caravan to

Mesched. As gold can purchase anything except virtue and health, understanding and beauty, I thought it might now administer to our safety. I therefore reserved a purse of one hundred and sixty crowns in gold, apprehending that the skilful application of it might ward off the danger which threatened us; but I afterwards found that our security was in our supposed poverty, for in near three weeks distress, I durst not show a single piece of gold, much less acknowledge that I had saved any money.'

He made up his mind to leave Astrabad as soon as possible, and, having obtained an acknowledgment of the value of his goods, at last set out with an escort of about two dozen armed men, under the command of a Hadji, or a holy man, who had made a pilgrimage to Mecca. Needless to say his escort were a pack of rogues, and it was by sheer good luck, and at some risk, that, at last, he fell in with some officers of the Shah, who were recruiting for forces wherewith to re-conquer Astrabad. They helped him to horses, although he complained of their quality. He got along somehow, although he lost his servants, and at last he reached Langarood, where the renegade Captain Elton lived, seven weeks after he had left Astrabad, and was received by Elton with open arms. Here he stayed some days to recruit, and then pushed on to Reshd.

A few days more of journeying, and he fell in with the Shah's camp, but failed to have an interview with that exalted potentate. Still his case was brought before Nadir Shah, and, the bill Hanway had received from Mohammed Hassan being produced as evidence, a decree was issued 'that I should give the particulars of the loss to Behbud Khan, the

Shah's general at Astrabad, who had orders to deliver to me whatever part of the goods might possibly be found, and to restore them in kind, and the deficiency to be paid out of the sequestered estates of the rebels to the last denier. This was not quite the thing which I wished for, because it laid me under a necessity of returning to that wretched place, Astrabad; however, I could not but acknowledge the highest obligation for so signal a mark of justice and clemency.'

This act of justice was somewhat unusual with Nadir Shah, of whose cruelty Hanway gives several examples. As, however, one perhaps outstrips its companions in brutality, I venture to give it in his words. 'I will give another example of Nadir's avarice and barbarity, which happened a little before I was in camp. The Shah, having appointed a certain general as governor of a province, imposed an exorbitant tax on it, to be levied in six months: at the expiration of the time the governor was sent for to the camp, and ordered to produce the account. He did so, but it amounted to only half the sum demanded. The Shah called him a rascal; and, telling him he had stolen the other half of the money, ordered the executioner to bastonade him to death: his estates also being confiscated, all his effects fell very short of the demands. The servants of the deceased were then ordered to come into the Shah's presence, and he inquired of them if there was anything left belonging to their master; to which they answered, *Only a dog.* He then commanded the dog to be brought before him; and observed that he appeared to be much honester than his master had been; however, that he should be led through the camp from tent to tent, and beaten with sticks, and wherever he expired, the master of such tent should pay the sum deficient. Accordingly the dog was carried to the tents of the ministers, successively, who, hearing the case, immediately gave sums of money, according to their abilities, to procure the removal of the dog: by which the whole sum the Shah demanded was raised in a few hours' time.'

On the 27th of March they set out on their return journey, accompanied by a small escort; they were detained for some time at Langarood, where Hanway had hoped to find a vessel, as the way by land was insecure. But, although a ship was sighted, she never put in; and the land journey was therefore, perforce, undertaken, and Astrabad was reached on the 16th of May. He saw the Shah's general, who said 'the decree must be obeyed.' Those who had insulted Hanway were most brutally punished—some of his cloth was recovered and given back to him, but there was a difficulty in raising the money for the missing portions, and he was pressed to take payment in women slaves. On his refusal, they begged of him to give them a receipt as if he had been paid, assuring him the money should be forthcoming in a very few days; but the British merchant was too wary to be caught in such a palpable trap. Eventually he got the greater part of it, and with it returned to Langarood, where he waited for some little while, and, at last, he recovered eighty-five per cent. of the value of his goods, according to his own valuation, so that, probably, he made a good sale.

At Langarood he fell ill of a low fever, but was cured by a French missionary, who administered Jesuit's bark (quinine) to him, and he then set out on his return journey, having invested all his cash in raw silk. He met with no particular adventures, and arrived safely at St. Petersburg on the 1st of January, 1745, 'having been absent a year and sixteen weeks, in which time I had travelled about four thousand English miles by land.'

In noticing this trip of Hanway's to the Caspian, it would be a pity if attention were not called to his description of Baku, now coming so much to the front (thanks to the industry and intelligence of the Messrs. Nobel) in providing the world with petroleum. This was the chief shrine of the followers of Zoroaster, who considered light, which was typified by fire, (which is bright both by day and night) as emblematical of all good, and they therefore worshipped Ormuzd, or the good god, whilst they regarded Ahriman, or darkness, as the evil god. Here, near Baku, the soil is so soaked and saturated with petroleum that a fire, natural and never-ceasing, could easily be obtained, and consequently, being perfectly unartificial, was looked upon as the personification of Ormuzd. Hanway writes, 'The earth round this place, for above two miles, has this surprizing property, that by taking up two or three inches of the surface and applying a live coal, the part which is so uncovered immediately takes fire, almost before the coal touches the earth . . . . . If a cane, or tube even of paper, be set about two inches in the ground, confined and closed with earth below, and the top of it touched with a live coal, and blown upon, immediately a flame issues without hurting either the cane or the paper, provided the edges be covered with clay, and this method they use for light in their houses, which have only the earth for the floor; three or four of these lighted canes will boil water in a pot; and thus they dress their victuals.'

Baku, the seat of this natural symbol of Ormuzd, was then a place of pilgrimage for the Parsees—and it is not so long since that fire-worship there has been discontinued. Mr. Charles Marvin (writing in 1884) commences his most interesting book, 'The Region of the Eternal Fire,' thus: 'A few years ago a solitary figure might have been daily seen on the shore of the Caspian Sea, worshipping a fire springing naturally from the petroleum gases in the ground. The devotee was a Parsee from India, the last of a series of priests who for more than two thousand five hundred years had tended the sacred flame upon the spot. Round about his crumbling temple was rising greasy derricks, and dingy distilleries—symbols of a fresh cult, the worship of mammon—but, absorbed in his devotions, the Parsee took no heed of the intruders. And so time passed on, and the last of the Fire-Worshippers died, and with him perished the flame that was older than history.'

He stayed some time in Russia, but undertook no more arduous journeys. Even when he did leave St. Petersburg, on the 9th of July, 1750, he travelled very leisurely overland, reaching Harwich on the 28th of October, 1750, after an absence from England of nearly eight years. He lived in London in a modest fashion, for his fortune was but modest—yet it was sufficient for him to keep a *solo* carriage, *i.e.*, only carrying one person, and on its panels was painted a device allusive to his dangers in Persia, especially of a somewhat perilous voyage on the Caspian. It consisted of 'a man dressed in the Persian habit, just landed in a storm on a rude coast, and leaning on his sword, his countenance calm and resigned. In the background was depicted a boat tossed about by the billows; in front, a shield charged with his arms leaning against a tree, and underneath the motto, in English, *Never Despair.*'

As a result of his eastern experiences,[1] on his return to England he used an umbrella, which at that time for a man to carry was considered somewhat effeminate. He is often credited with having introduced that useful article into England; but it had been generally used by women for fifty years previously—nay, there is in the British Museum (Harl. 630 fol. 15b,) an Anglo-Saxon MS. of the eleventh century—unmistakeably English in its drawing—wherein is an illustration of an umbrella being held (by an attendant) over the head of a king, or nobleman. It is a veritable 'Sangster,' and, as far as form goes, it would pass muster now. From this time the use of the umbrella became familiar, and in general use among men—probably because he introduced them of pure silk, whereas hitherto they had been cumbrous and heavy, being made of oiled paper, muslin, or silk.

He had enough to live on, and, as in those days no one cared about making a colossal fortune, he lived contentedly on his competence, and wrote a long description of his travels, which was very well illustrated, and which cost him £700 to produce his first edition of one thousand two hundred copies, after which he disposed of the copyright, and second, third, and fourth editions were published. Still, the

[1] Gay, in his 'Trivia,' book i, says,
'Let *Persian* Dames th' *Umbrella's* Ribs display,
To guard their Beauties from the Sunny Ray.'

climate of Russia had not agreed with him, and he had to go to the then fashionable Spa, Tunbridge Wells, and afterwards to Paris, thence to Brussels, Antwerp, and Amsterdam.

He returned to Tunbridge Wells, where he wrote (in 1753) a treatise against the Naturalisation of the Jews,[1] which was a question then being agitated. One can scarcely imagine a man with large sympathies, as was Jonas Hanway, a travelled man, also, of great experience of men, taking the narrow view of such a question of social polity. After a severe fight the Bill was carried (26 Geo. 2) and his Majesty gave his consent on the 7th of June, 1753,[2] but the opposition to it was so great that when Parliament next met (15th of November, 1753) the very first business after the address (which only occupied half-an hour or so—a valuable hint to present M.P.'s) was to bring in a bill repealing the privilege of Naturalization to the Jews. Popular clamour on its behalf was senseless, as it usually is, but it was too strong to resist, and in the debate thereon, on the 27th of November, 1753, William Pitt (all honour to him) said, 'Thus, sir, though we repeal this law, out of complaisance to the people, yet we ought to let them know that we do not altogether approve of what they ask.'[3] The Bill was carried on the 28th of November, and received the Royal Assent on the 20th of December, the same year, and consequently an

---

[1] 'A Review of the proposed Naturalization of the Jews.'
[2] Among other Bills which then received the Royal Assent was one for purchasing Sloane Museum and the Harleian MSS., and for providing a general repository for the same—by means of a lottery—the commencement of the British Museum.
[3] 'Parliamentary History,' Hansard, vol. xv, p. 154.

injustice was for some time done to some of the loyalest, quietest, and most law-abiding citizens we have. Hanway, however, thought so strongly on the subject that he wrote four tractates upon it, which, as the question is now happily settled, may be dismissed with this brief notice.

He was naturally of a busy turn of mind, and could not sit still. He wrote about anything—it did not much matter what—of the paving, etc. of Westminster and its adjacent parishes; he even wrote a big book, beautifully illustrated, on a little trip he took, when travelling was not so common as now, 'A Journal of Eight days' Journey from Portsmouth to Kingston-on-Thames,' (1756) a second edition of which was published in two volumes in 1757, with the addition of 'An Essay on Tea, considered as pernicious to Health, obstructing Industry, and impoverishing the Nation.' So we see he took strong views on things in general, which have since, by experience, been modified.

His scribbling propensities probably did some good, for in 1757 we find him taking up the cause of that very meritorious charity, the Marine Society, to which he was a subscriber to the extent of fifteen guineas. This society, whose house is in Bishopsgate Street, is still alive, and, what is more, flourishing. About this he wrote four or five pamphlets and books. This seems only to have served as a whet to his appetite for philanthropy, for in 1758 he paid £50 to qualify himself as a Life-Governor of the Foundling Hospital. This, naturally, led him to think upon the source whence the foundlings principally came: and he turned his attention towards the foundation of a Magdalen (?) Hospital, which was, with the co-operation of several gentlemen, established in London in 1758, in Great Prescott Street, Goodman's Fields (the site of which is now, or used to be, called Magdalen Row).

Many more books and pamphlets on the above subjects, the Foundling Hospital, the Marine and Stepney Societies, the Encouragement of British Troops, etc., occupied his leisure until 1760, when he took in hand the social question of giving fees, or *vails*, to servants, and wrote two pamphlets on the subject. In one of them are some very humorous stories of this absurd custom, one, especially, which from its raciness has become somewhat hackneyed.[1] 'It is a more *humorous* Story they tell of —— after he had dined with ——. The Servants with assiduous duty had taken the best care of his friend's *Hat, Sword, Cane, Cloak,* and among the rest his *Gloves* also. When he came to demand them, every Servant, with the most submissive respect, brought his part of the Old Gentleman's *personal furniture,* and so many *Shillings* were distributed with his usual liberality; but, as he was going away without his *Gloves,* one of the Servants reminded him of it, to which he answered, " *No matter, friend, you may keep the Gloves, they are not worth a Shilling.*" '

Hanway tried to do away with this social tax, which, however, remains to this day. But a very good story is told of Robert Hamilton of Kilbrachmont.[2] 'After a party at Kellie Castle the guests were passing through the Hall where the servants

---

[1] 'Eight Letters to his Grace—Duke of Newcastle—on the custom of Vails-giving in England, &c.,' 1760, p. 20.

[2] 'The East Neuk of Fife,' by Rev. Walter Wood. Edinburgh, 1862, p. 208.

were drawn up to receive their vails, in those days a customary exaction at great houses. The gifts of those who preceded "Robbie" (as the Laird was commonly called) drew forth no expression of gratitude, not even a smile, but when his turn came for performing the ceremony their features were at once lighted up with something even approaching to a laugh.

'"What did you give the fellows, Robbie?" said his friends, when they got outside; "they looked as sour as vinegar till your turn came."

'"Deil a bawbee they got frae me," said Robbie, 'I just kittled their loof."'[1]

This system of feeing servants received a crushing blow on the production (in 1759) of the Rev. James Townley's farce of 'High Life below Stairs,' which probably led to Hanway's writing his two pamphlets on the subject.

He used occasionally to go to Court—but never solicited any place for himself; still it was thought that his philanthropic exertions should be rewarded, more especially as he had by no means a large fortune. So a deputation of five prominent citizens of London, amongst whom was Hoare the banker, waited on Lord Bute (who was then Prime Minister), and asked that some substantial recognition of his services should made. Their representations had weight, and, in July, 1762, he was appointed one of the commissioners for victualling the Navy.

He was now in easy circumstances, and his official duties could not have been very heavy, for in that year he wrote four pamphlets on ' Meditations on Life, &c.,' 'Registration of the Parish Poor, and Ventila-

[1] Tickled the palms of their hands.

tion,' his pet Magdalens, and a 'Disquisition on Peace and War:' themes so diverse that they show the variety of subjects that occupied his serious attention. In fact, he scribbled on an infinity of things—all having for their aim the benefit of mankind. He had a financial scheme 'for saving from Seventy Thousand Pounds to One Hundred and Fifty Thousand Pounds to the Public;' he wrote on the 'Uses and Advantages of Music;' the 'Case of the Canadians at Montreal;' 'The Soldier's Faithful Friend, being Moral and Religious Advice to private Men in the Army and Militia;' the 'Registration of the Children of the Poor;' another pamphlet on the rising generation of the labouring poor; and, not content with addressing the private soldier, he must needs write 'The Christian Officer, addressed to the Officers of his Majesty's forces, &c.'

About this time he was evidently most *goody-goody*. He wrote 'Moral and Religious Instruction to young Persons,' 'Moral and Religious Instructions, intended for Apprentices among the lower Classes of the People;' 'Letters to the Guardians of the Infant Poor;' 'Rules and Regulations of the Magdalene Hospital, with Prayers, &c.;' 'Advice to a Daughter, on her going to Service, &c.;' 'Advice from a Farmer to his Daughter;' 'Observations on the Causes of the Dissoluteness which reigns among the lower Classes of the People.'

He could not even leave to Mrs. Elizabeth Montague of the 'Blue-Stocking Club' notoriety, her championship and patronage of the poor little climbing boys—and he fired off a pamphlet on 'The State of Chimney-Sweepers' young Apprentices, &c.' These poor little friendless mortals excited his pity, and his first efforts in their behalf were to get them regularly bound apprentices, so as to bring them under the cognizance of the magistracy; he advocated and inaugurated a subscription to defray the expense, and supply them with clothes. And this movement was attended with considerable success, for many boys were bound apprentices, and some of the masters were prosecuted for cruelty to their boys.

Then, to show the diversity of his talents, he wrote two pamphlets on bread, and a book in two volumes on ' Virtue in humble life, &c.' In 1775 he published a large quarto volume on ' The Defects of Police, the Causes of Immorality, &c.,' and in the copy which I have before me, is written, ' TO THE KING, *with the Author's most humble Duty.*' In this book, among other things, he advocated solitary, or rather isolated confinement—permitting the prisoners to work, and giving them an increased dietary according to their labour. This was followed in 1776 by a pamphlet on ' Solitude in Imprisonment, with proper labour, &c.'

He was now sixty-four years of age, but he was as bodily active as he was mentally, and in February, 1776, he had to go over to Hamburg in connection with his duties as one of the commissioners of the Victualling Board. In 1777, 1778, and 1782, he wrote three books on the Lord's Supper—and from that time he wrote, until he died in 1786, on all sorts of subjects, religious, social, and political, a list of which would only be wearisome. In the summer of 1786 his health gave way, and he was evidently sinking, but he lingered until the 5th of September, when he calmly passed away—perfectly prepared for the great change, putting on a fine ruffled shirt, giving up his keys, disposing of some trinkets, and having his will read to him. Death came easily to him, and he expired with the word 'Christ' upon his lips.

Such was the life, and such was the death, of Jonas Hanway, whose biography is not half well enough known.

A HOLY VOYAGE TO RAMSGATE A HUNDRED YEARS AGO.

THIS little story, which I very much condense, is most amusing, and is the work of 'Henry Blaine, Minister of the Gospel at Tring, Herts.' I only give it as showing the dread with which any country-bred man, at that time, put his precious body at the mercy of Father Neptune. Steam has changed all our habits, but then there were no 'Globe Trotters,'—few, if any, climbed the Alps for amusement; the Dolomites were unknown; people had no steam-yachts and went in pursuit of perpetual summer; a cruise to the Pacific Islands and Japan was never dreamt of; there was no Mudie's library to scatter broadcast holiday tours, for they never existed—so that we must look upon this relation of an inland-bred 'Minister of the Gospel' (whose long and extremely pious, but wearisome, exordia I omit) with very different eyes, to a similar one published in the present day.

It is a tract of fifty-four pages, and commences, 'In hopes of recovering that invaluable blessing, health, on Friday, August 10, 1787, I embarked on board the ship FRIENDS bound for RAMSGATE, in KENT. I had heard there was such a place; and many had raised my expectations by their reports of the efficacy of sea-bathing; and others encouraged my hopes by repeating their own experience of benefit received. By these means I was induced to determine on this little voyage. It reminded me of the never-to-be-forgotten season, when, urged by some motives, and impelled by a power unseen, but not unfelt, I entered on board that stately vessel which the Lord's prophet saw in a storm. *Isaiah* 54.—11.'

This is a sample of the tract. He then goes on to say: 'While we waited for the time of sailing (for different purposes, I suppose), many came on board, and appeared, to me at least, as if they intended to embark with us: but they left not the harbour, but, urged by other occasions and inducements, they took leave of their friends and departed; while we, who were bound for a distant place, kept steady to our purpose, turned our backs upon home and waited patiently for the gentle breeze and driving tide to convey us to the desired port.'

We can well imagine the good man, when he got back to Tring, giving, for a long time, his soul-harrowing experiences of that memorable voyage. He should have lived in our days and have been 'Our Special Correspondent' on whom the editor of the newspaper relies to fill so many columns—for every detail is taken, evidently note-book in hand. Witness this: 'When our sails were displayed, and our cable unloosed, assisted by a gentle gale, we began by degrees to view the lofty towers, the aspiring churches, and all the grandeurs of London at a distance behind us: in hopes of finding something we could not find in town, we turned our attention from the pleasures, and riches, and pomps of London; we bid farewel, for a time, to our dearest friends; we laid aside our daily and domestic cares, and cheerfully forsook the dear delights of home.'

At length they were fairly started on their voyage, which from the crowded state of the river, and the excessive timidity of the writer, must have been vastly perilous. 'Our vessel, though it set sail with a fair wind, and gently fell down the river towards her destined port, yet once or twice was nearly striking against other vessels in the river, to her own injury; but, by the care of the steersman and sailors, she was timely prevented ..... There was no spectacle more affecting, in all the little voyage, than the bodies of those unhappy malefactors which were hung up, *in terrorem*, on the margin of the river Thames. Surely these was some of the execrable characters whom Justice pursued, who, though "they escaped the sea, yet vengeance suffered not to live. *Acts* 28.—4." ..... Having passed these spectacles of horror, a fair wind and flowing tide smoothly carried us towards the boundless ocean ......

'When we drew towards the conflux of the river Thames there were two objects that attracted our notice: the one, the King's guardship, placed there for the purposes of good œconomy, the other a large painted vessel which floated on the surface of the water, and is called a buoy. While we were passing the king's ship, I heard the report of a cannon, and saw the flash of the charge at some distance; and, on inquiring the reason of such a circumstance, was informed it was customary for every ship which passed, by way of obedience, to lower her topsail; but the firing of the gun made them hasten to show their obedience, for fear of a more unfavourable salute; for, though a flash of powder might give us some alarm, the discharge of a ball might make us *feel* the effects of disobedience . . . . Hitherto the generality of our company appeared to carry jollity and mirth in their countenances; but now we began to see the blushing rose die in the sickly cheek, and several of our passengers began to feel the sickening effects of the rolling sea; they withdrew from their mirth, and in pleasure crept into a corner, and silently mourned their lost pleasures in solitude . . . . Thrice happy the souls who are by divine grace made sick of unsatisfying delights, and compelled to withdraw from unsatisfying objects, and seek and find permanent bliss in the friendship of Immanuel!

'There had been the appearance of affability and good-humour kept up among the passengers of our vessel, and a reciprocal exchange of civilities had passed between them; our bad tempers were for awhile laid aside, and we seemed mutually agreed to make each other as innocently happy as our present. If the same mode of conduct was observed through the whole of our department, how would the ills of life be softened, and the ties of society sweetened! . . . . . .

'The eyelid of the day was now nearly closed upon us, and the gloom of darkness began to surround us, which, together with the hollow bellowing of the wind, and dashing waves, had a tendency to create very solemn ideas in the mind; and I, being a stranger to such scenes, had my mind exercised upon things of greater importance . . . .

'About ten o'clock on Friday night we were brought safely into the harbour of Margate, and then cast anchor in order to set a great number of our passengers on shore, who were bound for that place of rendezvous. How great are the advantages of navigation! By the skill and care of three men and a boy, a number of persons were in safety conveyed from one part to another of the kingdom . . . . .

'When we had safely landed our passengers at Margate, we weighed anchor at eleven o'clock at night, in order to sail round the North Foreland for Ramsgate. The North Foreland is a point of land which stretches out some way into the sea, and is the extreme part of our country on the right hand, when we sail down the river Thames; and sailing round the point into the British Channel is esteemed by sailors rather dangerous. However, there was danger enough to awaken the apprehensions of a freshwater sailor. Yet here with some degree of confidence in Him who exercises His power over the sea and dry land, I laid me down and slept in quietness, while the rattling waves drove against the sides of our vessel, and the rustling winds shook our sails, and made our yielding masts to speak. I was led to reflect that now there was but a feeble plank between me and the bottomless deep, yet, by a reliance on the divine goodness, my fears were hushed, and a divine calm prevailed within. "Thou will keep him in perfect peace whose mind is staid on thee." *Isaiah* 26.—3.

'On Saturday morning I awoke and heard a peaceful sound from shore, which informed me it was two o'clock: and, inquiring where we were, I found we were safe anchored within the commodious harbour of Ramsgate. Being so early an hour, we again composed ourselves to sleep, and lay till five o'clock; then leaving our sleeping apartment, and mounting the peaceful deck—not like the frighted sailor, who leaves the horrid hulk to view a thousand deaths from winds, and waves, and rocks, without a friendly shore in view—but to see one of the finest retreats from all these dangers, which Providence has provided for the safety of those who are exposed to the violence and rage of angry elements. The commodious Pier of Ramsgate seems admirably calculated to shelter and protect vessels which are threatened with destruction from winds and waves. This beautiful piece of architecture is built in the form of a Crescent, or half-moon, the points of which join to the land .... The whole of this building of utility appeared to bear a clear resemblance to the glorious Mediator in his offices, who is appointed for a refuge from the storm ....

'By six in the morning we went on shore, and joyfully met our friends, who were brought down the day before; but in their passage were overtaken by a violent storm of thunder and lightning, whilst our voyage was smooth and prosperous; but, in the morning, we all met in peace and safety. Thus we sat down to a friendly breakfast, and cheerfully talked over the adventures of the little voyage. Something like this, I think, may take place in the state of blessedness ...... While we were thus employed, we consulted how to dispose of ourselves while we continued at Ramsgate; we mutually agreed to form ourselves into a little family, and though we could not all lodge, yet we wished to board together in the same house.' This is a pleasing instance of *bonne camaraderie* engendered, in a short time, among agreeable companions.

'In order to pursue the design of our coming, some of our company mixed among the bathers at the sea-side. The convenience of bathing, the coolness of a fine summer's morning, the agreeable appearance of company so early, and the novelty of the scene, had a very pleasing effect . . . . . We began to look around us; and though we were not presented with objects of taste and elegance, yet the town and environs afforded us some rural prospects, which yielded both instruction and pleasure. Upon our left hand, as we ascended from the sea-side, stands the seat of observation, erected on a point of land, and commanding an extensive prospect over that part of the sea called the Downs, where you behold a number of ships lying at anchor, or on their passage to different parts of the world. From thence you may likewise see the lofty cliffs of France, and reverberating the light of the sun; while, at the same time, you may, by way of amusement, watch the motions of every boat coming in and going out of the harbour; and, as the sea is always varying, its appearance altogether affords an agreeable amusement. Here the Company frequently stop to rest themselves after a morning's or an evening's walk, and are sweetly regaled by the cool refreshing breezes of the sea . . .

'It might be thought strange was I to say nothing of Margate, that being the chief resort for bathers, and of growing repute. The town of Margate is in a very increasing state, and its principal ornaments consist of its late additions. The chief concern of the publick seems to render it as much a place for pleasure as utility, as, under colour of utility, persons can pursue pleasure without censure. A mother, for instance, might be highly blamed by her acquaintance for leaving her family for a month, and going to spend her husband's money; but who can blame her when her health requires it? They are modelling it according to the taste of the times. They have, indeed, built one place of worship, but a playhouse nearly four times as large. Thus, when ill-health does not interrupt the company's pursuit of amusement, they are likely soon to be accommodated to their minds. Such is the provision already made, that the consumptive cough of a delicate lady may be furnished with the relief of the fumes of a smoking hot assembly-room, and the embarrassed citizen may drown his anxiety in the amusements of the Card-table . . . . .

'The libraries are decently furnished, and may serve as a kind of lounging Exchange, where persons overburdened with money and time may ease themselves with great facility. The most healthful amusement, and best suited to invalids, that is pursued at Margate, is that of the bowling-green, where, upon the top of a hill, and in full prospect of the sea, in a free open air, gentlemen may exercise their bodies, and unbend their minds; this, if pursued for the benefit of health and innocent recreation, with a serious friend, appears to have no more criminality in it than Peter's going a fishing . . . . .

'Having staid as long at Ramsgate as our affairs at home would, with prudence, admit; we went on board the same ship, and re-embarked for London. In order, I suppose, to take the better advantage, we sailed some leagues right out to sea; but, it being a dead calm, we hardly experienced any other motion than was occasioned by the tide and swell of the sea for that night. The cry of the sailors, Blow! Blow! reminded me of that pathetick exclamation of the ancient Church! The next day proved equally calm, so that we had little else to divert us but walk about the deck, and watch the rolling of the porpoises in the sea. We had an old sailor on board, whose patience being tired, declared he preferred being at sea in a storm to being becalmed on the ocean, which struck me with the propriety of the observation, when applied to Christian experience; for a storm, under Divine direction, is often made the means of hastening the Christian's progress, while a dead calm is useless and unsafe.'

It took them two days to get to Margate, and another day to reach Gravesend. On their way they passed a vessel cast on shore, which 'cut a dismal figure, such as they make, to an enlightened eye, who make shipwreck of faith, whom Christians see, as they pursue their course, run aground, and dash to pieces.'

By the time they came to Gravesend some of the passengers had had enough of the Hoy—so they hired a boat and four men to row them to London, but the wind getting up, the river became rough, and the boat being over-loaded, the boatmen begged them to get on board a fishing-smack, which they did, and arrived at Billingsgate safely. We can hardly imagine, in these days of steam, that a journey from Ramsgate to London would last from Monday morning to Wednesday night, but people did not hurry themselves too much in those days.

QUACKS OF THE CENTURY.

N all ages there have been pretenders to medical science, and it has been reserved to the present century to elevate the healing art into a real science, based on proper physiological facts, aided by the searching analyses of modern chemistry. The old alchemists had died out, yet they had some pretensions to learning, but the pharmacopœia at the commencement of the eighteenth century was in a deplorable condition. Surgery, for rough purposes, had existed since the earliest ages, because accidents would happen, then as now; and, moreover, there were wars, which necessitated the amputation of limbs, etc., but medicine, except in the knowledge of the virtue of herbs and simples, was in more than a primitive state. Anyone who chose, could dub himself Doctor, and, naturally, the privilege was largely taken advantage of.

The name of quack, or quacksalver, does not seem to have been much used before the seventeenth century, and its derivation has not been distinctly settled. In the 'Antiquities of Egypt,' etc., by William Osburn, junior, London, 1847, p. 94, he says: 'The idea of a physician is frequently represented by a species of duck, the name of which is CHIN: the

Egyptian word for physician was also CHINI.' But neither Pierret, in his 'Vocabulaire Hieroglyphique,' nor Bunsen, in ' Egypt's Place in Universal History,' endorse this statement. Still the Egyptian equivalent for cackling, or the noise of a goose, was *Ka ka*, and in Coptic *Ouok*, pronounced very much like quack.

The Germans also use the word *Quacksalber,* and the Dutch *Kwaksalver*, a term which Bilderdijk, in his ' Geslachtijst der Naamworden,' (derivation or gender of men's names) says, ought more properly to be *Kwabsalver*, from *Kwab*, a wen, and *Salver*, to anoint. Be this as it may, the English word quack certainly means an illegitimate medical practitioner, a pretender to medical science, whose pretensions are not warranted by his knowledge.

The seventeenth century was prolific in quacks— a notable example being John Wilmot, Earl of Rochester. Both Bishop Burnet and De Gramont agree that, during one of his banishments from Court, he lived in Tower Street (next door to the sign of the 'Black Swan,' at a goldsmith's house), and there practised as a quack doctor, as one Alexander Bendo, newly arrived from Germany. There is a famous mountebank speech of his extant, copies of which exist not only in broad sheets, but in some of the jest-books of the seventeenth century, which, genuine or not, is very amusing. It is far too long to transcribe here, but perhaps I may be pardoned if I give a short extract.

' The knowledge of these secrets I gathered in my travels abroad (where I have spent my time ever since I was fifteen years old to this, my nine and twentieth year) in France and Italy. Those that have travelled in Italy will tell you what a miracle

of art does there assist nature in the preservation of
beauty: how women of forty bear the same countenance with them of fifteen: ages are no way
distinguished by faces; whereas, here in England,
look a horse in the mouth and a woman in the face,
you presently know both their ages to a year. I
will, therefore, give you such remedies that, without
destroying your complexion (as most of your paints
and daubings do) shall render them perfectly fair;
clearing and preserving them from all spots, freckles,
heats, pimples, and marks of the small-pox, or any
other accidental ones, so that the face be not seamed
or scarred.

'I will also cleanse and preserve your *teeth* white
and round as pearls, fastening them that are loose:
your gums shall be kept entire, as red as coral; your
lips of the same colour, and soft as you could wish
your lawful kisses.

'I will likewise administer that which shall cure
the worst of breaths, provided the lungs be not
totally perished and imposthumated; as also certain
and infallible remedies for those whose breaths are
yet untainted; so that nothing but either a very
long sickness, or old age itself, shall ever be able to
spoil them.

'I will, besides, (if it be desired) *take away* from
their fatness who have over much, and *add* flesh to
those that want it, without the least detriment to
their constitutions.'

By his plausible manners and good address, he
soon gathered round him a large *clientèle* of servants,
etc., for he told fortunes as well as cured diseases.
These told their mistresses, and they too came to
consult the wise man. Even the Court ladies came

incognito to see him, and *la belle* Jennings, sister to the famous Sarah, first Duchess of Marlborough, went, with the beautiful Miss Price, to have their fortunes told, disguised as orange-wenches, and in all probability their visit would never have been heard of, had they not met with a disagreeable adventure with a somewhat dissolute gentleman named Brounker, who was gentleman of the chamber to the Duke of York, and brother to Viscount Brounker, President of the Royal Society.

John Cotgrave[1] thus describes the quack of his time:

' My name is Pulse-feel, a poor Doctor of Physick,
That does wear three pile Velvet in his Hat,
Has paid a quarter's Rent of his house before-hand,
And (simple as he stands here) was made Doctor beyond sea.
I vow, as I am Right worshipful, the taking
Of my Degree cost me twelve French Crowns, and
Thirty-five pounds of Butter in upper *Germany*.
I can make your beauty and preserve it,
Rectifie your body and maintaine it,
Clarifie your blood, surfle[2] your cheeks, perfume
Your skin, tinct your hair, enliven your eye,
Heighten your Appetite; and, as for Jellies,
Dentifrizes, Dyets, Minerals, Fucusses,[3]
Pomatums, Fumes, Italia Masks to sleep in,
Either to moisten or dry the superficies, *Paugh, Galen*
Was a Goose, and *Paracelsus* a patch
To Doctor *Pulse-feel*.'

Then there was that arch quack and empiric, Sir

[1] 'The English Treasury of Wit and Language,' etc., ed. 1655, pp. 223, 224.

[2] Or surfel—to wash the cheeks with mercurial or sulphur water.

[3] Face-washes and ointments.

Kenelm Digby, with his 'sympathetic powder,' etc., and Dr. Saffold, originally a weaver, who distributed his handbills broadcast, advertising his ability to cure every disease under the sun.

Also in this century is a poem called 'The Dispensary,'[1] by Sir Samuel Garth, who lived in Queen Anne's time, which gives the following account of a quack and his surroundings:

' So truly *Horoscope* its Virtues knows,
To this bright Idol[2] 'tis, alone, he bows;
And fancies that a Thousand Pound supplies
The want of twenty Thousand Qualities.
Long has he been of that amphibious Fry,
Bold to prescribe, and busie to apply.
His Shop the gazing Vulgar's Eyes employs
With forreign Trinkets, and domestick Toys.
Here *Mummies* lay, most reverently stale,
And there, the *Tortois* hung her Coat o' Mail;
Not far from some huge *Shark's* devouring Head,
The flying Fish their finny Pinions spread.
Aloft in rows large Poppy Heads were strung,
And near, a scaly Alligator hung.
In this place, Drugs in Musty heaps decay'd,
In that, dry'd Bladders, and drawn Teeth were laid.
An inner Room receives the numerous Shoals
Of such as pay to be reputed Fools.
Globes stand by Globes, Volumns on Volumns lie,
And Planitary Schemes amuse the eye
The Sage, in Velvet Chair, here lolls at ease,
To promise future Health for present Fees.

---

[1] Edition 1699, p. 19. The poem had reference to the College of Physicians, establishing a dispensary of their own, owing to the excessive charges of the apothecaries. The institution did not last very long.

[2] Gold.

> Then, as from *Tripod*, solemn shams reveals,
> And what the Stars know nothing of, reveals.'

Medicine in the last century was very crude. Bleeding and purging were matters of course; but some of the remedies in the pharmacopœia were very curious. Happy the patient who knew not the composition of his dose. Take the following:[1]

'Or sometimes a quarter of a pint of the following decoction may be drank alone four times a day:

'Take a fresh viper, freed from the head, skin, and intestines, cut in pieces; candied eryngo root, sliced, two ounces. Boil them gently in three pints of water, to a pint and three-quarters, and to the strained liquor add simple and spiritous cinnamon waters, of each two ounces. Mix them together, to be taken as above directed.

'The following viper broth (taken from the London Dispensatory) is a very nutritous and proper restorative food in this case, and seems to be one of the best preparations of the viper: for all the benefit that can be expected from that animal is by this means obtained:

'Take a middle-sized viper, freed from head, skin, and intestines; and two pints of water. Boil them to a pint and a half; then remove the vessel from the fire; and when the liquor is grown cold, let the fat, which congeals upon the surface, if the viper was fresh, be taken off. Into this broth, whilst warm, put a pullet of a moderate size, drawn and freed from the skin, and all the fat, but with the flesh intire. Set the vessel on the fire again, that the liquor may boil;

---

[1] 'The Female Physician, &c.,' by John Ball, M.D.—London, 1770, pp. 76, 77.

then remove it from the fire, take out the chicken, and immediately chop its flesh into little pieces : put these into the liquor again, set it over the fire, and as soon as it boils up, pour out the broth, first carefully taking off the scum.

'Of this broth let the patient take half a pint every morning, at two of the clock in the afternoon, and at supper-time.'

In the same book, also (p. 97), we find the following remedy for cancer :

'Dr. Heister, professor of physic and surgery in the university of *Helmstadt* in *Germany*, with many others, greatly extols the virtue of millepedes, or wood-lice, in this case; and, perhaps, the best way of administering them is as follows :

'Take of live wood-lice, one ounce ; fine sugar, two drams ; a little powder of nutmeg ; and half a pint of alexeterial water. Let the wood-lice and sugar, with the nutmeg, be ground together in a marble mortar, then gradually add the water, which being well mixed, strain it with hard pressing. Two ounces of this expression are to be taken twice a day, shaking the vessel, so that no part of it may be lost.'

And it also seems that much virtue was attached to the great number of component parts in a medicine, as may be seen in the recipe for *Arquebusade Water*[1] (from the same book, p. 101).

'Take of comfrey leaves and root, sage, mugwort, bugloss, each four handfulls ; betony, sanicle, ox-eye daisy, common daisy, greater figwort, plantane, agrimony, vervain, wormwood, fennel, each two

---

[1] This water, as its name implies, was supposed to be a sovereign remedy for gunshot wounds. It was also called *aqua vulneraria, aqua sclopetaria,* and *aqua catapultarum.*

handfulls; St. John's wort, long birthwort, orpine, veronica, lesser centaury, milfoil, tobacco, mouse-ear, mint, hyssop, each one handfull; wine twenty-four pounds. Having cut and bruised the herbs, pour on them the wine, and let them stand together, in digestion, in horse dung, or any other equivalent heat, for three days: afterwards distill in an alembic with a moderate fire.

'This celebrated water has for some time been held in great esteem, in contusions, for resolving coagulated blood, discussing the tumors that arise on fractures and dislocations, for preventing the progress of gangrenes, and cleansing and healing ulcers and wounds, particularly gunshot wounds . . . .'

Amongst the empyrical medicines, the following is much cried up by many people, as an infallible remedy:

'Take two ounces of the worts that grow dangling to the hinder heels of a stone horse,[1] wash them in common water, then infuse them in white wine all night, and afterwards let them be dried, and reduced to powder. The dose is half a dram twice a day, in any proper vehicle. A dram of Venice soap given twice a day, either in pills, or dissolved in some proper liquor, is likewise said to cure a Cancer.'

In the early part of the eighteenth century, the regular physicians were very ignorant. Ward[2] thus describes them, and, although his language was coarse, he was a keen observer.

'They rail mightily in their Writings against the ignorance of *Quacks* and *Mountebanks*, yet, for the sake of *Lucre*, they Licence all the Cozening Pretenders about Town, or they could not Practise;

---

[1] Now called an *entire horse*, or *stallion*.
[2] 'The London Spy,' ed. 1703, p. 124.

which shows it is by their Toleration that the People are Cheated out of their Lives and Money; and yet they think themselves so Honest, as to be no ways answerable for this Publick Injury; as if they could not kill People fast enough themselves, but must depute all the Knaves in the Town to be Death's Journeymen. Thus do they License what they ought carefully to Suppress; and Practise themselves what they Blame and Condemn in others; And that the Town may not be deceived by *Apothecaries*, they have made themselves *Medicine-Mongers*,[1] under a pretence of serving the Publick with more faithful preparations; in order to perswade the World to a belief of which, they have publish'd Bills, where, in the true *Quack's* Dialect, they tell you the Poor shall be supply'd for nothing; but whoever is so Needy as to make a Challenge of their promise empty-handed, will find, according to the *Mountebank's* saying, *No Money, No Cure*. The disposal of their Medicines they leave to a Boy's management, who scarce knows *Mercurius Dulcis* from *White Sugar*, or *Mint Water* from *Aqua Fortis*: So that People are likely to be well serv'd, or Prescriptions truly observed by such an Agent.'

If this was a faithful portrait of a physician in the commencement of the century, what must a charlatan have been? They sowed their hand-bills broadcast. Gay, in his 'Trivia,' book ii., says,

'If the pale Walker pants with weak'ning Ills,
His sickly Hand is stor'd with Friendly Bills:

[1] An allusion to the dispensary which the College of Physicians set up in the latter part of the seventeeth century, and which was the subject of Sir S. Garth's satirical poem, called ' The Dispensary.'

From hence he learns the seventh born[1] Doctor's Fame,
From hence he learns the cheapest Tailor's name.'

So universal was this practice of advertising that, to quote Ward[2] once more, when talking of the Royal Exchange, he says,

'The Wainscote was adorn'd with Quacks' Bills, instead of Pictures; never an Emperick in the Town, but had his Name in a Lacquered Frame, containing a fair Invitation for a Fool and his Money to be soon parted.'

The newspapers teemed with quack advertisements. These, of course, we have; but we also have preserved to us a quantity of the ephemeral hand-bills, which, presumably, were kept on account of the intrinsic merits they possessed. They are a curious study. There was the 'Oxford Doctor at the Fleet Prison, near Fleet Bridge, London,' who would sell ten pills in a box for sixpence, warranted a cure for the '*Scurvy, Dropsie,* and *Colt-evil,*' would provide a remedy for '*Headach, Sore Eyes, Toothach, Stomach-ach, Bleeding, Scorbutick Gums, Black, Yellow, foul Teeth, Cramp, Worms, Itch, Kibes,* and *Chilblains;* the Price of each proper Specifick, Twopence. Teeth or stumps of Teeth, Drawn with Ease and Safety, Let Blood neatly, Issues or Setons Curiously made; *For Two Pence each, and welcome.* By the Doctor that puts forth this paper, you may be Taught Writing, Arithmetick, Latin, Greek, and Hebrew, at reasonable Rates by the great, *Or Two Pence each of them by the Week.*' Presumably, as he does not advertise it, he

---

[1] A seventh son of a seventh son is supposed to be endowed with extraordinary faculties of healing, and many of these quacks pretended to such a descent.

[2] 'The London Spy,' ed. 1703, p. 64.

could not teach manners at the same traditional price.

There was another who sold the *Elixir Stomachum* which was sold at the various coffee-houses about town, and he complains thus: '☞ Garrowaye, the Apple-man at the Exchange, who had it of me, to sell, for five or six years, I have lately found out, is Counterfeiting it, and have removed mine from him; and what he now sells is a Counterfeit sort, and not the Right, as was formerly Sold there.'

There was a man, living in Blackfriars, who was so modest that he veiled his identity under the initials R.C., who, from two in the afternoon till night, 'will give to all People a Secret how they may utterly destroy *Buggs* without injury to their Goods, at reasonable rates; do as you are Taught, and if any be doubtful of the truth of it, they may have full satisfaction of them that have Experienced it.'

Here is a gentleman who gives a minute address. ' In *Petty France, Westminster, at a house with a black dore*, and a Red Knocker, between the Sign of the *Rose and Crown* and *Jacob's Well*, is a *German* who hath a Powder which, with the blessing of God upon it, certainly cures the Stone, &c. . . . . If any person of known Integrity will affirm that upon following their directions the cure is not perfected, they shall have their Money returned. Therefore be not unwilling to come for help, but suspend your Judgment till you have try'd, and then speak as you find.'

There is another, which may belong to the previous century—but it is so hard to tell, either by means of type or wood blocks—put forth by '*Salvator Winter,* an *Italian* of the City of *Naples*, Aged 98 years, Yet, by the Blessing of God, finds himself in health, and as strong as anyone of Fifty, as to the Sensitive part; Which first he attributes to God, and then to his *Elixir Vitæ*, which he always carries in his pocket adayes, and at Night under his pillow; And when he finds himself distemper'd, he taketh a Spoonful or two, according as need requireth.' It is needless to say that the *Elixir* was warranted to cure every evil under the sun, including such diverse maladies as catarrhs, sore eyes, hardness of hearing, toothache, sore throat, consumption, obstructions in the stomach, and worms. The net was arranged to catch every kind of fish. In fact, his business was so profitable that he had a successor, '*Salvator Winter, Junior*,' who says thus: 'My father, aged 98 years, yet enjoys his perfect health, which, next to the blessing of God, he attributes to the *Elixir Vitæ* having alway a bottle of it in his pocket, drinking a spoonful thereof four or five times a day; snuffing it very strongly up his Nostrils, and bathing his Temples; thus by prevention, he fortifies his vital Spirits.'

Nor did the sterner sex monopolise the profession of quackdom, for 'At the *Blew-Ball* in *Grays-Inn Lane*, near *Holborn Barrs*, next Door to a *Tallow-Chandler*, where you may see my Name upon a Board over the Door, *liveth* Elizabeth Maris, *the True German Gentlewoman* lately arrived.' It seems that we were much indebted to Germany for our quacks, for 'At the *Boot* and *Spatter dash*,[1] next Door but One to the *Vine Tavern*, in *Long-Acre*, near *Drury Lane*, Liveth a German D^{r.} and Surgeon, Who by the blessing of GOD on his great Pains, Travels and Experience, hath had wonderful Success in the Cure of the Diseases following,' &c. There was also ' *Cornelius à Tilbourg*, Sworn Chirurgeon in *Ordinary* to K. *Charles*

---

[1] A covering, or gaiter, to protect the legs from dirt or wet.

the II., to our late Sovereign K. *William,* as also to Her present Majesty Queen *Ann.*'

A certain *John Choke,* whose motto was ' NOTHING WITHOUT GOD,' and was ' an approved Physician; and farther, Priviledged by his Majesty,' advertised ' an Arcane which I had in *Germany,* from the Famous and most Learned *Baptista Van Helmont,* of worthy Memory (whose Daughter I Wedded), and whose Prœscripts most Physicians follow.'

Curative and magical powers seem to have extended from seventh sons of seventh sons to women —for I find an advertisement, ' At the Sign of the *Blew-Ball,* at the upper end of *Labour in vain-Street,* next *Shadwell-New-Market,* Liveth a Seventh Daughter, who learn'd her Skill by one of the ablest Physicians in *England* (her uncle was one of K. Charles's and K. James's twelve Doctors), who resolves all manner of Questions, and interprets Dreams to admiration, and hath never fail'd (with God's Blessing) what she took in hand.' Also there was a book published late in the seventeenth century, called ' The WOMAN'S PROPHECY, or the Rare and Wonderful DOCTRESS, foretelling a Thousand strange monstrous things that shall come to pass before New Year's day next, or afterwards—. She likewise undertakes to cure the most desperate Diseases of the Female Sex, as the *Glim'ring of the Gizzard,* the *Quavering of the Kidneys,* the *Wambling Trot,* &c.' A man who lived at the ' Three Compasses ' in Maiden Lane, also issued a hand bill that he would infallibly cure ' several strange diseases, which (though as yet not known to the world) he will plainly demonstrate to any Ingenious Artist to be the greatest Causes of the most common Distempers incident to the Body of Man. The Names of which take as follow: The *Strong Fives*, the *Marthambles*, the *Moon-Pall*, the *Hockogrocle*.'

Then there was a medicine which was administered to children even in my young days, 'DAFFY'S *famous* ELIXIR SALUTIS, prepared by *Katharine Daffy*. The finest now exposed to Sale, prepar'd from the best Druggs, according to Art, and the Original Receipt, which my Father, Mr. *Thomas Daffy*, late Rector of *Redmile*, in the Valley of *Belvoir*, having experienc'd the Virtues of it, imparted to his Kinsman, Mr. *Anthony Daffy*, who publish'd the same to the Benefit of the Community, and his own great Advantage. This very Original Receipt is now in my possession, left to me by my father aforesaid, under his own Hand. My own Brother, Mr. *Daniel Daffy*, formerly Apothecary in *Nottingham*, made this ELIXIR from the same Receipt, and Sold it there during his Life. Those, who know me, will believe what I Declare; and those who do not, may be convinc'd that I am no Countefeit, by the Colour, Tast, Smell, and just Operation of my ELIXIR.' This was, however, disputed by one John Harrison—and the rivals of nearly two centuries ago, remind us forcibly of the claimants to the original recipe of Bond's Marking Ink.

A man sold a useful medicine. 'A most excellent Eye Water, which cures in a very short time all Distempers relating to the Eyes, from whatever Cause soever they proceed, even tho' they have been of seven, eight, nine, or ten Years' continuance .... This excellent Water effectually takes away all Rebies or Pimples in the face, or any Part of the Body; it also dissolves any small, or new-come Wens or Bunches under the Skin, so easily that it can hardly be perceived.'

One quack blossomed forth in verse, and thus describes himself: ' *In* Cripplegate Parish, *in* Whitecross Street, *almost at the farther End, near* Old Street *(turning in by the sign of the* Black Croe, *in* Goat Alley, *straightforward down three steps, at the sign of the* Blew Ball), *liveth one of above Forty Years' Experience, who with God's Blessing performeth these cures following:*

> ' To all that please to come, he will and can
> Cure most Diseases incident to Man.
> The Leprosie, the Cholic, and the Spleen,
> And most Diseases common to be seen.
> Although not cured by Quack Doctors' proud,
> And yet their Name doth ring and range aloud,
> With Riches, and for Cures which others do,
> Which they could not perform, and this is true.
> This Doctor he performeth without doubt,
> The Ileak Passion, Scurvy, and the gout,
> Even to those the Hospitals turn out.'

Such ground as one did not cover, another did. Take, for instance, the following : ' In *Surry-Street*, in the *Strand*, at the Corner House with a White-Balcony and Blue-Flower pots, liveth a Gentlewoman, who

' Hath a most excellent Wash to beautifie the Face, which cures all Redness, Flushings, or Pimples. Takes off any Yellowness, Morpheu, Sunburn, or Spots on the Skin, and takes away Wrinckles and Driness, caused too often by Mercurial Poysonous Washes, rendring the worst of Faces fair and tender, and preserves 'em so. You may have from half a Crown to five Pound a Bottle. You may also have Night Masks, Forehead Pieces, incomparable white-pots, and Red Pomatum for the lips, which keeps them all the Year plump and smooth, and of a delicate natural colour. She has an admirable Paste to smooth and whiten the Hands, with a very good Tooth powder, which cleanses and whitens the Teeth. And a Water to wash the Mouth, which prevents the Scurvy in the Gums and cures where 'tis already come.

'You may have a Plaster and Water which takes off Hair from any part of the Body, so that it shall never come again. She has also a most excellent Secret to prevent the Hair from falling, causing it to grow where it is wanting in any part of the Head. She also shapes the Eye-brows, making them perfectly beautiful, without any pain, and raises low Foreheads as high as you please. And colours Grey or Red Hair to a lovely Brown, which never decays, changes, or smoots the Linnen. She has excellent Cosmeticks to anoint the Face after the *Small Pox*, which wears out any Scars, Marks, or Redness; and has great skill in all manner of sore Eyes.

'She has a most excellent Dyet Drink which cures the worst of Consumptions, or any Impurity of the Blood: And an Antiscorbutick spirit, which, being taken one spoonful in the Morning, and another at Night, with moderate Exercise, cures the *Scurvy*, tho' never so far gone, and all broke out in Blotches: with many other Secrets in Physick, which you may be satisfied in when you speak with her . . . She has an approved Remedy for Barrenness in Women.'

Very late in the preceding century (he died May 12, 1691), there was a most famous quack, Dr. Thomas Saffold, one of whose handbills I give as a curiosity:

> 'Dear Friends, let your Disease be what God will,
> Pray to Him for a Cure—try *Saffold's* Skill,
> Who may be such a healing Instrument
> As will Cure you to your own Heart's Content.
> His Medicines are Cheap, and truly Good,
> Being full as safe as your daily Food.
> Saffold he can do what may be done, by
> Either Physick or true Astrology :
> His Best Pills, Rare Elixirs, and Powder,
> Do each Day Praise him Lowder and Lowder.
> Dear Country-men, I pray be you so Wise,
> When Men Back-bite him, believe not their Lyes,
> But go see him and believe your own Eyes ;
> Then he will say you are Honest and Kind,
> Try before you Judge, and Speak as you Find.

'By *Thomas Saffold*, an Approved and Licensed Physician and Student in Astrology, who (through God's Mercy), to do good, still liveth at the *Black Ball* and Old *Lilly's Head*, next Door to the Feather-Shops that are within *Black-fryers* Gate-way, which is over against *Ludgate* Church, just by *Ludgate* in *London*. Of him the Poor, Sore, Sick, and Lame may have Advice for nothing, and proper Medicines for every particular Distemper, at reasonable Rates ready prepared, with plain Directions how to use them, to cure either Men, Women, or Children of any Disease or Diseases afflicting any Body, whether inward or outward, of what Name or Nature soever (if Curable); Also of this you may be sure, he hath Medicines to prevent as well as Cure.

'Lastly, He doth with great certainty and privacy: Resolve all manner of Lawful Questions, according to the Rules of Christian Astrology, and more than Twenty One Years' Experience.'

Talk of modern quacks—they are but second-rate to Saffold! His *Pillulæ Londinenses*, or London pills, were advertised that 'not only the meaner sort of all Ages and each Sex, but people of Eminence, both for their Rank in the World and their parts, have found admirable success in taking these Pills.'

This *panacea* was warranted to cure 'Gout, Dropsy, Coma, Lethargy, Caries, Apoplexy, Palsy, Convulsions, Falling Sickness, Vertigo, Madness, Catarrhs, Headache, Scald, and Sore Heads, sore Eyes, Deafness, Toothache, sore Mouth, sore and swollen Throat, foul Stomach, bad Digestion, Vomiting, Pain at the Stomach, sour Belching, Colic, Twisting of the Guts, Looseness, Worms, all Obstructions of the Pancreas, of the Mesaraic Veins, of the passages of the Chyle, and of the Liver and Spleen, the Jaundice, Cachexy, Hypochondriac Melancholy, Agues, Itch, Boils, Rheumatism, Pains and Aches, Surfeits by Eating and Hard Drinking, or by Heats and Colds (as some call them).'

Then there comes a charming bit of candour almost sufficient to disarm the unwary: 'They are also good in taking the Waters. I would not advise them by any means in the Bloody Flux, nor in continual Fevers, but they are good to purge after either of those Diseases is over, or to carry off the Humor aforehand. They must also be foreborn by Women with Child. Otherwise they are good for any Constitution, and in any Clime. They are Durable many years, and good at Sea as well as on Land.'

Thomas Saffold knew well the value of advertising, and scattered his very varied handbills broadcast. Presumably, like modern quacks, he made money.

Of course he died, and his epitaph is as follows (he originally was a weaver):

> 'Here lies the Corpse of Thomas Saffold,
> By Death, in spite of Physick, baffled;
> Who, leaving off his working loom,
> Did learned doctor soon become.
> To poetry he made pretence,
> Too plain to any man's own sense;
> But he when living thought it sin
> To hide his talent in napkin;
> Now Death does Doctor (poet) crowd
> Within the limits of a shroud.'

There was a harmless remedy advertised, even though it was a fraud—and this was the loan, or sale, of necklaces to be worn by children in teething.

THE FAMOUS AND VIRTUOUS NECKLACES.

'One of them being of no greater weight than a small *Nutmeg*, absolutely easing Children in Breeding Teeth without *Pain;* thereby preventing *Feavers, Ruptures, Convulsions, Rickets,* and such attendant Distempers, to the Admiration of thousands of the City of *London*, and Counties adjoining, who have experienced the same, to their great comfort and satisfaction of the Parents of the Children who have used them. Besides the Decrease in the *Bills of Mortality*, apparent (within this Year and a half) of above one half of what formerly Dyed; and are now Exposed to sale for the Publick good, at *five shillings* each *Necklace*, &c.'

Then there was a far higher-priced necklace, but, as it also operated on adults, it was perhaps stronger and more efficacious. 'A necklace that cures all sorts or fits in children, occasioned by Teeth or any other Cause; as also Fits in Men and Women. To be had at Mr. Larance's in Somerset Court, near Northumberland House in the Strand; price ten shillings for eight days, though the cure will be performed immediately.' And there was the famous '*Anodyne Necklace.*'

In the preceding century there were some famous quacks, notably Sir Kenelm Digby, who, with his sympathetic powder, worked wonders, especially one instance, an account of which he read to a learned society at Montpellier. He recounted how a certain learned gentleman, named Howell, found two of his friends engaged in a duel with swords, how he rushed to part them, and catching hold of one of their blades, his hand was severely cut, the other antagonist cutting him severely on the back of his hand. Seeing the mischief they had done, they bound up his hand with his garter, and took him home. Mr. Howell was of such note that the King sent his own physician to him, but without avail; and there was expectation that the hand would mortify and have to be amputated. Here Sir Kenelm, who knew him, stepped in, and, being applied to by his friend to try his remedies, consented. Let him tell his own tale.

'I asked him then for anything that had blood upon it; so he presently sent for his garter, wherewith his hand was first bound, and as I called for a basin of water, as if I would wash my hands, I took a handful of powder of vitriol, which I had in my study, and presently dissolved it. As soon as the bloody garter was brought me, I put it in the basin, observing, in the interim, what Mr. Howell did, who stood talking with a gentleman in a corner of my chamber, not regarding at all what I was doing. He started suddenly, as if he had found some strange alteration in himself. I asked him what he ailed.

'" I know not what ails me; but I feel no more pain. Methinks that a pleasing kind of freshness, as it were a wet cold napkin, did spread over my hand, which hath taken away the inflammation that tormented me before."

'I replied, " Since, then, you feel already so much good of my medicament, I advise you to cast away all your plasters; only keep the wound clean, and in a moderate temper, betwixt heat and cold."

' This was presently reported to the Duke of Buckingham, and, a little after, to the King, who were both very curious to know the circumstances of the business; which was, that after dinner, I took the garter out of the water, and put it to dry before a great fire. It was scarce dry before Mr. Howell's servant came running, and saying that his master felt as much burning as ever he had done, if not more; for the heat was such as if his hand were betwixt coals of fire. I answered that although that had happened at present, yet he should find ease in a short time; for I knew the reason of this new accident, and would provide accordingly; for his master should be free from that inflammation, it might be, before he could possibly return to him; but, in case he found no ease, I wished him to come presently back again; if not, he might forbear coming. Thereupon he went; and, at the instant, I did put the garter again into the water; thereupon he found his master without any pain at all. To be brief, there was no sense of pain afterwards; but within five or six days the wounds were cicatrized, and entirely healed.'

Faith worked wonders, and a credulous imagination formed an excellent foundation for healing. Take another instance in the same century—the case of Valentine Greatraks (who cured by the imposition of hands), who was nearly contemporary with Sir Kenelm. It would serve no good purpose to go minutely into his history: suffice it to say that he was an Irishman of good family, and, as a young man, served under Cromwell. After the disbandment of the army he was made Clerk of the Peace for the County of Cork, Registrar for Transplantation (ejection of Papists who would not go to church) and Justice of the Peace, so that we see he occupied a respectable position in society.

After Greatraks settled down in his civil capacity, he seems to have been a blameless member of society; but his religious convictions were extremely rabid, and strong on the Protestant side. Writing in 1668, he says: 'About four years since I had an Impulse, or a strange perswasion, in my own mind (of which I am not able to give any rational account to another) which did very frequently suggest to me that there was bestowed on me the gift of curing the King's Evil: which, for the extraordinariness of it, I thought fit to conceal for some time, but at length I communicated this to my Wife, and told her, That I did verily believe that God had given me the blessing of curing the King's Evil; for, whether I were in private or publick, sleeping or waking, still I had the same Impulse; but her reply was to me, That she conceived this was a strange imagination: but, to prove the contrary, a few daies after there was one *William Maher* of *Salterbridge*, in the Parish of *Lissmore*, that brought his Son *William Maher* to my house, desiring my Wife to cure him, who was a person ready to afford her Charity to her Neighbours, according to her small skill in Chirurgery; on which my Wife told me there was one that had the King's Evil very grievously in the Eyes, Cheek, and Throat; whereupon I told her that she should now see whether this were a bare fancy, or imagination, as she thought it, or the Dictates of God's Spirit on my heart; and thereupon I laid my hands on the places affected, and prayed to God for Jesus' sake to heal him, and then I bid the Parent two or three days afterwards to bring the Child to me again, which accordingly he did, and then I saw the Eye was almost quite whole, and the Node, which was almost as big as a Pullet's Egg, was suppurated, and the throat strangely amended, and, to be brief (to God's glory I speak it), within a month discharged itself quite, and was perfectly healed, and so continues, God be praised.'

This may be taken as a sample of his cures, albeit his first; and, although he excited the enmity of the licensed medical profession, he seems to have cured the Countess of Conway of an inveterate head-ache, which greatly enhanced his reputation. He died no one knows when, but some time early in the century.

And in our time, too, have been the quacks, the Zouave Jacob and Dr. Newton, who pretended to have the miraculous gift of healing by the imposition of hands, so that we can scarcely wonder that, in an age when the dissemination of accurate and scientific knowledge as the present is (imperfect though it be), a man like Valentine Greatraks was believed in as of almost divine authority at the period at which he lived. But it is a very curious thing that some men either imagine that they have, or feign to have a miraculous gift of healing. Witness in our own day the 'Peculiar People,' who base their peculiar gift of healing on a text from the Epistle of St. James, chap. 5, v. 14—'Is any sick among you? let him call upon the elders of the Church; and let them pray over him, anointing him with oil in the name of the Lord.'

So also the *Catholic and Apostolic Church* (Irvingites) teach this practice as a dogma, vide their catechism,[1] 'What are the benefits to be derived from this rite?' 'St. James teaches us again that the prayer of faith shall save the sick, and the Lord shall raise him up; and, if he have committed sins, they shall be forgiven him.' After this, who can say that the age of faith is passed away?

With them, also, is a great function for the benediction of oil for anointing the sick; the rubric for which is as follows:[2] 'In the Celebration of the Holy Eucharist on a Week-day, immediately before the elements are brought up and placed on the Altar, the Elder or Elders present shall bring the vessel containing the oil to the Angel, who shall present it uncovered upon the Altar; and then kneeling down at the Altar, and the Elders kneeling down at the access to the Sanctuary, the Angel shall say this PRAYER OF BENEDICTION.'

Here follows a not very long prayer, in which the Almighty is intreated to impart to the oil the virtue which is dogmatically asserted that it possesses, in the catechism. The rubric then continues, 'The oil which has been blessed shall remain on the Altar until

[1] 'The Liturgy and other Divine Offices of the Church.' London, Bosworth, 1880, p. 638.
[2] 'The Liturgy and other Divine Offices of the Church,' p. 584.

after the Service, and shall then be delivered by the Angel to the senior Elder, that it may be reverently carried to the Sacristy, and there deposited in the proper place by the Angel.'

In the 'Order for anointing the Sick' (p. 602), the rubric says: 'This rite shall be administered only to such as have, in time past, received the Holy Communion, or to whom it is intended presently to administer the Communion; also, only in such cases of sickness as are of a serious or dangerous character. In order to the receiving of the rite, opportunity should, if possible, be previously given to the sick person to make confession of his sins.

'A table should be provided in the sick person's room, with a clean cloth thereon, upon which may be placed the vessel of holy oil .... The Elder in charge shall be accompanied, when possible, by the other Elders, the Pastor, and the Deacon.'

A somewhat lengthy service follows, and in the middle is this rubric: 'Then the Elders present shall anoint the sick person with the oil on the head or forehead, and, if the sick person request it, also on any part affected.' And it winds up with the subjoined direction, 'All the holy oil that shall remain after the anointing shall be forthwith consumed by Fire.'

I had intended to confine my subject entirely to English quacks, but the name of Mesmer is so allied to quackery in England that I must needs refer to him. He was born at Merseburg in Germany on May 23, 1733, and died at the same place March 5, 1815. He studied medicine, and took a doctor's degree in 1766. He started his extraordinary theory in 1772 by publishing a tract entitled, ' *De Planetarium*

Influxu,' in which he upheld that tides exist in the air as in the sea, and were similarly produced. He maintained that the sun and the moon acted upon an etherial fluid which penetrated everything, and this force he termed *Animal Magnetism*. But there is every reason to believe that he was indebted for his discovery to a Jesuit father named Hel, who was professor of astronomy at Vienna. Hel used peculiarly made steel plates, which he applied to different portions of his patient's body. Hel and Mesmer subsequently quarrelling about the prior discovery of each, the latter discontinued the use of the plates, and substituted his fingers. Then he found it was unnecessary to touch his patient, but that the same magnetic influence could be induced by waving his hands, and making what are called *mesmeric passes* at a distance.

But the Viennese are a practical race, and his failures to cure, notably in one case, that of Mademoiselle Paradis (a singer), who was blind, caused charges of deceit to be brought against him, and he was told to leave Vienna at a day's notice. He obeyed, and went to Paris, where he set up a superb establishment, fitted up most luxuriously. The novelty-loving Parisians soon visited him, and here, in a dimly lit room, with pseudo-scientific apparatus to excite the imagination, and a great deal of corporal manipulation, tending to the same purpose, to the accompaniment of soft music or singing, hysterical women went into convulsive fits, and laughed, sobbed, and shrieked, according to their different temperaments.

Having reached this stage, Mesmer made his appearance, clad in a gold embroidered robe of violet silk, holding in his hand a magnetic rod of wondrous power. With slow and solemn steps he approached his patients, and the exceeding gravity of his deportment, added to their ignorance of what might be coming next, generally calmed and subdued those who were not insensible. Those who had lost their senses he awoke by stroking them, and tracing figures upon their bodies with his magnetic wand, and, on their recovery, they used to testify to the great good his treatment had done them.

A commission of scientific and medical men sat to make inquiry into 'Animal Magnetism,' and they reported adversely. He then endeavoured to get a pecuniary recognition of his services from the French Government, but this being declined, he retired to Spa, where, the bubble having been pricked, he lived for some time in comparative obscurity.

Mesmerism was introduced into England in the year 1788, by a Dr. De Mainauduc, who, on his arrival at Bristol, delivered lectures on 'Animal Magnetism'; and, as his somewhat cautious biographer, Dr. George Winter, observes, he 'was reported to have cured diseased persons, *even* without the aid of medicines, and of his having the power of treating and curing diseased persons at a distance.' He found many dupes, for the said authority remarks, 'On looking over the lists of Students that had been, or then were under the Doctor's tuition, it appeared that there was 1 Duke—1 Duchess—1 Marchioness—2 Countesses—1 Earl—1 Lord—3 Ladies—1 Bishop—5 Right Honourable Gentlemen and Ladies—2 Baronets—7 Members of Parliament—1 Clergyman—2 Physicians—7 Surgeons—exclusive of 92 Gentlemen and Ladies of respectability, in the whole 127.

'Naturally fond of study, and my thirst after knowledge being insatiable, I also was allured to do myself the honour of adding my name to the list; and to investigate this very extraordinary Science: and, according to the general terms, I paid 25 Guineas to the Doctor, and 5 Guineas for the use of the Room ; I also signed a bond for £10,000, and took an affidavit that I would not discover the secrets of the Science *during the Doctor's natural life.*'

So we see that this wonderful power had a market value of no mean consideration, and, indeed, an anonymous authority, who wrote on 'Animal Magnetism,' states that Dr. Mainauduc realised £100,000. So lucrative was its practice, that many pretenders sprung up, notable one Holloway who gave lectures at the rate of five guineas the course, besides Miss Prescott, Mrs. Pratt, Monsieur de Loutherbourg the painter, Mr. Parker, and Dr. Yeldal; but the chief of these quacks was Dr. Loutherbourg, who was assisted in his operations by his wife. A book about his wonderful cures was written by one of his believers, Mary Pratt, 'A lover of the Lamb of God,' in which he is described as ' A Gentleman of superior abilities, well known in the scientific and polite Assemblies for his brilliancy of talents as a Philosopher, and Painter : this Gentleman is no other than Mr. De Loutherbourg, who with his Lady, Mrs. De Loutherbourg, have been made by the Almighty power of the Lord Jehovah, proper Recipients to receive divine Manuductions, which heavenly and divine Influx coming from the Radix *God*, his divine Majesty has most graciously condescended to bestow on them (*his blessing*) to diffuse healing to *all* who have faith in the Lord as mediator, be they Deaf, Dumb, Lame, Halt, or Blind.'

That thousands flocked to these charlatans is undoubted, for Dr. George Winter (above quoted) says, 'It was credibly reported that 3,000 persons have attended at one time, to get admission at Mr. Loutherbourg's, at Hammersmith; and that some persons sold their tickets for from One, to Three Guineas each.' And this is corroborated by crazy Mary Pratt. 'Report says three Thousand People have waited for Tickets at a time. For my own part, the Croud was so immense that I could with difficulty gain the Door on Healing Days, and I suppose, upon conviction, Report spoke Truth.' De Loutherbourg charged nothing for his cures, and Mary Pratt is extremely scandalized at those who, having received a ticket gratis, sold them from two to five guineas.

Many cases are given in her book of the cures effected by this benevolent couple; how the blind were made to see, the deaf to hear, the lame to walk, or the dumb to speak—nay, could even cast out devils—as the following testimonial will show.

'The second case I shall mention is that of a woman possessed with Evil Spirits, her name Pennier, lives at No. 33 Ogle Street, Mary-le-bone, near Portland-Chapel; her husband lives with the French Ambassador: her case was too terrific to describe; her eyes and mouth distorted, she was like a Lunatic in every sense of the word; she used to say that it was not her voice that spoke, but the devil in her. In short, her case was most truly distressing, not only to her family, but the neighbourhood; she used to invite people in with apparent civility, then bite them, and scratch like a cat; nay, she would beg a pin of women, and then scratch them with it, &c., &c., &c.'

'Mrs. De Loutherbourg, a lady of most exquisite

sensibility and tenderness, administered to this Mrs. Pennier; she daily amended, and is now in her right mind, praising God, who has through his servant performed such an amazing cure, to the astonishment of hundreds who saw her and heard her.'

Mrs. De Lutherbourg's system of cure was extremely simple, as this example will show: 'Mrs. Hook, Stable Yard, St. James's, has two daughters, born Deaf and Dumb. She waited on the Lady above mentioned, who looked on them with an eye of benignity, and healed them. (I heard both of them speak.)'

Her husband's plan was rather more clumsy. He imposed hands. 'A News-Carrier at Chelsea cured of an Abscess in his Side. Mr. De Loutherbourg held his hand on the Abscess half a minute, and it broke immediately.'

Perhaps these cures were not permanent, for ' Mr. De Loutherbourg told me he had cured by the blessing of God, two Thousand since Christmas. But, as our Lord said, of the ten healed, one only returned to thank him; so many hundreds have acted, that have never returned to Mr. De Loutherbourg.'

One of the most impudent of these quacks was named Benjamin Douglas Perkins, whose father claimed to be the inventor of the metallic tractors, which were rods made either of a combination of copper, zinc, and gold, or of iron, silver, and platinum, and he explains, in the specification to his patent, that 'the point of the instrument thus formed, I apply to those parts of the body which are affected with diseases, and draw them off on the skin, to a distance from the complaint, and usually towards the extremities.'

He charged the moderate sum of five guineas a set for these precious instruments, and made a good thing out of them. He was a member of the Society of Friends, and, as a proof that his charlatanism was believed in, this benevolent society subscribed largely, and built for him the *Perkinean Institution*, an hospital where the poor could be treated on his system, free of cost.

He was an adept in the art of puffing, and his 'Testimonials' are quite equal to those of modern times. I will only cite two. ' My little infant child was *scalded* with hot tea on the forehead, about three and a half inches in length, and three-fourths of an inch in breadth, which raised a vesicle before I had time to apply anything to it. The *Tractors* were solely used, and the whole redness disappeared. The Blister broke, &c.'

' A lady fell from her horse, and *dislocated* her ancle, which remained several hours before it was reduced, by which it became very much *swelled, inflamed*, and *painful*. Two or three applications of the *Tractor* relieved the pain, and in a day or two she walked the house, and had no further complaint.'

Then also was Dominicetti, who, in 1765, established a house in Cheyne Walk, Chelsea, for medicated baths, but he hardly belongs to the magnetisers. Then there was Katterfelto, but he, too, hovers on the borderland of quackism—vide the following one of hundreds of advertisements.[1]

' By particular Desire of many of the First Nobility.
  This PRESENT EVENING and TO-MORROW,
  At late Cox's MUSEUM, Spring Gardens,
  A SON of the late Colonel KATTERFELTO of the

[1] *General Advertiser*, March 26, 1782.

Death's Head Hussars, belonging to the King of Prussia, is to exhibit the same variety of Performances as he did exhibit on Wednesday the 13th of March, before many Foreign Ministers, with great applause.

Mr. Katterfelto

Has had the honour in his travels to exhibit before the Empress of Russia, the Queen of Hungary, the Kings of Prussia, Sweden, Denmark, and Poland.

Mr. Katterfelto's

Lectures are Philosophical, Mathematical, Optical, Magnetical, Electrical, Physical, Chymical, Pneumatic, Hydraulic, Hydrostatic, Styangraphic, Palenchic, and Caprimantic Art.

Mr. Katterfelto

Will deliver a different Lecture every night in the week, and show various uncommon experiments, and his apparatus are very numerous, and elegantly finished: all are on the newest construction, many of which are not to be equalled in Europe.

Mr. Katterfelto

Will, after his Philosophical Lecture, discover various arts by which many persons lose their fortunes by Dice, Cards, Billiards, and E.O. Tables, &c.'

He was a charlatan *pur et simple*, and to his other attractions he added a performing black cat,[1] ' but Colonel Katterfelto is very sorry that many persons will have it that he and his famous BLACK CAT were DEVILS but such suspicion only arises through his various wonderful and uncommon performances: he only professes to be a moral and divine Philosopher, and he says, that all persons on earth live in darkness,

[1] *General Advertiser*, May 1, 1783.

if they are able, but won't see that most enterprizing extraordinary, astonishing, wonderful, and uncommon exhibition on the Solar Microscope. He will this day, and every day this week, show, from eight in the morning till five in the afternoon, his various new Occult Secrets, which have surprized the King and the whole Royal Family: and his evening lecture begins this, and every night, precisely at eight o'clock; but no person will be admitted after eight; and after his lecture he will exhibit many new deceptions. His Black Cat will also make her appearance this evening at No. 24, Piccadilly. His exhibition of the Solar Microscope has caused him lately very grand houses; also his wonderful Black Cat at night; many thousands could not receive admission lately for want of room, and Katterfelto expects to clear at least above £30,000, in a year's time, through his Solar Microscope and surprizing Black Cat.'

He also invented a sort of lucifer-match.[1] 'Dr. Katterfelto will also, for 2/6d. sell such a quantity of his new invented *Alarum*, which is better than £20 worth of Phosphorus matches, and is better in a house or ship than £20,000, as many lives may be saved by it, and is more useful to the Nation than 30,000 Air Balloons. It will light 900 candles, pistols or cannons, and never misses. He also sells the very best Solid, Liquid, and Powder Phosphorus, Phosphorus Matches, Diamond Beetles, &c.' Katterfelto died at Bedale, in Yorkshire, 25th of November, 1799.

There also lived Dr. Graham, who was not heard of before 1780, and he was an arch quack. About that year he took a mansion in the Royal Terrace, Adelphi, which he fitted up sumptuously. It was

[1] *General Advertiser*, February 13, 1784.

inscribed 'Templum Æsculapio Sacrum,' and was called both the 'Temple of Health,' and the 'Hymeneal Temple' Here, in air heavy with incense, he lectured on electricity and magnetism. He was a past master in the art of puffing, and published several books in glorification of himself. In one, called 'MEDICAL TRANSACTIONS at the Temple of Health in London, in the course of the years 1781 & 1782,' he gives a wonderful list of cures worked by his 'Electrical Æther, Nervous Æthereal Balsam, Imperial Pills, Liquid Amber, British Pills,' and his 'Bracing, or Restorative Balsam,' which, in order to bring within the reach of ordinary people, he kindly consented to sell at half-price, namely, 'that the bottles marked, and formerly sold at one guinea, may *now* be had at only half-a-guinea; the half-guinea bottles at five shillings and threepence; the five shilling at half-a-crown, and the two-and-sixpenny vials at *only one shilling and threepence.*'

In this book, too, are some choice specimens of poetry, all laudatory of Dr. Graham, one of which is worth repeating, as a specimen—

'*An* ACROSTIC, *by a* LADY.

D EIGN to accept the tribute which I owe,
O ne grateful, joyful tear, permit to flow;
C an I be silent when good health is given?
T hat first—that best—that richest gift of heaven!
O Muse! descend, in most exalted lays,
R eplete with softest notes, attune his praise.

G en'rous by nature, matchless in thy skill!
R ich in the God-like art—to ease—to heal;
A ll bless thy gifts! the sick—the lame—the blind,
H ail thee with rapture for the cure they find!
A rm'd by the DEITY with power divine,
M ortals revere HIS attributes in thine.'

In this temple of 'Health and Hymen' he had a wonderful 'Celestial Bed,' which he pretended cost sixty thousand pounds. He guaranteed that the sleepers therein, although hitherto childless, should become prolific; but it was somewhat costly, for the fee for its use for a single night was one hundred pounds. Still, he had some magneto-electric beds, which, probably, were as efficacious, at a lower rate, only fifty pounds nightly. The title-page of a pamphlet on his establishment is noteworthy.

'Il Convito Amoroso,
Or a Serio—comico—philosophical
Lecture
on the
Causes, Nature, and Effects of Love and Beauty,
At the Different Periods of Human Life, in Persons, and Personages, Male, Female, and Demi-Charactêre;
And in Praise of the Genial and Prolific Influences of the
Celestial Bed!
As Delivered by Hebe Vestina,
The Rosy Goddess of Youth and of Health!
from the
Electrical Throne! in the Great Apollo-Chamber,
At the Temple of Hymen, in London,
Before a glowing and brilliant Audience of near Three Hundred Ladies and Gentlemen, who were commanded by Venus, Cupid, and Hymen! to assist, in joyous Assembly, at the Grand Feast of very Fat Things, which was held at their Temple, on Monday Evening, the 25th of November, 1782; but which was interrupted by the rude and unexpected Arrival of his Worship Midas Neutersex, Esq$^{re.}$ . . . . just as the Dessert was about to be served up.

Published at the earnest Desire of many of the Company, and to gratify the impatient and very intense longings of Thousands of Adepts, Hibernian and British;—of the Cognoscenti;—et de les Amateur ardens des *delices exquise* de Venus!

To which is subjoined, a description of the Stupendous Nature and Effects of the Celebrated
CELESTIAL BED!'

The ' VESTINA, or Goddess of Health,' was no mean person. She began life as a domestic servant, and was named Emma Lyons. She was a good-looking, florid, buxom wench, and, after having played her part as priestess at the 'Temple of Health and Hymen,' became the wife of the dilletante Sir William Hamilton, English Minister at Naples, and was afterwards notorious for her connection with Lord Nelson.

Graham wrote in 1790, ' A short Treatise on the All cleansing—all healing—and all invigorating Qualities of the SIMPLE EARTH, when long and repeatedly applied to the naked Human Body and Lungs, for the safe, speedy, and radical Cure of all Diseases, internal as well as external, which are, in their Nature or Stage, susceptible of being cured;— for the preservation of the Health, Vigour, Bloom, and Beauty of Body and of Mind; for rejuvenating the aged and decaying Human Body;—and for prolonging Life to the very longest possible Period, &c.'

For the benefit of those who would try the doctor's earth-cure, I extract the following: ' I generally, or always, prefer the sides or tops of hills or mountains, as the air and the earth are the more pure and salubrious; but the air and earth of ordinary pasture or corn-fields, especially those that are called upland, and even good clean garden-ground, or the higher commons, especially fallow corn-fields, are all salutary and good.

'As to the colour and nature of the earth or soil, I prefer a good brown or reddish blooming mould, and light, sandy, crumbly, mellow and marrowy earth; or that which feels when I am in it, and crumbling with my hands and fingers, like bits of marrow among fine Flour; and that which has a strong, sweet, earthly smell——'

So that my readers now know exactly what to do.

He had a fairly comprehensive idea of modern hygiene, as will be seen from the following extract from 'General Instructions to the persons who consult Dr. Graham as a Physician':

'It will be unreasonable for Dr. Graham's Patients to expect a complete and a lasting cure, or even great alleviation of their peculiar maladies, unless they keep the body and limbs most perfectly clean with very frequent washings,—breathe fresh, open air day and night,—be simple in the quality and moderate in the quantity of their food and drink,—and totally give up using the deadly poisons and weakeners of both body and soul, and the cankerworm of estates called foreign Tea and Coffee, Red Port Wine, Spirituous Liquors, Tobacco and Snuff, gaming and late hours, and all sinful, unnatural, and excessive indulgence of the animal appetites, and of the diabolical and degrading mental passions. On practising the above rules—on a widely open window day and night—and on washing with cold water, and going to bed every night by eight or nine, and rising by four or five, depends the very perfection of bodily and mental health, strength and happiness.'

He wrote many pamphlets, some of them on religious matters, and the fools who patronised him paid him large fees; yet his expenses were very heavy, and his manner of living luxurious, so that we experience but little wonder when we find the 'Temple of Health' sold up, and that Graham himself died poor—either in, or near, Glasgow.

Early in the century there were (in surgery) two noted quacks, namely, Dr. (afterwards Sir William) Read, and Roger, or, as he called himself, Doctor, Grant—both oculists. Read originally was a tailor, and Grant had been a tinker and Anabaptist preacher. The list of cures of both are marvellous—Grant even advertising in the *Daily Courant*, of July 20, 1709, that he had cured, in five minutes, a young man that had been born blind. But at that time, when people believed in their sovereign being able to cure scrofula by touching the patient with a gold coin, a little faith went a long way.

But quackery was not confined to the masculine gender—the ladies competed with them in the field. Notably Mrs. Map, the bone-setter of Epsom, of whom Mr. Pulteney writes so amusingly to Swift on December 21, 1736: 'I must tell you a ridiculous incident; perhaps you have not heard it. One Mrs. Mapp, a famous she bone-setter and mountebank, coming to town with a coach and six horses, on the Kentish road, was met by a rabble of people, who, seeing her very oddly and tawdrily dressed, took her for a foreigner, and concluded she must be a certain great person's mistress. Upon this they followed the coach, bawling out, "No Hanover w——! No Hanover w——!" The lady within the coach was much offended, let down the glass, and screamed louder than any of them, "She was no Hanover w——! she was an English one!" Upon which they cried out, "God bless your ladyship!" quitted the pursuit, and wished her a good journey.'

This woman sprang into notoriety all at once. The first authentic account of her is on page 457 of the *London Magazine* for 1836, under the date of August 2 : 'The Town has been surprized lately with the fame of a young woman at *Epsom*, who, tho' not very regular, it is said, in her Conduct, has wrought such Cures that seem miraculous in the Bone-setting way. The Concourse of People to *Epsom* on this occasion is incredible, and 'tis reckon'd she gets near 20 Guineas a Day, she executing what she does in a very quick Manner: She has strength enough to put in any Man's Shoulder without any assistance; and this her strength makes the following Story the more credible. A Man came to her, sent, as 'tis supposed, by some Surgeons, on purpose to try her Skill, with his Hand bound up, and pretended his Wrist was put out, which upon Examination she found to be false; but, to be even with him for his Imposition, she gave it a Wrench, and really put it out, and bad him *go to the Fools who sent him, and get it set again*, or, if he would come to her that day month, she would do it herself.

'This remarkable person is Daughter to one *Wallin*, a Bone-setter of *Hindon*, *Wilts*. Upon some family Quarrel, she left her Father, and Wander'd up and down the Country in a very miserable Manner, calling herself *Crazy Salley*. Since she became thus famous, she married one Mr. *Hill Mapp*, late servant to a Mercer on *Ludgate Hill*, who, 'tis said, soon left her, and carried off £100 of her Money.'

She was not long making her way in the world, for we read in the same magazine, under date, September 19, 1736: 'Mrs. *Mapp*, the famous Bone-setter at *Epsom*, continues making extraordinary Cures. She has now set up an Equipage, and this Day came to *Kensington* and waited on her Majesty.'

The *Gentleman's Magazine*, under date of August 31, 1736, gives a similar account of her private life, adding that her husband did not stay with her above a fortnight, but adds that she was wonderfully clever in her calling, having 'cured Persons who have been above 20 years disabled, and has given incredible Relief in most difficult cases.'

'Mrs. *Mapp* the Bone-setter, with Dr. Taylor the Oculist, being present at the Playhouse in *Lincoln's Inns Fields*, to see a Comedy call'd the Husband's Relief, with the Female Bone-setter, and Worm Doctor; it occasioned a full House, and the following

Epigram.

'While *Mapp* to th' Actors shew'd a kind regard,
On one side *Taylor* sat, on t'other *Ward*:
When their mock Persons of the Drama came,
Both *Ward* and *Taylor* thought it hurt their *fame*;
Wonder'd how *Mapp* cou'd in good Humour be—
Zoons, crys the Manly Dame, it hurts not *me*;
Quacks without Arts may either blind or kill,
But *Demonstration* shews that mine is *Skill*.

And the following was sung upon y[e] Stage:

You Surgeons of *London* who puzzle your Pates,
To ride in your Coaches, and purchase Estates,
Give over, for Shame, for your Pride has a Fall,
And y[e] Doctress of *Epsom* has outdone you all.

> What signifies Learning, or going to school,
> When a Woman can do without Reason or Rule,
> What puts you to Non-plus, and baffles your Art,
> For Petticoat-Practice has now got the Start.
>
> In Physick, as well as in Fashions, we find
> The newest has always its Run with Mankind;
> Forgot is the bustle 'bout Taylor and Ward,
> Now *Mapp's* all ye Cry, and her Fame's on Record.
>
> Dame Nature has giv'n her a Doctor's Degree,
> She gets all ye Patients, and pockets the Fee;
> So if you don't instantly prove her a Cheat,
> She'll loll in her Chariot while you walk ye Street.'[1]

At this time she was at her acme—but if an anonymous writer in the *Cornhill Magazine* for March, 1873, p. 82, is to be believed, she died December, 1837, 'at her lodgings near Seven Dials, so miserably poor, that the parish was obliged to bury her.'

In No. 572 of the *Spectator*, July 26, 1714,[2] is a very amusing article on the quacks of Queen Anne's time: 'There is scarce a city in Great Britain but has one of this tribe, who takes it into his protection, and on the market-day harangues the good people of the place with aphorisms and receipts. You may depend upon it he comes not there for his own private interest, but out of a particular affection to the town. I remember one of these public-spirited artists at Hammersmith, who told his audience that he had been born and bred there, and that, having a special regard for the place of his nativity, he was determined to make a present of five shillings to as many as would accept of it. The whole crowd stood agape

---

[1] *Gentleman's Magazine*, 1736, pp. 617–618.
[2] By Dr. Zachary Pearce, Bishop of Rochester.

and ready to take the doctor at his word; when, putting his hand into a long bag, as everyone was expecting his crown piece, he drew out a handful of little packets, each of which, he informed the spectators, was constantly sold at five shillings and sixpence, but that he would bate the odd five shillings to every inhabitant of that place; the whole assembly immediately closed with this generous offer, and took off all his physick, after the doctor had made them vouch for one another, that there were no foreigners among them, but that they were all Hammersmith men.

'There is another branch of pretenders to this art, who, without either horse or pickle herring,[1] lie snug in a garret, and send down notice to the world of their extraordinary parts and abilities by printed bills and advertisements. These seem to have derived their custom from an eastern nation which Herodotus speaks of, among whom it was a law that whenever any cure was to be performed, both the method of the cure, and an account of the distemper, should be fixed in some public place; but, as customs will corrupt, these, our moderns, provide themselves with persons to attest the cure before they publish or make an experiment of the prescription. I have heard of a porter, who serves as a Knight of the post[2] under one of these operators, and, though he was never sick in his life, has been cured of all the diseases in the Dispensary. These are the men whose sagacity has invented elixirs of all sorts, pills and lozenges, and

---

[1] A pickle herring was a Merry-Andrew or clown, and this means that the quack was too poor to afford either horse or attendant.

[2] A false witness—one who would swear to anything for a trifle.

take it as an affront if you come to them before you have been given over by everybody else. Their medicines are infallible, and never fail of success; that is, of enriching the doctor, and setting the patient effectually at rest.

'I lately dropt into a coffee-house at Westminster, where I found the room hung round with ornaments of this nature. There were Elixirs, Tinctures, the Anodyne Fotus, English Pills, Electuaries, and, in short, more remedies than I believe there are diseases. At the sight of so many inventions, I could not but imagine myself in a kind of arsenal or magazine, where a store of arms was deposited against any sudden invasion. Should you be attacked by the enemy sideways, here was an infallible piece of defensive armour to cure the pleurisy; should a distemper beat up your head-quarters, here you might purchase an impenetrable helmet, or, in the language of the artist, a cephalic tincture; if your main body be assaulted, here are various kinds of armour in case of various onsets. I began to congratulate the present age upon the happiness man might reasonably hope for in life, when death was thus in a manner defeated, and when pain itself would be of so short a duration, that it would just serve to enhance the value of pleasure.

'While I was in these thoughts, I unluckily called to mind a story of an ingenious gentleman of the last age, who, lying violently afflicted with the gout, a person came and offered his services to cure him by a method which, he assured him, was infallible; the servant who received the message carried it up to his master, who, inquiring whether the person came on foot or in a chariot, and being informed that he was on foot: "Go," says he, "send the knave about his business; was his method infallible as he pretends, he would, long before now, have been in his coach and six." In like manner I concluded that, had all these advertisers arrived to that skill they pretend to, they would have no need, for so many years successively, to publish to the world the place of their abode, and the virtues of their medicines. One of these gentlemen, indeed, pretends to an effectual cure for leanness: what effects it may have had upon those who have tried it, I cannot tell; but I am credibly informed that the call for it has been so great, that it has effectually cured the doctor himself of that distemper. Could each of them produce so good an instance of the success of his medicines, they might soon persuade the world into an opinion of them.

'I observe that most of the bills agree in one expression, viz., that, "with God's blessing," they perform such and such cures: this expression is certainly very proper and emphatical, for that is all they have for it. And, if ever a cure is performed on a patient where they are concerned, they can claim a greater share than Virgils IAPIS in the curing of ÆNEAS; he tried his skill, was very assiduous about the wound, and, indeed, was the only visible means that relieved the hero, but the poet assures us it was the particular assistance of a deity that speeded the whole operation.'

There was another female quack in 1738, one Mrs. Stephens, and in the *Gentleman's Magazine* for that year, p. 218, we read that 'Mrs. *Stephens* has proposed to make her Medicines for the Stone publick, on Consideration of the sum of £5,000 to be rais'd by

Contribution, and lodged with Mr. *Drummond, Banker.* He has receiv'd since the 11th of this month (April) about £500 on that Account.' She advertised her cures very fully, and she obtained and acknowledged, as subscriptions from April 11 to the end of December, 1738, the receipt of £1,356 3s. (*Gentleman's Magazine*, 1739, p. 49). And the subscribers were of no mean quality; they included five bishops, three dukes, two duchesses, four earls, two countesses, five lords, and of smaller fry a vast quantity. But this did not satisfy her; she had influence enough to get a short Act of Parliament passed in her favour (Cap. 23, 12, Geo. II., 1739), entitled:

'*An Act for providing a reward* to Joanna Stephens *upon a proper discovery to be made by her for the use of the publick, of the medicines prepared by her for the cure of the stone.*

'WHEREAS *Joanna Stevens* (sic) of the City of *Westminster*, spinster, hath acquired the knowledge of medicines, and the skill of preparing them, which by a dissolving power seem capable of removing the cause of the painful distemper of the stone, and may be improved, and more successfully applied when the same shall be discovered to persons learned in the science of physick; now, for encouraging the said *Joanna Stephens* to make discovery thereof, and for providing her a recompence in case the said medicines shall be submitted to the examination of proper judges, and by them be found worthy of the reward hereby provided; may it please your Majesty, that it be enacted, etc.

'£5,000 granted out of the supplies for the discovery of Mrs. Stephens's medicines. Treasury to issue the said sum on a proper certificate.'

A committee of twenty scientists investigated her medicines, and reported favourably on them. They were trifold. A powder, a draught, and a pill—and what think you they were made of? The powder was made of egg-shells and snails, both burnt; the draught was made of Alicante soap, swine's cresses burnt, and honey. This was made into a ball, which was afterwards sliced and dissolved in a broth composed of green camomile, or camomile flowers, sweet fennel, parsley, and burdock leaves, boiled in water and sweetened with honey; whilst the pill was compounded of snails, wild carrot seeds, burdock seeds, ashen keys, hips and haws, all burnt to blackness, and then mixed with Alicante soap! These were the famous remedies for which a grateful nation paid such a large sum ! ! !

CAGLIOSTRO IN LONDON.

CARLYLE, in a very diffuse essay on this adventurer, thus introduces him: 'The Count Alessandro di Cagliostro, Pupil of the sage Althotas, Foster-child of the Scherif of Mecca, probable Son of the last King of Trebisond; named also Acharat, and unfortunate child of Nature; by profession healer of diseases, abolisher of wrinkles, friend of the poor and impotent, grand-master of the Egyptian Mason Lodge of High Science, Spirit Summoner, Gold Cook, Grand Cophta, Prophet, Priest, and thaumaturgic moralist and swindler; really a Liar of the first magnitude, thorough-paced in all provinces of Lying, what one may call the King of Liars.

'Mendez Pinto, Baron Munchaüsen, and others are celebrated in this art, and not without some colour of justice; yet must it in candour remain doubtful whether any of these comparatively were much more than liars from the teeth onwards: a perfect character of the species in question, who lied not in word only, but continually in thought, word, and act; and, so to speak, lived wholly in an element of lying, and from birth to death did nothing but lie—was still a desideratum. Of which desideratum Count Alessandro offers, we say, if not the fulfilment, perhaps as near an approach to it as the limited human faculties permit.'

And yet this man made a name, and was famous in his time, and even afterwards. Lives, novels, and romances, notably being immortalized by Alexandre Dumas in his 'Memoires d'un Médecin,' nay, even plays, have been written about this clever rogue, who rose from a poor man's son to be the talk of Europe, and his connection with the famous diamond necklace, made him of almost political importance, sufficient to warrant his incarceration in the Bastille.

I do not propose to write the life of Cagliostro—enough and to spare has been written on this subject,[1] but simply to treat of him in London; yet at the same time it is necessary to say when and where he was born—the more especially because he always professed ignorance of his birth, and, when examined in a French court of justice in relation to the famous diamond necklace on January 30, 1786, the question was put to him, 'How old are you?' *Answer*—'Thirty-seven or thirty-eight years.' *Question*—'Your name?' *Answer*—'Alessandro Cagliostro.' *Question*—'Where born?' *Answer*—'I cannot say for certain, whether it was at Malta or at Medina; I have lived under the tuition of a governor, who told me that I was of noble birth, that I was left an orphan when only three months old,' etc.

But in a French book,[2] of which an English transla-

---

[1] I have before me now twelve lives of him, and that is by no means an exhaustive list.

[2] 'Memoire pour le Comte de Cagliostro, accusé: contre Monsieur le Procureur-General, accusateur; en presence de Monsieur le Cardinal de Rohan, de la Comtesse de la Motte, et autres co-accusés.' Paris, 1786, 4to.

tion was made in 1786, Cagliostro is made to say, 'I cannot speak positively as to the place of my nativity, nor to the parents who gave me birth. From various circumstances of my life I have conceived some doubts, in which the reader perhaps will join with me. But I repeat it: all my inquiries have ended only in giving me some great notions, it is true, but altogether vague and uncertain concerning my family.

'I spent the years of my childhood in the city ot Medina, in Arabia. There I was brought up under the name of Acharat, which I preserved during my progress through Africa and Asia. I had apartments in the palace of the Muphti Salahaym. It is needless to add that the Muphti is the chief of the Mahometan Religion, and that his constant residence is at Medina.

'I recollect perfectly that I had then four persons in my service; a governor, between 55 and 60 years of age, whose name was Althotas, and three servants, a white one, who attended me as valet-de-Chambre, and two blacks, one of whom was constantly about me night and day.

'My Governor always told me that I had been left an orphan when only three months old; that my parents were Christians, and nobly born; but he left me absolutely in the dark about their names, and the place of my nativity: a few words which he dropped by chance have induced me to suspect that I was born at Malta; but this circumstance I have never been able to ascertain.'

Althotas was a great sage, and imparted to his young pupil all the scientific knowledge he possessed, and that awful person, the Grand Muphti himself, would deign to converse with the boy on the lore and history of ancient Egypt. At this time he says he dressed as a Mussulman, and conformed to their rites; but was all the time at heart a true Christian.

At the mature age of twelve, he felt a strong desire to travel, and Althotas indulged him by joining a caravan going to Mecca, and here comes an attempt to fasten his paternity upon the Cherif of that place.

'On our arrival at Mecca, we alighted at the palace of the Cherif, who is the sovereign of Mecca, and of all Arabia, and always chosen from amongst the descendants of Mahomet. I here altered my dress, from a simple one, which I had worn hitherto, to one more splendid. On the third day after our arrival, I was, by my Governor, presented to the Cherif, who honoured me with the most endearing caresses. At sight of this prince, my senses experienced a sudden emotion, which it is not in the power of words to express; my eyes dropped the most delicious tears I ever shed in my life. His, I perceived, he could hardly restrain . . . .

'I remained at Mecca for the space of three years; not one day passed without my being admitted to the Sovereign's presence, and every hour increased his attachment and added to my gratitude. I sometimes surprized his eyes rivetted upon me, and then looking up to heaven, with every expression of pity and commiseration. Thoughtful, I would go from him, a prey to an ever fruitless curiosity. I dared not ask any question of my Governor, who always rebuked me with great severity, as if it had been a crime in me to wish for some information concerning my parents, and the place where I was born . . . .

'One day as I was alone, the prince entered my apartment; so great a favour struck me with amazement; he strained me to his bosom with more than usual tenderness, bade me never cease to adore the Almighty, telling me that, as long as I should persist in serving God faithfully, I should at last be happy, and come to the knowledge of my real destiny; then he added, bedewing my cheeks with tears, "Adieu, thou nature's unfortunate child." . . . .'

This is one side of the question—his own. It is romantic, and in all probability a lie. There is another side; but the evidence, although far more within the bounds of reason, is unsupported by corroboration. The authority is from an Italian book of one hundred and eighty-nine pages, entitled: 'Compendio della Vita, et delle Gesta di GUISEPPE BALSAMO, denominato Il CONTE CAGLIOSTRO. *Che si è estratto dal Processo contro di lui formato in Roma l'Anno*, 1790. *E che può servire di scorta per conoscere l'indole della Setta de* LIBERI MURATORI. In Roma 1791.' This book purports to be printed in the Vatican, 'from the Printing press of the Reverend Apostolic Chamber.'[1]

In the preface of this book is the following sentence, which is intended to vouch for the facts it contains: 'Thence comes the justice of that observation, that these Charlatans especially acquire credit, renown, and riches, in those countries where the least religion is found, where philosophy is most fashionable. Rome is not a place that agrees with them, because error cannot throw out its roots, in the centre, the capital, of the true faith. The life of Count Cagliostro is a shining proof of this truth. It is for this reason that it has been thought proper to

[1] Of this work there was a French translation published in 1791 at Paris and Strasbourg, under the title of 'Vie de Joseph Balsamo, connu sous le nom de Comte Cagliostro,' &c. 2nd edition.

compose this compendium, faithfully extracted from the proceedings taken against him, a short while since, at Rome; this is evidence which the critic cannot attack. In order to effect this, the Sovereign Pontifical Authority has deigned to dispense with the law of inviolable secrecy, which always accompanies, with as much justice as prudence, the proceedings of the Holy Inquisition.'

And the account of his life opens thus: 'Joseph Balsamo was born at Palermo on the 8th of June, 1743. His parents were Pietro Balsamo and Felice Braconieri, both of mean extraction. His father, who was a shopkeeper, dying when he was still a baby, his maternal uncles took care of him,' &c.

In another book, 'The Life of the Count Cagliostro,' &c., London, 1787, there is a foot-note to the first page: 'Some authors are of opinion that he is the offspring of the grand Master of Malta, by a Turkish lady, made captive by a Maltese galley. Others that he is the only surviving son of that prince who, about thirty-five years ago, swayed the precarious sceptre of Trebisond, at which period, a revolution taking place, the reigning prince was massacred by his seditious subjects, and his infant son, the Count Cagliostro, conveyed by a trusty friend to Medina, where the Cherif had the unprejudiced generosity to have him educated ln the faith of his Christian parents.'

I do not follow his career, but the most marvellous stories were current about him, *vide* the following extract from a book already quoted (see foot-note page 334): 'The Comtesse de la Motte dares to assert that one of my men makes a boast of having been 150 years in my service. That I sometimes acknowledge myself to be only 300 years old; at others that I brag of having been present at the nuptials in Cana, and that it was to burlesque the Holy Sacrament of the Eucharist, the transubstantiation, that I had imagined to multiply the necklace, taken to pieces, into a hundred different manners, and yet it was delivered, as it is said, in its full complement to the august Queen.

'That I am by turns a Portuguese Jew, a Greek, an Egyptian of Alexandria, from whence I have imported into France hyeroglyphics and sorcery.

'That I am one of those infatuated Rosicrucians, who have the power of making the dead converse with the living; that I attend the poor gratis, but that I sell for *something*, to the rich, the gifts of immortality.'

But it is not of these things I wish to treat; it is of the facts connected with his residence in London. Two or three accounts say that he visited London in 1772, where he swindled a Doctor Benemore, who had rescued him from prison, under pretence of painting his country house, and his enemy, De Morande, of the *Courier de l'Europe*, who, in No.'s 16, 17, and 18 of that journal, made frightful accusations against Cagliostro, reiterates the story of his being here in 1772. In page xiv. of the preface to 'The Life of the Count Cagliostro,' 1787, there occurs the following passage: 'M. de Morande is at infinite pains to persuade us that the Count resided in London in 1772, under the name of Balsamo, in extreme poverty, from which he was relieved by Sir Edward Hales. That Baronet professes, indeed, to recollect an *Italian* of that name; but, as M. de Morande positively assures us that the Count is a *Calabrois*, a *Neapolitan*, or a *Sicilian*, we can desire no better argument to prove the fallacy of his information.'

In a pamphlet entitled, 'Lettre du Comte Cagliostro au Peuple Anglois pour servir de suite à ses Memoires,' 1786, p. 7, he says distinctly: 'Nous sommes arrivés, ma femme et moi, en Angleterre, pour la première fois de ma vie, au mois de Juillet, 1776,' and on p. 70 of the same work is the following (translated):

'The greatest part of the long diatribe of M. Morande is used to prove that I came to London in 1772, under the name of *Balsamo*. In view of the efforts which M. Morande makes, in order to arrive at such proof, an attempt is made to show that the *Balsamo* with whom they attempt to identify me ought to have been hung, or, at all events, he rendered himself guilty of some dishonourable actions. Nothing of the sort. This *Balsamo*, if the *Courier de l'Europe* can be believed, was a mediocre painter, who lived by his brush. A man named *Benamore*, either agent, or interpreter, or chargé d'affaires to the King of Morocco, had commissioned him to paint some pictures, and had not paid for them. *Balsamo* issued a writ against him for £47 sterling, which he said was due to him, admitting that he had received two guineas on account. Besides, this Balsamo was so poor that his wife was obliged to go into town herself, in order to sell the pictures which her husband painted. Such is the portrait which M. de Morande draws of the *Balsamo* of London, a portrait which no one will accuse him of having flattered, and from which the sensible reader will draw the conclusion that the *Balsamo* of London was an honest artist who gained a livelihood by hard work.

'I might then admit without blushing that I had lived in London in 1772 under the name of *Balsamo*, on the product of my feeble talents in painting; that the course of events and circumstances had reduced me to this extremity, etc. . . .

'I am ignorant whether the law-suit between *Balsamo* and *Benamore* is real or supposed: one thing is certain, that in London exists a regular physician of irreproachable probity, named Benamore. He is versed in oriental languages: he was formerly attached, as interpreter, to the Moroccan Embassy, and he is, at this date, employed, in the same capacity, by the ambassador of Tripoli. He will bear witness to all who wish to know that, during the 30 years he has been established in London, he has never known another Benamore than himself, and that he has never had a law-suit with anyone bearing the name of *Balsamo*.'

Now take Carlyle, with whom dogmatism stood in stead of research, and judge for yourselves. ' There is one briefest but authentic-looking glimpse of him presents itself in England, in the year 1772 : no Count is he here, but mere Signor Balsamo again, engaged in house-painting, for which he has a peculiar talent. Was it true that he painted the country house of a "Doctor Benemore;" and, not having painted, but only smeared it, was refused payment, and got a lawsuit with expenses instead? If Doctor Benemore have left any representatives in the Earth, they are desired to speak out. We add only, that if young Beppo had one of the prettiest of wives, old Benemore had one of the ugliest daughters; and so, putting one thing to another, matters might not be so bad.'

Who set this story afloat, about Cagliostro being in London in 1772? Why, Monsieur de Morande, the editor of the *Courier de l'Europe*, and of his veracity we may judge by an advertisement in the *London Evening Post* of November 27 to 30, 1773, p. 4, col. 4, (translated).

'Monsieur Le Comte de Lauraguais has kindly consented, after the humble apologies I have made to him, to forego the action commenced against me for having defamed him in some verses full of untruths, injurious both to his honour and his reputation, of which I was the author, and which I caused to be inserted in the *Morning Chronicle* of 24 and 25 June last, entitled: "Answer of the Gazetteer Cuirassé." I therefore beg you, Mr. Woodfall,[1] to publish through the same channel by which I made my verses public, —my sincere repentance for having so injuriously libelled Monsieur le Comte, and my very humble thanks for his having accepted my apologies, and stopping all action in the matter.

'De Morande.

'Nov. 26, 1773.'

This is what in law would be called *a tainted witness*, as, about that time he was, on his own confession, given to lying.

According to his own account he came to London in July, 1776, possessed of a capital of about three thousand pounds in plate, jewels, and specie, and hired apartments in Whitcomb Street, Pall Mall East, and here he fell into evil company. The story is not very lucid—but it seems that his wife's companion, a Portuguese woman named Blavary, and his secretary and interpreter, Vitellini, introduced to him a certain

[1] Editor of the *Morning Chronicle*, 1772—89.

Lord Scot. They were a lot of sharpers all round. Scot introduced a woman as his wife—Lady Scot, if you please—(in reality Miss Fry), who got money and clothes from the countess, and Cagliostro lent my lord two hundred pounds on his simple note of hand.

He declares that he gave them lucky numbers for the lottery, and that they gained much money thereby—on one occasion, when he gave Miss Fry the number eight, she won the sum of fifteen hundred guineas; but she was requested by Cagliostro not to visit, or bother himself, or his wife again. He moved into Suffolk Street in January, 1777, but the persevering Miss Fry took lodgings in the same house. She attempted to borrow money, and to get lucky numbers, but, failing in both, she had him arrested on the 7th of February for a pretended debt of one hundred and ninety pounds. He recovered his liberty the next day, by depositing in the hands of the sheriff's officer, jewels worth double the amount.

Then a warrant was taken out against him and his wife, signed by one Justice Miller—on the charge of practising witchcraft. This does not, however, seem to have been acted on, but he was frequently harassed by actions for debt brought against him by Miss Fry, and he became well acquainted with the inside of a spunging-house. On the 24th of May he was taken into custody for a debt of two hundred pounds, at the suit of Miss Fry, but he managed to find bail. The case was tried before Lord Mansfield, in the Court of Queen's Bench, on the 27th of June, but his lordship suggested that it was a case for arbitration, which was agreed to.

The arbitration took place on the 4th of July, when

Cagliostro's lawyer deserted him, and the decision was that the count had lost his case, and must pay all costs. As if this was not bad enough, as he was leaving the court he was arrested at the suit of one Aylett, who had lodged a detainer against him for a debt of ten pounds and upwards, by the name of Melisa Cagliostro, otherwise Joseph Balsamo, which debt he said was due to him from Balsamo, who had employed him in 1772 to recover a debt from Dr. Benamore. He got bail, but, as his money was getting scarce, it was at the cost of 'two soup-ladles, two candlesticks, two salt-cellars, two pepper-castors, six forks, six table spoons, nine knife handles with blades, a pair of snuffers and stand, all of silver.' He had, however, suffered six weeks' imprisonment, as he was not liberated from the King's Bench till the 24th of September, 1777.

In vain his friends endeavoured to stir him up to commence actions for fraud and perjury against all concerned, but either his cause was not just, or he had had enough law to last him some time—and he refused. He paid up his debts and left England, with only fifty guineas and a few jewels in his possession.

Rightly or wrongly, he was connected with the 'Diamond Necklace' affair, and suffered incarceration in the Bastile. If he can be at all believed, the police plundered him and his wife right royally. He says he lost fifteen rouleaux, each containing fifty double louis, sealed with his seal; one thousand two hundred and thirty-three sequins (Venetian and Roman): one rouleau of twenty-four Spanish quadruples, sealed also; and forty-seven billets of one thousand livres each on the Caisse d'Escompte. They also took papers which were to him of inestimable value; and, as to diamonds and jewellery, he knew not what was taken, besides plate, porcelain, and linen, etc. After an examination, he was acquitted, but he had to leave France, and came to London, where he lived in Sloane Street. Here he became acquainted with Lord George Gordon, and this acquaintance afterwards cost him dearly, when he was arrested at Rome. To show the intimacy between the two, I will quote from the *Public Advertiser* of the 22nd of August, 1786, p. 2, col. 3.

'M. Barthelemy, who conducts the affairs of France in the absence of Comte Dazimer, having sent M. Daragon with a message to Comte de Cagliostro, in Sloane Street, intimating that he had received orders from the Court of Versailles to communicate to Comte de Cagliostro that he now had permission to return to France; yesterday morning, the Comte, accompanied by Lord George Gordon and M. Bergeret de Frouville, waited upon M. Barthelemy at the "Hotel of France," in Piccadilly, for an eclaireissement upon the subject of this message from the Court of France, delivered by M. Barthelemy, relative to the permission granted to the Comte de Cagliostro to return to Paris. M. Barthelemy, the Comte de Cambise, and M. Daragon seemed much surprised to see Comte de Cagliostro arrive in Lord George Gordon's coach, with his Lordship, and M. Frouville, and, having expressed their desire that the Comte de Cagliostro *alone* should speak with M. Barthelemy, they were informed that Lord Gordon and M. Bergeret de Frouville were there on purpose to attend their friend, and that Comte de Cagliostro would not dispense with Lord George Gordon's absence from the Conference. Will any friend to liberty blame Comte de Cagliostro, after ten months' imprisonment in a dungeon, for having his friends near him, when insidious proposals are made to him by the faction of Breteuil and the supporters of the Bastile? Men who have already sought his destruction, and, after his innocence was declared by the judgment of the Parliament of Paris, embezzled a great part of his fortune, and exiled him from France? M. Barthelemy (seeing the determination of the Comte's friends) then read the letter from M. Breteuil; but, upon the Comte de Cagliostro desiring a copy, M. Barthelemy refused it. A great deal of conversation then ensued upon the subject, which in all probability will give rise to a full representation to the King of France, who is certainly very much imposed on. The Queen's party is still violent against Comte de Cagliostro, the friend of mankind; and De Breteuil—le Sieur De Launey—Titon—De Brunières—Maître Chesnon—Barthelemy and Dazimer are mere instruments of that faction. The honour of the King of France, the justice and judgment of the Parliament of Paris, the good faith of the Citizens, and the good name of the nation, are all attainted by the pillage and detention of the property of Comte de Cagliostro.'

And again, in the same paper, 24th of August, 1786, p. 2, col. 3, is another paragraph respecting him:

'Comte de Cagliostro has declared he will hold no intercourse with any of Le Sieur Breteuil's messengers from France, except in the presence of Lord George Gordon. The gang of French spies in London, who are linked in with M. de Morande, and the Sieurs Barthelemy, Dazimer, Cambise, and the Queen's Bastile party at Paris, are trying the most insiduous arts to entrap the Comte and Comtesse, and have the effrontery and audaciousness to persecute them publicly, and vilify them even in this free country, where these noble Strangers are come to seek protection in the arms of a generous people. The friendship and benevolence of Comte de Cagliostro, in advising the poor Prince Louis de Rohan to be upon his guard against the Comtesse de Valois, and the intrigues of the Queen's faction, (who still seek the destruction of that noble Prince) has brought upon the Comte and his amiable Comtesse the hateful revenge of a tyrannical Government. The story of the Diamonds has never been properly explained to the Public in France. It would discover too much of the base arts practised to destroy Prince Louis, and involve in guilt persons not safe to name in an arbitrary kingdom.'

This airing of private grief in public extorted some strictures in a letter in the *Morning Post*, of 29th of August, 1786, in which it was suggested, generally, that foreigners should wash their dirty linen at home. But Monsieur de Morande, editor of the *Courier de l'Europe*, published many assertions, be they facts, or fiction, relative to Cagliostro, and he once more blossomed out into print in his old champion, the *Public Advertiser* (vide that newspaper, 5th of September, 1786, p. 2. col. 1), translated in the number of 7th September. In this curious letter, he adverts to his adversaries' slanders, and the following singular passages occur:

'Of all the very good stories which you relate at my expense, the best, without comparison, is that of the pig fed with arsenic, which poisoned the lions, tygers, and leopards of the forests of Medina. I am going, Mr. Railer, to give you an opportunity of being witty on a perfect comprehension of the fact. You know that, in physics and chymistry, reasoning proves but little, ridicule nothing, and that experiment is all. Permit me, then, to propose a small experiment to you, of which the issue will divert the public, either at your expense, or mine. I invite you to breakfast with me on the 9th of November next, at nine o'clock in the morning. You shall furnish the wine, and the appendages. For myself, I shall only furnish a single dish, after my own fashion—it shall be a sucking pig, fattened after my method. Two hours before breakfast, I shall present you the pig alive, fat and healthy. You shall order it to be killed as you please, and prepared, and I shall not approach until it is served at the table. You shall cut it into four equal parts, you shall chuse that which most flatters your appetite, and I shall take that which you please. The day after that of our breakfast, one or more of four things will happen. Either both of us shall die, or we neither of us shall die, or you shall die and I survive, or I shall die and you survive. Of these four chances I give you three, and I bet you 5000 guineas, that, on the day after our breakfast, you shall die, and I be perfectly well. You must either accept of this Challenge, or acknowledge that you are an ignorant fellow, and that yon have foolishly ridiculed a thing which is totally out of your knowledge,

'If you accept of this Challenge, I shall instantly deposit the 5000 guineas with any banker that you please. You shall do the same in five days, during which time you shall have leave to make your supporters Contribute,' &c.

Monsieur de Morande's reply was published immediately following the above letter. It is, like Cagliostro's, too long for insertion; but its gist is, that he intends to unmask the pretender, and that he utterly declines to attend a poisoning match. He writes:

'I solemnly defy you to contradict them' (*i.e.*, his assertions as to Cagliostro's quackeries and adventures); 'and that I even offer, without croupiers or supporters, to make you another wager of five thousand guineas that I shall compleatly unmask you.

'But, *Monsieur le Comte*, I shall not put my foot in your house, and shall not breakfast with you myself. I am neither abject enough to keep you company, nor will let it be suspected for a single moment.

'You clearly conceive that such an interview ought not, nor can be, within your doors; you would be liable to be found guilty of criminal practises, in case of accident. This your *Council* had not foreseen.

'As no tavern would permit such infamous scenes to pass under its roof as those you propose, you must, *Monsieur le* Comte, return once more to the *booth;* and worthy disciple of LOCUSTA,[1] choose in London a public place to make an open-air exhibition of your talents.'

And like the scorpion, which carries its sting in its tail, he adds a foot-note, which refers to the heading of his letter:

'*M. de Morande's Answer to Don Joseph Balsamo,*

---

[1] Locusta, or, more correctly, Lucusta, was a celebrated poisoner. She was employed by Aggripina to poison the Emperor Claudius, and by Nero to kill Britannicus. For this she was most handsomely rewarded by Nero; but was executed for her crimes by Galba.

self-created Count of Cagliostro, Colonel in the Service of all the Sovereign Powers in Europe.'

'If it was not the case, it would be very singular to have seen, in the year 1777, M. Cagliostro calling himself in England Colonel of the Third Regiment of Brandenbourg, and, afterwards, in Russia, Colonel in the Spanish Service; for which, however, he was reprimanded by the magistrates of Petersburgh. Having forgot to take his Commission with him, he could not exhibit proofs, and was obliged to put down his regimentals. This check on his conduct made him abscond from Petersburgh. Every Russian nobleman in London knows this anecdote, and, without presuming to mention names, we trust that this will be found to be the case upon enquiry.'

To this letter Cagliostro replied with another in the *Public Advertiser* (p. 2, col. 1) of September 9, 1786, in which he repeats his challenge, and declines to sit down to breakfast with a carnivorous animal.

De Morande, of course, could not be silent, and replied in the *Public Advertiser* (p. 2, col. 1) of September 12, 1786. He reiterated the charges he made against Cagliostro in the *Courier de l'Europe*, saying, among other things, 'I have said that you were in England in the year 1771, under the name of *Balsamo*, and that you were then a needy, as well as a *very indifferent* painter; that twenty persons, at least, are ready to prove it. You take no notice of this second assertion, which becomes serious, *by the oath you have taken under that name*, of which I have a legal copy in my possession.

'I have said that you have made your appearance under another name, THAT OF CAGLIOSTRO, in the year 1777. I have several *affidavits*, amongst which there are some of your own, which authenticate very curious anecdotes concerning you; to this you have replied nothing.

'I have said that you falsely pretended then to be a *Colonel of the third regiment* of Brandenbourg; that you had, at that time, a law-suit in the Court of Queen's Bench, *about a certain necklace, and a gold snuff-box*, which you asserted to have been given MADAME LA COMTESSE, but which you were obliged to return, and pay all Costs, on the Clear proofs given by your adverse party, that you obtained them *under false pretences*. No reply has been made to this.

'I have added that, were you curious to try the same experiment now, a new Act of Parliament, which you and your fellow-adventurers have rendered *very necessary*, would certainly have caused you to be sent to the Thames.[1] To that direct and very clear observation you have not replied a single word.

'I have said that you were ordered by the Police in Russia, not to presume to take the name of a Colonel in the Spanish service, and to strip off your Spanish regimentals. I have given you an opportunity to vindicate yourself, by giving to understand, that there is not a Russian nobleman in London who would not certify this fact. I might have added that I have in my possession *the most respectable authority* to say so. What have you said in reply to this?

'I have roundly asserted that I am in possession of proofs, that you are an impostor under every possible denomination; that you have not only no pretension

---

[1] *i.e.*, to serve on the convict hulks there, to dredge the Thames. The treatment on board was based on good principles; those convicts who were well-behaved had remission of sentence, those who were recalcitrant had unmerciful punishment.

to any title, but not even to the rank of a sergeant. Shall this remain likewise unanswered?

. . . .

'I am sorry to be obliged once more to name Messrs. B. & C. Bankers, to prove that your pretensions to lay a wager of 5000 guineas, are as well grounded as your pretensions to the title of a COUNT, or an *Alchemist*. It is a fact, that you *humbly* offered to pledge in their hands the watch, of which the too long, and too much, deluded Cardinal de Rohan made you a present. It is likewise a fact *that they disdainfully refused it*. Your proposing, after this, a wager of 5000 guineas is probably no more than a new pretence to obtain credit, as you have formerly (in pretending to make great quantities of gold) obtained small sums, and little diamonds to make larger, which you afterwards declared had been given to MADAME LA COMTESSE. Those proofs, I repeat to you, *are in my possession;* they are all fully authenticated, and I will make good every one of my assertions.' And he winds up his letter with expressing 'the satisfaction I feel in having furnished the world with sufficient proofs to convince them that you are THE GREATEST IMPOSTOR OF THIS OR ANY OTHER AGE.'

This ended the correspondence, for the general public were beginning to meddle in it, and the editor of the *Public Advertiser* would only open his pages to the principals in this duel. This finished Cagliostro's career in England. He had tried to sell his quack medicines, his Egyptian pills, but the charm was broken, and he quitted England for the Continent in May, 1787, leaving his wife behind, with sufficient means, under the guardianship of the De

Loutherbourgs. She afterwards sold all up, and joined him in June.

By this time his good genius had forsaken him, and for teaching freemasonry, then even more repugnant to the Roman Catholic hierarchy than at present, he was arrested, and imprisoned in the Castle of St. Angelo, November 27, 1789. He never again enjoyed freedom, but was found dead in his cell at St. Leo. Even the date of his death is uncertain, most authorities giving 1795; but some say 1794 and 1797. His wife, too, shared his fate; she was convicted of sorcery and witchcraft, and was shut up in a convent, where she died in 1794.

His portraits represent him as by no means bad-looking, although the full eye, the puffed cheeks, and weak mouth betray a sensuality of feeling.

THE END.

Soc
DA
485
A79
1972